WHAT IS A CLASSIC IN HISTORY?

The Making of a Historical Canon

JAUME AURELL

University of Navarra

CAMBRIDGE
UNIVERSITY PRESS

Shaftesbury Road, Cambridge CB2 8EA, United Kingdom

One Liberty Plaza, 20th Floor, New York, NY 10006, USA

477 Williamstown Road, Port Melbourne, VIC 3207, Australia

314–321, 3rd Floor, Plot 3, Splendor Forum, Jasola District Centre,
New Delhi – 110025, India

103 Penang Road, #05–06/07, Visioncrest Commercial, Singapore 238467

Cambridge University Press is part of Cambridge University Press & Assessment,
a department of the University of Cambridge.

We share the University's mission to contribute to society through the pursuit of
education, learning and research at the highest international levels of excellence.

www.cambridge.org
Information on this title: www.cambridge.org/9781009469968

DOI: 10.1017/9781009469937

© Jaume Aurell 2024

First published 2024

A catalogue record for this publication is available from the British Library

*A Cataloging-in-Publication data record for this book is available from the
Library of Congress*

ISBN 978-1-009-46996-8 Hardback
ISBN 978-1-009-46995-1 Paperback

WHAT IS A CLASSIC IN HISTORY?

What is a classic in historical writing? How do we explain the continued interest in certain historical narratives, even when their accounts and interpretations of particular periods have been displaced or revised by newer generations of historians? How do these texts help to maintain the historiographical canon? Jaume Aurell's innovative study ranges from the heroic writings of ancient Greek historians such as Herodotus to the twentieth-century microhistories of Carlo Ginzburg and gender and postcolonial historiography. The book explores how certain texts have been able to stand the test of time, gain their status as historiographical classics, and capture the imaginations of readers across generations. Investigating the processes of permanence and change in both historiography and history, Aurell further examines the creation of historical genres and canons. Taking influence from methodologies including sociology, literary criticism, theology, and postcolonial studies, *What Is a Classic in History?* encourages readers to re-evaluate their ideas of history and historiography alike.

JAUME AURELL is Professor of Medieval History at the University of Navarra. He specializes in medieval and modern historiography. His previous publications include *Medieval Self-Coronations: The History and Symbolism of a Ritual* (Cambridge University Press, 2020), *Theoretical Perspectives on Historians' Autobiographies* (Routledge, 2016), and *Authoring the Past: History, Autobiography, and Politics in Medieval Catalonia* (University of Chicago Press, 2012).

CONTENTS

v

ACKNOWLEDGEMENTS

All historians, and I think all scholars as well, know that some research subjects lead to others, in a dynamic that has something of scientific logic, but also of serendipity. My interest in the concepts developed in this book grew as I worked on a monograph about some 450 historians' autobiographies, finally published as *Theoretical Perspectives on Historians' Autobiographies: From Documentation to Intervention* (Routledge, 2016). During that long process of research, I became fascinated by the many ways in which historians can convey their approach to the past, which may go far beyond conventional academic genres such as the monograph or the paper.

This led me to think about the different ways – from the variety of the genres deployed to the diversity of platforms used and the different rhetoric in play – through which historians transmit the reality of the past, something often relegated to the background in historiographical analyses, which tends to centre on heuristic, methodological, and epistemological questions. At first, I thought that researching the 'classic' and its associated concepts would be a lonely journey. However, as my research progressed, I realized, as so often happens in our work, that others were also examining these issues. In recent decades, critical historians of history with deep training in literary criticism, or literary critics with a special historiographical sensibility, such as Lionel Gossman, Leo Braudy,

ACKNOWLEDGEMENTS

Peter Gay, John Clive, Jack Hexter, Ann Rigney, and Philippe Carrard, have opened up the field of 'historical criticism', the disciplinary context for this book.

Among these critics of history, I owe special recognition to Hayden White, one of whose quotations led me to systematically consider the questions raised in this book:

> The content of the historiographical discourse is indistinguishable from its discursive form. That this is so is confirmed by the fact that classic historiographical works have continued to be valued for their literary qualities long after their information has become outdated and their explanations have been consigned to the status of commonplaces of the cultural moment in which they were written. … It is the metaphoric nature of the great classics of historiography that explains why none of them has ever wrapped up a historical problem definitively; rather, they have always opened up a prospect on the past that inspires more study.[1]

However, half a century has passed since the publication of Hayden White's *Metahistory* and the subsequent theoretical revolution associated with it. As a consequence, considering myself a historian and a critic of history at the same time, I thought that historiography demanded new themes, approaches, and perspectives.

With all these questions and reflections already in my mind, the first specific impetus for this research came in the form of an invitation to participate in the conference 'Writing as

[1] Hayden V. White, 'Literary Theory and Historical Writing', in *Figural Realism* (Baltimore, MD: Johns Hopkins University Press, 1998), 5–7.

Historical Practice: A History & Theory Workshop', held at the Center for the Humanities, Vanderbilt University, Nashville, in May 2017, organized by Laura Stark. The second impulse arrived a year later when I was invited by Kalle Pihlainen to give a seminar at the Institute of Historical Research at the University of London in March 2018. During the intense discussions that followed these presentations, I realized that the topic I proposed, which has since given rise to this book, was clearly counter-cultural. However, beyond the polemic that it might provoke – especially concerning the (dubious) idea of normativity that might arise from the concepts of the classic and the canon – I had no doubt that the topic would interest not only my fellow historians but also literary critics and other theorists from other social and scientific disciplines.

As a result, as I work on a project that goes against the prevailing trends, I have particularly appreciated the collaboration and encouragement of some colleagues who have followed the development of the book with interest during its long digesting, making, and writing. The most relevant source of inspiration and gratitude for the ideas in this book corresponds to the research group on 'Religion and Civil Society', in the Institute for Culture and Society at the University of Navarra. This project is an example of interdisciplinary dialogue, without which it is simply impossible to think in depth about the key questions of the past or present. I especially appreciated the valuable suggestions and encouragement received from the director of this group, Montserrat Herrero.

I have also appreciated the comments and suggestions on early drafts of this book made by Gary Shaw, Hans Kellner, Miri Rubin, Laura Stark, Gabrielle M. Spiegel,

Peter Burke, Juan Pablo Domínguez, Philippe Carrard, Robert A. Rosenstone, Edoardo Tortarolo, Rocío G. Davis, Jill K. Conway, Hayden V. White, Carlos Eire, Jouni-Matti Kuukkanen, Ethan Kleinberg, Patrick Finney, and Kalle Pihlainen.

Finally, I am particularly grateful to my editor, Liz Friend-Smith. I had already had a great experience during the process of publishing my *Medieval Self-Coronations: The History and Symbolism of a Ritual* (Cambridge University Press, 2020), which has been confirmed with this new book. I also thank the anonymous readers of the first manuscript for their comments and suggestions: more specifically, the insight and inexhaustible scholarship of one of them ennobles the hidden task of the generous reviewers.

I hope this book will interest those who believe that history is a noble activity that may become an inspiring form of narrative and is being constantly revitalized through the rise of new methodologies, genres, and forms of transmitting the reality of the past. Accordingly, this book is devoted to those who have achieved sublime historical writing in the past and deserve the respect and admiration of the historians that have succeeded them.

Introduction

Tradition is not the worship of ashes,
but the preservation of fire.

Gustav Mahler

What is *the* classic in history? What is *a* classic in historical writing? How do we explain the enduring interest in certain historical narratives, even when their accounts and interpretations of particular periods have been displaced or revised by newer generations of historians, and new data have enriched historical understanding? Why are particular texts repeatedly chosen by historians of historiography as the basis for their accounts? Why are they thought of as models of historical writing in classes? Why do learned audiences show an interest in them? Can we speak of the existence of a canon *in* history and, therefore, draw up a canon *of* history? How are historical genres relevant for historiography? Why is the concept of genealogy, recovered by modern criticism, related to that of the classic and the canon?

Very few historians have addressed these questions and, more specifically, the question of the classic and the canon in history/historiography. When they have, discussions remain brief. Nevertheless, inquiry into these concepts leads us to acknowledge the peculiar ambivalence in historical texts between science and art, content and form, scientific and narrative language, analysis and synthesis, particularity

1

and generality, metaphor and metonymy, past and present.[1] This duality makes history different from literature and science, requires a careful analysis of the interaction between historical content and narrative form, locates the discipline in a peculiar epistemic space between the humanities and social sciences, and demands a specific engagement with the condition and features of the concept of the classic.

In seeking to answer these questions, this book will explore the conditions that have enabled some historical books to stand the test of time and achieve durability (Chapter 1), and be counted among the classics of historiography (Chapter 2). By becoming durable, these books have entered a canon – more or less explicit, variable and flexible – passed on from generation to generation among professional historians, teachers of history and their students, and general readers of history (Chapter 3). A careful observation of all these rhetorical phenomena reveals the interconnection between the classics in historiography and the generation or consolidation of historical genres (Chapter 4). Finally, the observation of the phenomenon of the continuity, permanence, and durability of these historical texts necessarily leads to an inquiry into genealogy, a key concept in understanding the processes of permanence and change – acting as a 'double agent' as the title of the chapter states – in both historiography and history (Chapter 5).

* * *

As the first step in this exploration, and considering the lack of historiographical discussion on the classic in history – and

---

[1] Lionel Gossman, *Between History and Literature* (Cambridge: Harvard University Press, 1990), 199.

of a systematic corpus of historical criticism – I turned to literary critics for advice. Though literary processes differ from historical progressions, certain parallels allow for a fruitful interdisciplinary approach. Locating these common features allows us to identify the specificities of the classic in both fields and examine their peculiarities.

There are three foundational articles on the literary classic. T. S. Eliot's 'What is a Classic?', the presidential address to the Virgil Society in 1944, persuaded his audience that this subject matters, because classics may redeem literature from provincialism, and only the permanent light of the classics could widen authoritative, authorial, and universal perspectives: '[M]y [Eliot's] concern here is only with the corrective to provincialism in literature.'[2] For 'provincial', Eliot means 'distortion of values, the exclusion of some, the exaggeration of others, which springs, not from lack of wide geographical perambulation, but from applying standards acquired within a limited area, to the whole of human experience; which confounds the contingent with the essential, the ephemeral with the permanent.'[3] Accordingly, Eliot was primarily concerned with the idea of universality conveyed by classical texts: 'When a work of literature has, beyond this comprehensiveness in

---

[2] T. S. Eliot, 'What is a Classic?', *On Poetry and Poets* (London: Faber and Faber, 1957), 53–71, here 69. See Tansu Acik, 'What is a Classic According to T. S. Eliot and H.-G. Gadamer?', *The International Journal of the Humanities* 8 (2010): 54–63; Hans Ulrich Gumbrecht, '"Phoenix from the Ashes" or: From Canon to Classic', *New Literary History* 20, 1 (1988): 141–163; Irmgard Wagner, 'Hans Robert Jauss and Classicity', *Comparative Literature* 99, 5 (1984): 1173–1184.

[3] Eliot, 'What is a Classic?', 67.

relation to its own language, and equal significance in relation to a number of foreign literatures, we may say that it has also *universality*.'[4] Eliot argues that the classic provides us with a measure: 'Without the constant application of the classical measure, which we owe to Virgil more than to any other one poet, we tend to become provincial.'[5]

Three decades later, Frank Kermode wrote a brief but dense essay entitled *The Classic: Literary Images of Permanence and Change* (1983), in which he focused on the sense of stability these texts provide. Unlike Eliot, who was concerned with provincialism, Kermode centres on the ability of the classic to traverse the new and the old – an aspect that illuminates the exploration of classics in historiography. The passage of time has not diminished the value of these texts, because they have kept their ability to dialogue with the times, and their openness to successive fruitful readings and interpretations. As Kermode explains, 'from day to day we must cope with the paradox that the classic changes, yet retains its identity. It would be not read, and so would not be a classic, if we could not in some way believe it to be capable of saying more than its authors meant.'[6]

As a result of this paradox, the classic itself confronts the past with the present, the old with the modern: 'What is begin contested is a received opinion as to the structure of the past and of its relation to the present. It is a question of how the works of the past may retain identity in

---

[4] Eliot, 'What is a Classic?', 69. The emphasis in the original.
[5] Eliot, 'What is a Classic?', 69.
[6] Frank Kermode, *The Classic: Literary Images of Permanence and Change* (London: Harvard University Press, 1983), 80.

4

change, of the mode in which the ancient presents itself to the modern.'[7]

Finally, in his 'What is a Classic?' (1993), John M. Coetzee takes up Eliot's and Kermode's reflections. Coetzee was persuaded of the relevance of this subject, especially in its meta-critical dimension, since 'the function of criticism is defined by the classic: criticism is that which is duty-bound to interrogate the classic'.[8] Listening to Bach's *Well-Tempered Clavier* made him reflect on the essence of a classic, and provided him with some of its basic features:

> Bach is a classic of music. Sense one: the classic is that which is not time bound, which retains meaning for succeeding ages, which 'lives'. Sense two: a proportion of Bach's music belongs to what are loosely called 'the classics', the part of European musical canon that is still widely played, if not particularly often or before particularly large audiences. The third sense, the sense that Bach does not satisfy, is that he does not belong to the revival of so-called classical values in European art starting in the second quarter of the eighteenth century.[9]

Yet Coetzee was aware of the complexities of the process, and he noted an important quality of the classic, which I will revisit later in this book: the classic is 'historically constituted, ... constituted by identifiable historical forces and within a specific historical context'. If critics take this into account, they may avoid 'facile notions of the classic as the timeless, as that

[7] Kermode, *The Classic*, 16.

[8] John M. Coetzee, 'What is a Classic?', in *Stranger Shores: Literary Essays* (New York: Viking, 2001), 1–16, here 19.

[9] Coetzee, 'What is a Classic?', 10.

which unproblematically speaks across all boundaries'.[10] When we acknowledge this historical relativization of the classic and its constructed nature, and when we do not fall into a radical essentialism in our approach to the classic, then we can start wondering at its ability to speak across the ages. Coetzee concludes that, rather than being the enemy of the classic, the sharpest critic is perhaps what the classic needs to define itself and ensure its survival. Yet, the evidence that the classic is historically constituted does not contradict the fact that there is 'something inherent' to *some* particular historical texts which provides them with enduring quality. I will describe this 'something inherent' as a 'surplus of meaning', applying the Paul Ricoeur's concept – originally designed for literary criticism – to historical criticism.[11]

The classic thus moves between the structural and the accidental, between the essential and the historical, and between the permanent and the constructed. The sociologist Pierre Bourdieu's reflection on the concept of *habitus*, which shows many analogies with that of the classic, helps to explain the relationship between the permanent and the changing: 'The habitus, the durably installed generative principle of regulated improvisations, produces practices which tend to reproduce the regularities immanent in the objective conditions of the production of their generative principle, while

[10] Coetzee, 'What is a Classic?', 10.

[11] Paul Ricoeur, *Interpretation Theory: Discourse and the Surplus of Meaning* (Forth Worth: The Texas Christian University Press, 1976). See also Theodoor Marius van Leeuwen, *The Surplus of Meaning: Ontology and Eschatology in the Philosophy of Paul Ricoeur* (Amsterdam: Brill, 1981) and Stephanie N. Arel and Dan R. Stiver (eds.), *Ideology and Utopia in the Twenty-First Century: The Surplus of Meaning in Ricoeur's Dialectical Concept* (Lanham: Lexington, 2019), 53–71.

adjusting to the demands inscribed as objective potentialities in the situation, as defined by the cognitive and motivating structures making up the habitus.'[12]

The concept of habitus explains that, while the classic generates models of writing, it can also adjust to the new circumstances of its context, which guarantees its durability and permanence beyond the changing world. This contextual and historically constructed dimension of the classic has been discussed more recently by Ankhi Mukherjee in her *What is a Classic?* (2014), which explores the postcolonial dimension of some classic works of literature. In recent decades, scholars from different disciplines practising postcolonial, ethnic, and feminist critiques have denounced the persistence of particular Western stereotypes which have dominated the world – and the critical interpretation of it – in the past. As a result, any attempt to read the classics in history should keep these perspectives in mind to avoid falling into the reductionism and anachronism that these recent critical approaches are challenging. Consequently, approaches to the classic in history should consider that 'the invention of modern classics is sustained by a dynamic and variable conversation between the past and the present …, as that conversation goes from being specifically Western to being worldwide'.[13] Mukherjee notes that a classic 'is easily mistaken for a snobbish and conservative question that signals entrenched cultural privilege and overreach.

[12] Pierre Bourdieu, *Outline of a Theory of Practice* (Cambridge: Cambridge University Press, 2009), 78.

[13] Ankhy Mukherjee, *What is a Classic?: Postcolonial Rewriting and Invention of the Canon* (Stanford: Stanford University Press, 2014), 8.

In the context of increasingly globalized structures of labour, trade, environment, warfare, and knowledge, however, the question of the classic is no longer bound to class imperatives, "cognitive acquirement," or the power-knowledge nexus of a colonial canon.'[14]

Following this approach, my intention to transcend the normative canon in my exploration of the classic derived from the recognition of the relevance of postcolonial and gender critiques, and the attempt to blend the universalist dimension of some of the Western historiographical classics I mention in this book with the recent *provincialization* of the West itself.

The historicity of the classic, as described by these critics, leads to the important idea of the 'gradualness' of the classic. Being a classic is not an absolute category. Certain literary and historical works are *more* or *less* classic than others if we consider endurance as their most basic feature, but there are no absolute classics. Horace explains this in quantitative terms: if a work is still around a hundred years after it was written, it must be a classic. Clearly, some historians succeed in achieving a 'surplus of meaning' better than others, but relegating the question of a classic to a given immovable canon or to simply a ranking would contradict the very historicity of the classic. This paradox accompanies the life of a classic: on the one hand, it defines itself by surviving, but on the other, it survives because it receives historical sanction from critics and readers. Its survival depends on criticism – as indeed this book aims to do.

[14] Mukherjee, *What is a Classic?*, 41.

INTRODUCTION

In his popular *Why Read the Classics* (1995), Italo Calvino summarizes most of the conditions and features that make a literary text a classic. Among the points he brings up, he refers to the text's longevity, that it says something about the human condition, implies continuance and consistency, has been enhanced by plagiarism and strengthened by satire, sustains its impact over time, expresses artistic quality, generates critical discourse around itself, allows for re-reading, and provokes thinking in our lives.[15] Calvino agrees with Eliot, Kermode, Coetzee, and Mukherjee regarding the complexity of this category, which, though critically constructed, remains a valid category, applicable to literary texts. Accordingly, the main question facing the research presented in this book is: can we historians apply this category – and its definition – to historical writings?

George Steiner has not touched on the subject of the classic as explicitly as the previous critics, but he highlights a central problem – the apparent neglect by modern historiography of the literary quality of its narratives:

> [M]uch of what passes for history at present is scarcely literate. … The illusion of science and the fashions of the academic tend to transform the young historian into a grey, lean ferret gnawing at the minute fact or figure. He dwells in footnotes and writes monographs in as illiterate a style as possible to demonstrate the scientific bias of his craft.[16]

Steiner's words constitute one of the major incentives for this book: the need historians have to propose, time

---

[15] Italo Calvino, *Perché leggere i classici* (Milano: Oscar Mondadori, 1995).
[16] George Steiner, 'The Retreat from the World', in *Language and Silence* (London: Faber and Faber, 1985), 36–37.

and again, to present our texts with the greatest possible literary quality, which is not incompatible with the transmission of knowledge of the past. Steiner himself quotes C. V. [Cicely Veronica] Wedgwood, a historian who aspired to literariness in her writing, who argued that there is no literary style that may not at some point take away something from the ascertainable outline of truth, which it is the task of scholarship to excavate and re-establish. Steiner concluded: 'But where such excavation abandons style altogether, or harbours the illusion of impartial exactitude, it will light only on dust.'[17]

These reflections lie at the root of my concern for the classic and have led me to write this book. If Eliot was concerned about excessive provincialism in literature, I am concerned with excessive academicism in history, moving from narrow specialization to narcissistic archaeologism. In fact, academia may have become for some historians a kind of straitjacket that precludes them from saying what they consider relevant for themselves and for the society. Professionalism does not guarantee historiographical classicism at all. Inversely, it may complicate it because of its tendency to formalism. It certainly provides the historian with the clues for gaining professional recognition and scholarship progression. It facilitates the struggle for objectivity, a collective enterprise after all – that 'noble dream' nicely described by Peter Novick.[18] It establishes the standards of proofs and

---

[17] Steiner, 'The Retreat', 36.
[18] Peter Novick, *That Noble Dream: The 'Objectivity Question' and the American Historical Profession* (Cambridge: Cambridge University Press, 1998).

presentation – 'the full footnote, the honest bibliography, the accurate citation'.[19] It serves to discriminate reality from imagination. But it puts history under the danger of formalism, of creating the spectre of an impeccable historical construction while perhaps deviating from the essential historical reality. The fight for objectivity is not necessarily the same as the fight for the truth. As the popular wisdom advises, the more are the trees in the woods, the more the general vision of the landscape may be distorted by them, turning the historical operation into a fragmentary or even contradictory narration.

I think these reflections on historical writing from literary critics might lead us away from the danger that E. H. Carr signalled: 'Gerald Brenan [the Hispanist author of *The Spanish Labyrinth* (1943)] once told me that he despaired of finding "truth" with the method of professional historians and that it could only be grasped by the unfettered imaginations in novels.'[20] History had already been declared inferior to literature in antiquity, because of the authority of Aristotle, who was persuaded that

> the distinction between the historian and the poet is not whether they give their accounts in verse or prose … The [real] difference is this: that the one [the historian] tells what happened, the other [the poet] tells the sort of things that can happen. That's why in fact poetry is a more speculative and more 'serious' business than history: for poetry deals with universals, history with particulars.[21]

[19] Peter Gay, *Style in History* (New York: Basic Books, 1974), 209.
[20] E. H. Carr, *Times Literary Supplement*, 23–29 June, 1989.
[21] Aristotle, *Poetics*, John Baxter and Patrick Atherton (eds.) (Montreal: McGill-Queen's University, 1997), 83 (Chapter 9). On the meaning of

Aristotle's warning echoes Eliot's concern with provincialism in literature, just as Brenan's warning comes from the departure of history from the narrative. These dangers are real in history since we should not think that content (the representation of the past through a historical narrative) and form (the structure and style of the narrative) can be dissociated in historiography. We have valuable critical literature at our disposal on issues related to the content of histories written by historians, especially those devoted to methodological, theoretical, and epistemological questions related to the writing of history. But, in contrast, we have very few studies on the formal and literary issues of historiography. This book aims to contribute to that discussion.

* * *

This project does not arise from a preconceived notion of the classic and a canon in historiography. Neither is it born out of an anxiety to delimit a canon of historical works, or to intend to impose my *own* canon, or to make a ranking of the best or worst. Rather, it aims to interrogate these concepts through historiographical analysis and to inquire whether they have always existed or, on the contrary, have been constructed by critics. Moreover, the concept of classic refers directly to the essential question of change and permanence in history, so this project is not simply historiographic, critical,

these Aristotle quotes for history, see Nancy Partner, 'The Fundamental Things Apply: Aristotle's Narrative Theory and the Classical Origins of the Postmodern History', in Nancy Partner and Sarah Foot (eds.), *The SAGE Handbook of Historical Theory* (Los Angeles: SAGE, 2013), 495–507.

or rhetorical, but also properly historical. In using the word 'history' instead of 'historiography' in the title of the book, I play on the double meaning that the word *history* has, in some languages such as English: it refers to both history as past and history as the narrative of the past.

My *longue-durée* approach in historical research, discerning the permanent and changing in the stories of the past, motivates this study on the classic in historiography. The classic is a privileged site for the encounter of permanence and change. Historical texts are also an ideal source for exploring this essential encounter since they continually verify the dynamic interplay between content and form. Historians have sought to recover the content of the past, but they have presented it in very different ways. In the medieval period, for example, the genres of annals, genealogies, autobiographical testimonies, chronicles, and universal and urban histories followed one another. Today, the hegemonic genre of historiography, the monograph, coexists with others of a more literary nature, such as biography and autobiography, and with the great variety resulting from digital platforms, from documentaries to computer games, as well as the performative spectacles of popular festivals. But this plurality of forms in which history has been transmitted is compatible with the unique content the historian tries to explore: the reality of the past.

Much of the historiography of the last half century, from Hayden White's *Metahistory* in 1973 to recent studies on the influence of digital platforms, centres on the question of *how* to convey the realities of the past. White articulated this tendency with the choice of the title of one of the collected volumes of his essays, *The Content of the Form* (1989). This trend emphasizes the study of issues that affect the changing shape of historiography, especially with regard to the question of historical narrative, assuming the theoretical postulates that come from literary criticism – from Northrop Frye and Mikhail Bakhtin to Michel de Certeau and Paul Ricoeur – and those from the theorists of historiography itself, from Frank Ankersmit to Alun Munslow.

However, the proposals presented in this book are, in some sense, countercultural, disruptive, and innovative. The tendency of current historiography – that always reflects the current intellectual and cultural trends – to emphasize discontinuities and ruptures, rather than continuities and permanence, has an explanation that is not only of a conjunctural nature. As Orest Ranum states, those of us who study the theory and practice of history are more inclined to discern change and discontinuity than permanence and continuity.[22] For this reason, I have always thought that attempting to delve into questions of permanence and continuity in historical discourse can balance the scales somewhat. For this purpose, it seemed to me particularly appropriate to locate and define the concepts that are most closely related to the continuity of historical discourse from antiquity to the present, such as durability, the classic, and the canon.

The stability of historical discourse conveyed by the classics might appear as an unintended continuity since

---

[22] Orest Ranum, *Artisans of Glory: Writers and Historical Thought in Seventeenth-Century France* (Chapel Hill: The University of North Carolina Press, 1980), 6.

historians more generally experience the ephemerality of our narratives. Our writings are always surpassed by the following generations' work, either by an enrichment of the available sources that make greater historical accuracy possible or by new perspectives better suited to historical circumstances. These elements shape the content of our narrations. However, contrary to this tendency towards ephemerality, history also shows how certain perspectives have overcome the necessary 'scientific' progressiveness of historical knowledge so that the permanence and durability of certain historical texts challenge the idea that the historical discipline is like a river that flows progressively. This can happen for two reasons, one related to the narrative and language, and the other to the historical content and meaning.

Firstly, because the narrative *form* of given historical texts is so significant that it continues to compel readers, even if new discoveries delegitimize part of its historical *content*, as in narrations by Thucydides, Edward Gibbon, Johan Huizinga, Georges Duby, and Natalie Zemon Davis. As Lionel Gossman has argued, 'As long as literary studies were dominated by rhetoric, the literary character of Buffon, Michelet, Carlyle, or Macaulay was recognized, and these authors were regularly studied as models of style to be followed or avoided.'[23]

Secondly, because the presentation and structuring of the content of the past become a model for future historical representations, as happens with some other modern classics

---

[23] Lionel Gossman, *The Empire Unpossess'd: An Essay on Gibbon's Decline and Fall* (Cambridge: Cambridge University Press, 1981), xiii.

such as texts by Leopold von Ranke (historicism), Fernand Braudel (structuralism), and Edward Thompson (Marxism). Hence Gossman concludes his argumentation: 'At the same time, in its particularity, each [historical] text is a singular utterance, emitted at a specific point in time, the engagement of and individual user of language and of texts with the world. Gibbon's *History*, it seems to me, does not simply convey information. It utilizes other texts, other histories, to create meaning and to bear testimony.'[24]

The inductive observation of this unintended continuity of some historical works generates some difficult questions, which I address in this book. To this end, I examine the five concepts that seem to me the key to a better understanding of this historiographical dynamic: durability, the classic, the canon, genre, and genealogy.

* * *

As in any historical research, I began with the question of primary sources. The project required that I examine narratives that have proven to be particularly long-lived in historiography. Considering that, unlike literature and art, no approximate list of supposedly classical and canonical works in historiography exists, I had to decide on the paradigms that would define my choice. The list of historical works systematically chosen by the available histories of historiography, from Benedetto Croce to Georg Iggers, served as a first step, and I soon saw the similarities among the historians and their works included in these selections.

---

[24] Gossman, *The Empire Unpossess'd*, xiii.

16

Along with this inductive criterion, I also heeded
Roland Barthes's notion that a book enters the pantheon of
classics for the simple reason that it is *there*. Obviously, the
historical works most often cited in this book are the result
of my own particular view of historiography, which is in turn
the result of my own particular historiographical education
and context. They are therefore the fruit of *my* historiographical canon. Nevertheless, without needing to dig much deeper,
any student of history could quote the most characteristic historians and works of the Western tradition: Herodotus' narratives on Persian wars, Thucydides' stories of Peloponnesian
conflicts, Polybius' storytelling of the Roman domination,
Plutarch's comparative biographies, Eusebius' *Ecclesiastical
History*, Augustine's *City of God*, Jean Froissart's chronicles of the Anglo-French Hundred Years' war, Francesco
Guicciardini's urban history of Florence, Edward Gibbon's
Decline and Fall of the Roman Empire, Jules Michelet's *History
of France*, Leopold von Ranke's *History of the Reformation*,
Jacob Burckhardt's *The Civilization of the Renaissance in Italy*,
Johan Huizinga's *The Waning of the Middle Ages*, Fernand
Braudel's *Mediterranean*, Edward Thompson's *The Making
of the English Working Class*, Carlo Ginzburg's *The Cheese
and the Worms*, Natalie Zemon Davis's *The Return of Martin
Guerre*, and Joan Scott's *Gender and the Politics of History*,
among others.

However, this list, like any other attempt at a canon,
satisfies no one, for two reasons. First, a project of these characteristics cannot escape this fate or paradox: it does not seek
to impose a canon, but at the same time it necessarily proposes one. Second, there are few fields more presentist than

the history of historiography, which implies that each period also has certain rules for the choice of a canon. The history of historiography reflects the changing mentalities, cultural sensibilities, and social trends of the time, which is perhaps what makes it so relevant as intellectual history. For instance, historiography today is being greatly enriched by global historiographies beyond the Western tradition. Although I will refer to them, I have not yet been able to use them systematically for my study, firstly because my analysis focuses on the Western tradition, but also because we do not yet have enough perspective to discern whether these new works will enjoy the durability that the others used as primary sources in my book do.

Along with these primary sources, I discovered throughout this project a rich corpus of critical literature, which constitutes the secondary sources of this research. The five concepts analysed in this book lead to philosophical, literary, and historical implications, since they directly refer to categories of temporality, periodization, destiny, continuity, change, and permanence. In addition, the concept of classic encapsulates everything required for its constitution as an event in itself, since, as Paul Ricoeur explains, 'all change enters the field of history as a quasi-event'.[25] For this reason, I argue that, even if philosophers and literary critics have traditionally appropriated these concepts, they also deserve a historicist/historiographical–critical approach. Nevertheless, since historians deal with a real past, they need to address the categories of philosophers at some point; and, since

---

[25] Paul Ricoeur, *Time and Narrative* (Chicago: The University of Chicago Press, 1990), II: 224.

they render their conclusions through the texts, they need to address the categories of literary critics too. This explains why I have turned to these different disciplines for the critical analysis of the historical narratives that I study in this book, as well as to obtain the hermeneutic keys necessary for the understanding of such complex concepts as the classic and the canon.

In this context, I classify the critical and interpretative sources on historical texts in this book into seven fields: (1) *philosophies of history*, the theoretical discussion of history; (2) *histories of historiography*, the historical development of histories which tends to focus on content rather than on form; (3) *critical histories*, which are concerned with the rhetorical conditions and formal aspects of historical writings; (4) *literary criticism*, applied to the analysis of historical narratives; (5) *philosophy*, devoted to the reflection on the concept of the classic and the canon; (6) *sociology*, as it reflects on its own classics; and (7) *biblical studies* – usually framed between literary criticism and theology – devoted specifically to the analysis of the exploration of the concept of the canon, essential to the understanding of the historical formation of the Scriptures.

The first three fields refer to the practice of history and its transformation into an academic discipline from the mid-nineteenth century onwards. These critical–historiographical subdisciplines are closely related, but each group has its own specific practices and roles. The first one, the theory of history, is the most consolidated, since it responds to what has traditionally been called the 'philosophy of history', with Augustine of Hippo, Joachim of Fiore, Giambattista Vico and Hegel considered classics in this subdiscipline. But in recent decades, historians have begun producing philosophy of history, with Benedetto Croce and Robin G. Collingwood leading the transition from philosophy to history.[26] Their works, published mostly during the interwar period and the immediate post-war period, brought the great philosophical debates on time and the past back to historians.

A period of particular significance in the formation of the new philosophy of history was the incorporation of analytic philosophy into the debates on narrative in history during the 1960s. W. B. Gallie justified the work of historians by the power of the temporal dimension of narrative.[27] Luis O. Mink argued that temporal succession did not in itself guarantee the essence of the narrative, but rather the authorial correlation of the various events of a story towards a common goal.[28] Arthur C. Danto, perhaps the most influential of them, created the concept of 'conceptual narrative', arguing that 'a "true" historical account of what actually happened in history would be one which remained on the levels of synchronic classification of the data on the one hand and of diachronic representation of them on the other'.[29]

[26] Benedetto Croce, *Theory and History of Historiography* (London: George G. Harrap, 1917) and Robin G. Collingwood, *The Idea of History* (Oxford: Oxford University Press, 1994 [1946]).

[27] W. B. Gallie, *Philosophy and the Historical Understanding* (New York: Schocken, 1964).

[28] Louis O. Mink, 'The Autonomy of Historical Understanding', *History and Theory* 5 (1966): 24–47.

[29] Hayden White, *Metahistory: The Historical Imagination of Nineteenth-Century Europe* (Baltimore: Johns Hopkins University Press, 1973), 275. Arthur C. Danto, *Analytical Philosophy of History* (Cambridge: Cambridge University Press, 1965).

These analytical philosophers of history were sensitive to the new trends linked with the linguistic turn and the debates around narrative in history. They foreshadowed the key work of Hayden White, *Metahistory* (1973), in which he emphasized the literary dimension of historical texts. Thus, in the decades since the publication of this work, the field of the theory of history has encouraged a rich exchange between philosophers and theorists of history, such as Frank Ankersmit, Alun Munslow, Keith Jenkins, François Hartog, Ethan Kleinberg, Kalle Pihlainen, and Jouni-Matti Kuukkanen.[30] To these historians it should be added the multidisciplinary figure of Michel Foucault, who has inspired the theorists of history too.[31] These scholars' backgrounds in philosophy allow them to engage with important aspects of the historical operation and the practice of history itself. In particular, their reflections on permanence and change in history

---

[30] White, *Metahistory*; Frank Ankersmit, *Sublime Historical Experience* (Stanford: Stanford University Press, 2005); Alun Munslow, *Narrative and History* (New York: Palgrave Macmillan, 2007); Keith Jenkins, *Re-thinking History* (London: Routledge, 2003); François Hartog, *Régimes d'historicité: présentisme et expériences du temps* (Paris: Seuil, 2003); Kalle Pihlainen, *The Work of History: Constructivism and a Politics of the Past* (New York: Routledge, 2019); Ethan Kleinberg, *Haunting History: For a Deconstructive Approach to the Past* (Stanford: Stanford University Press, 2017); Jouni-Matti Kuukkanen, *Postnarrativist Philosophy of Historiography* (New York: Palgrave Macmillan, 2015).

[31] Michel Foucault, *The Archaeology of Knowledge* (New York: Harper, 1972); Foucault, *The Order of Things* (New York: 1973); Foucault, 'Nietzsche, Genealogy, History', in *Language, Counter-Memory, Practice* (Ithaca: Cornell University Press, 1977), 139–164.

INTRODUCTION

and historiography have provided me with a solid theoretical foundation for addressing the question of the classic and the canon, as well as the related concepts of durability, genre, and genealogy.

For the second historical–critical field, the history of historiography, two historiographers of antiquity, Dionysius of Halicarnassus and Lucian of Samosata, have been key to deciphering the codes of the dynamics of the classic and the canon in antiquity, as Gervase of Canterbury did for the Middle Ages. In the mid-twentieth century, Harry Elmer Barnes's and James Westfall Thompson's histories of historical writing acted as forerunners although, admittedly, reduced to the English, German, and French historiographical traditions.[32] But the field has developed since the 1970s, encouraged by the increasing presence of courses on the 'history of historiography' at universities, and has provided me with the necessary heuristic basis for selecting the primary sources for this book, as well as the necessary diachrony to address the question of the classic in historiography. Modern scholars have addressed the history of a discipline based on the historical texts of each period. Some of these historiographers are Arnaldo Momigliano and Peter Brown for the historiography of antiquity[33]; Gabrielle M. Spiegel and Jaume Aurell for

[32] Harry Elmer Barnes, *A History of Historical Writing* (Norman: University of Oklahoma Press, 1938) and James Westfall Thompson, *A History of Historical Writing* (New York: Macmillan, 1942).

[33] Arnaldo Momigliano, *Essays in Ancient and Modern Historiography* (Oxford, 1977); Peter Brown, *Society and the Holy in Late Antiquity* (Los Angeles: University of California Press, 1982).

medieval historiography[34]; Peter Burke, Anthony Grafton, and John Burrow for the Early Modern historiography[35]; Stefan Berger and Georg G. Iggers for nineteenth-century historiography[36]; and Donald Kelley, Daniel Woolf (both early modernists but also modern historiographers), Ernst Breisach, Peter Novick, for twentieth-century historiography.[37] This subgenre is very relevant for my research since it provides the most basic source for it: the catalogue of the

[34] Gabrielle M. Spiegel, *The Past as Text: The Theory and Practice of Medieval Historiography* (Baltimore: The Johns Hopkins University Press, 1994); Jaume Aurell, *Authoring the Past: History, Politics, and Autobiography in Medieval Catalonia* (Chicago: The University of Chicago Press, 2012).

[35] Peter Burke, *The Renaissance Sense of the Past* (New York: St. Martin Press, 1969); Anthony Grafton, *What Was History? The Art of History in Early Modern Europe* (Cambridge: Cambridge University Press, 2007); John W. Burrow, *A History of Histories* (London: Allen Lane, 2007).

[36] Stefan Berger, *Writing National Histories: Western Europe since 1800* (New York: Routledge, 1999); Georg G. Iggers, *The German Conception of History* (Middletown: Wesleyan University Press, 1968).

[37] Donald R. Kelley, *Faces of History: Historical Inquiry from Herodotus to Herder* (New Haven: Yale University Press, 1998); Donald R. Kelley, *Fortunes of History: Historical Inquiry from Herder to Huizinga* (New Haven: Yale University Press, 2003); Donald R. Kelley, *Frontiers of History: Historical Inquiry in the Twentieth Century* (New Haven: Yale University Press, 2006); Ernst A. Breisach, *Historiography: Ancient, Medieval, & Modern* (Chicago: University of Chicago Press, 1983); Georg G. Iggers, *Historiography in the Twentieth Century: From Scientific Objectivity to the Postmodern Challenge* (Middletown: Wesleyan University Press, 2012); Novick, *That Noble Dream*; Daniel Woolf, *A Global History of History* (Cambridge: Cambridge University Press, 2012); Georg G. Iggers, Q. Edward Wang, and Supriya Mukherjee, *A Global History of Modern Historiography* (London: Routledge, 2017).

works of history considered the most representative and qualified of them.

These two traditional critical fields – the 'theory of history' and the 'history of historiography' – have been enriched by a third, which has progressively established itself in the academic literature devoted specifically to the critical analysis of historical texts. In the last forty years, some critics have tried to explore the artistic and literary elements of historical works. Antonis Liakos has explained the intellectual and historiographical conditions that have led to the new critical studies on the rhetorical dimension of history: 'What was new in the final decades of the century was the shift from the epistemology of history to the poetics of history, and from the question of how our knowledge of the past could be reliable, to the question of how we represent history.'[38]

These critics, thus, explore the rhetorical or formal aspects of historical narratives and have introduced into the discourse concepts that include 'narrative form in history' (Leo Braudy), 'style in history' (Peter Gay, John Clive), the 'rhetoric of historical representation' (Jack Hexter, Ann Rigney), 'the rule of metaphor' (Paul Ricoeur), 'melancholy in history' (Peter Fritzsche), 'experimental history' (Alun Munslow and Robert A. Rosenstone), 'history and tropology' (Frank Ankersmit) and 'poetics of history' (Philippe Carrard, Hayden White).[39] These 'critical historians of history' – as

[38] Antonis Liakos, 'Historicising Twentieth-Century Historiography', *Historein* 16 (2017): 139–148, here 145.

[39] Leo Braudy, *Narrative Form in History and Fiction: Hume, Fielding & Gibbon* (Ann Arbor: University Microfilms International, 1970); Gay, *Style in History*; John Clive, *Not by Fact Alone: Essays on the Writing*

Lionel Gossman, himself one of its most prominent practitioners, once called them – have opened the door to a better understanding of historical *writing*, particularly in its literary and narrative dimensions. These new approaches support the consideration of the concept of a classic in historiography, without necessarily borrowing the theoretical concepts and epistemological tools from literature or philosophy. These critics have *rescued* the historiographical criticism of the great historians – Herodotus, Thucydides, Eusebius, Gibbon, Michelet, Burckhardt – for historiographical criticism. Gossman, for example, explains that,

> In the 1930s the literature on Gibbon took the form of
> biography. ... The student of Gibbon in our time [1980s],
> professional and academic, has generally abandoned
> the biographical mode in favour of scholarly analysis of
> Gibbon's place in the history of ideas and the history of
> historiography and of the rhetoric and narrative art of the
> *Decline and Fall*. ... The text of the *Decline and Fall* itself,

and Reading of History (New York: Alfred A. Knopf, 1989); Jack H.
Hexter, *On Historians* (Cambridge: Harvard University Press, 1979);
Ann Rigney, *The Rhetoric of Historical Representation* (Cambridge:
Cambridge University Press, 1990); Paul Ricoeur, *The Rule of Metaphor*
(Toronto: University of Toronto Press, 1977); Peter Fritzsche, *Stranded
in the Present: Modern Time and the Melancholy of History* (Cambridge:
Harvard University Press, 2004); Alun Munslow and Robert A.
Rosenstone (eds.), *Experiments in Rethinking History* (London, 2004);
Frank Ankersmit, *History and Tropology: The Rise and Fall of Metaphor*
(Berkeley: University of California Press, 1994); Philippe Carrard,
*Poetics of the New History: French Historical Discourse from Braudel to
Chartier* (Baltimore: The Johns Hopkins University Press, 1992); White,
Metahistory.

the intellectual and ideological context in which it was produced, and the literary conventions by which it was shaped are now the focus of interest.[40]

In addition to these three historiographical fields, my discussion draws from the reflections of a number of literary critics, mentioned at the beginning of this introduction, who have devoted themselves specifically to the question of the classic in literature, such as Eliot, Kermode, Steiner, Calvino, and Coetzee, to which should be added Erich Auerbach, Northrop Frye, Hans Robert Jauss, and Mikhail Bakhtin.[41]

I have also turned to the philosophers who have addressed the question of the classic, attracted by the semantic and hermeneutic richness of this concept. Their reflections can therefore illuminate more traditional fields, such as literature and art, and other rhetorical activities, such as history. My main sources of inspiration in this direction have been Reinhart Koselleck, Paul Ricoeur, and Hans-Georg Gadamer.[42]

The sixth source of data and inspiration comes from theoretical studies in sociology. An abundant and qualified

[40] Gossman, *The Empire Unpossess'd*, ix.

[41] Erich Auerbach, *Mimesis: The Representation of Reality in Western Civilization* (New York: Doubleday, 1953); Northrop Frye, *Anatomy of Criticism* (Princeton: Princeton University Press, 1957); Hans R. Jauss, *Toward an Aesthetic of Reception* (Minneapolis: University of Minnesota Press, 1982); Mikhail Bakhtin, *The Dialogic Imagination* (Austin: University of Texas Press, 1981).

[42] Reinhart Koselleck, *Futures Past: On the Semantics of Historical Time* (New York: Columbia University Press, 2004); Ricoeur, *Time and Narrative*; Hans-Georg Gadamer, *Truth and Method* (London: Sheed & Ward, 1989).

bibliography on the classics of sociology reflects on whether the concept itself can apply to this social discipline.[43] In their exploration of their own recent classics, sociologists might be spurred by the need to consolidate a very recent social discipline. In its efforts to define itself as an academic discipline, sociology gradually detached from philosophy at the beginning of the twentieth century, especially through its empirical turn. Sociologists' reflections on the classics of their discipline are of particular interest to my own inquiry into the classics of historiography since these are two disciplines that have had to combine scientific, inductive, quantitative, and statistical research with discourse and narration.

The critical bibliography around the classics of sociology has also provided me with key insights, through specific metaphors, on this process. Niklas Luhmann, considered a classic scholar by his colleagues, had, in the beginning, little appreciation for the classics of sociology when he described his own research as 'exegetical gnawing of old theoretical bones'.[44] However, sociologists seem to be very interested

[43] One of the first sociologists (a classic in his discipline himself) to address this question was Robert K. Merton, 'On the "History" and "Systematics" of Sociological Theory', in *On Theoretical Sociology* (New York: Free Press, 1967), 1–37. See also Robert A. Jones, 'On Understanding a Sociological Classic', *American Journal of Sociology* 83 (1977): 279–319; Jeffrey C. Alexander, 'The Centrality of the Classics', in Anthony Giddens and Jonathan Turner (eds.), *Social Theory Today* (Stanford: Stanford University Press, 1987), 11–57; Peter Baehr, *Founders, Classics, Canons, Modern Disputes over the Origins and Appraisal of Sociology's Heritage* (New York: Routledge, 2002).
[44] Niklas Luhmann, 'Neuere Entwicklungen in der Systemtheorie', *Merkur* 42 (1988): 292–300, here 292.

in their old bones. Bones are, after all, something basic to
hold on to. And just as a healthy body needs a stable skeleton, the bolder theoretical edifices that sociologists construct
for themselves also need a skeleton to which to attach free-
floating thoughts. These sociologists, reflecting on the classics of their own discipline, have shown me that in times of
rapid changes in thinking when the half-life of new thoughts
seems to be getting shorter and shorter, the classics offer a
safe haven.

Dirk Kaesler offers another metaphor as he compares
sociology to an old house continually under construction.
Over time, the building becomes a large complex with many
floors, corridors, tunnels, and windows of many kinds. In this
house, however, there is a large common kitchen where the
residents meet regularly and which supplies the house with
energy. The works of the classics of sociology or, more precisely, their concepts, terms, hypotheses, and research results,
provide the energy for the heart of sociological research in the
present and the future.[45]

Finally, the chapter devoted to the analysis of the
canon is theoretically based on the rich critical output of
biblical theology, the basis of the creation of history as a scientific discipline in mid-nineteenth-century Germany.[46] As
historians and their discipline do not have a magisterium

[45] Dirk Kaesler (ed.), *Klassiker der Soziologie*, 2 vols. (München: C. H.
Beck 1999).
[46] Robert Alter, *Canon and Creativity. Modern Writing and the Authority
of Scripture* (New Haven: Yale University Press, 2000) and Aviezer
Tucker, *Our Knowledge of the Past: A Philosophy of Historiography*
(Cambridge: Cambridge University Press, 2004), 53–59.

that generates a closed list of canonical books, critical biblical studies can enrich theoretical perspectives on the creation and fixation of a canon, but not so much on its historical dynamics. Indeed, in the course of this research, I have come to realize that many of the criticisms levelled against the canon as hegemonic or rigid stem from a misguided projection of the logics of biblical criticism onto historical criticism.

In my approach to the classics of history, I have also kept in mind the apophatic method. This is a form of theological thinking and religious practice which attempts to approach the Divine by negation, to speak only in terms of what may not be said about the perfect goodness that is God: it cannot be affirmed, but neither can it be denied.[47] Especially at the beginning of my research, I was confronted with the same well-known dilemma of St. Augustine regarding the definition of time: 'For what is time? Who could find any quick or easy answer to that? Who could even grasp it in his thought clearly enough to put the matter into words? ... What, then, is time? If no one asks me, I know; if I want to explain it to someone who asks me, I do not know.'[48]

In this context, the classic and the canon would function as an *aporia*, as François Hartog has described it recently in his research on the *chronos*.[49] I do not deny that in the

---

[47] William Franke, *On the Universality of What Is Not: The Apophatic Turn in Critical Thinking* (Notre Dame: University of Notre Dame Press, 2020).

[48] Saint Augustine of Hippo, *The Confessions 11.14.17*, David Vincent Meconi (ed.) (San Francisco: Ignatius, 2012), 343.

[49] François Hartog, *Chronos: The West Confronts Time* (New York: Columbia University Press, 2022), 1.

future someone may take the same approach to the classic
or the canon of historiography from the apophatic method
but, in the end, I had to put it aside, in order to focus on the
arguments of historical and literary critics and hermeneutic
philosophers.

In the end, my reflection on the classic in history
centres on the data, ideas, and interpretations of these seven
groups: theorists of history, historiographers, history critics, literary critics, philosophers, sociologists, and scholars coming from the critical analysis of Scripture. They deal
with both the content and the form of historical narrations
to a greater or lesser extent. Since some of them can focus
on the formal aspects of history, they may give more clues to
the understanding of the historical classic – and, crucially, to
what distinguishes the classics of history from the classics of
literature – since 'history is ultimately determined by formal
and rhetorical structures', as Susan Gearhart puts it.[50] As a
consequence, this book analyses historiographically, proceeds
critically, and searches for philosophical explanations.

* * *

The five concepts chosen for this historiographical–critical
exploration are durability, classic, canon, genre, and genealogy. These concepts, analysed in each chapter, convey
different spheres of literary and historical reality, providing clues to understanding the dynamics of permanence
and change. They reveal the essential tension between

---

[50] Susan Gearhart, *The Open Boundary of History and Fiction* (Princeton:
Princeton University Press, 1984), 7.

continuities/discontinuities and content/form, which I try
to disentangle in this book. All of them have traditionally
served as tools for the interpretation of historical texts *and*
historical reality.

The first chapter focuses on the concept of durabil-
ity. When we think in terms of the durability of historical
texts, some works instantly come to mind, from Herodotus',
Thucydides', and Polybius' war narratives to Jules Michelet's
History of France, Leopold von Ranke's *History of the
Reformation*, Jacob Burckhardt's *The Civilization of the
Renaissance in Italy*, Fernand Braudel's *Mediterranean*, and
Edward Thompson's *The Making of the English Working
Class*. Historians generally perceive them as durable texts,
part of a canon of history and historiography. I examine
the conditions that might be considered necessary for historical writing to achieve durability, justify why these and
other historical texts support the potential for durability,
speculate regarding the conditions of creation and reception that enabled this longevity, and discuss the practical
lessons we might obtain from this inquiry. I try to establish the specific conditions for durability of historical texts,
focusing on what I call the 'effect of contemporaneity' and
the connections between the concepts of durability and the
'practical past'.

Following the logic of my inductive proceeding in
the book, I locate the analysis of durability in the first chapter
because it is the most visible of the five concepts. Its experience does not depend on critics' consensus or readers'
agreement. Rather, the notion of durability conveys the empirical fact that the memory of these texts remains not only in

our readings but also in historians' imagination, teachings, examples, and quotations. Historiographical durability is the empirical quality of preservation, longevity, and perpetuation of certain historical texts which have overcome the passage of time. Its factual quality enables historical–empirical observation, as its intrinsic relation with time itself encourages historiographical–theoretical speculation. That a historical text is durable does not mean that its meaning and interpretations are closed and univocal. On the contrary, durable historical writings are usually susceptible – and this lies at the heart of their durability – to multiple readings, criticisms, and interpretations.

I engage durability in Chapter 1 to gain understanding of what a classic in history is (Chapter 2) and how the logic of the canon functions (Chapter 3). The classic and the canon 'involve the dimension of criticism, or interpretive traditions that contest the definition of literary value'.[51] Durability is primarily related to temporal validation, the classic refers to what is new and old in history, and the canon requires external verification by critical observation and consensual agreement. Certain historical works might certainly fall under these three categories simultaneously – everybody would include Herodotus' *Histories* in a list of durable, classic, and canonical works – but this is compatible with the fact these three concepts deserve diverse approaches, examinations, definitions, and analyses of internal rules because they respond to very different epistemic and rhetorical realities.

---

[51] Mukherjee, *What is a Classic?*, 31.

Chapter 2 deals with the analysis of the complex reality of the classic, a central inquiry in this book. What is the classic in history? How do we define a classic in historical writing? I discuss in this chapter to what extent historians should engage the concept of the classic. If one assumes that the historical text is not only a referential account but also a literary narrative, then the concept of the classic becomes one of the keys to understanding the historical text – and may improve our understanding not only of historiography but of history itself.

I argue in this chapter that it is possible to identify a category of a classic text in some historical writings, precisely because of the 'literariness' they possess without losing their specific historical condition. Because of their narrative element, some historical texts share some of the features assigned to classic literary texts – that is, endurance, timelessness, universal meaningfulness, resistance to historical criticism, susceptibility to multiple interpretations, and ability to function as models. Yet, since historical texts do not construct imaginary worlds but reflect external realities, they also have to achieve some specific features according to this referential content and without damaging the pastness of the past – that is, surplus of meaning, historical use of metaphors, and a certain effect of contemporaneity and appropriation of 'literariness'.

As I try to show in Chapter 2, the concept of the classic is probably the most comprehensive of the five concepts – and the reason I foreground it as the title of this book. A classic embodies both permanence and change, being durable and historical at the same time, conveying convention and novelty, able to share essentiality and contextuality, merging history and systematics, becoming a source of permanent inspiration, looking to the past and the future as the cover image suggests, and functioning as a paradigmatic model for future art and writing. In historiography, classics have created multiple and diverse interpretations without losing their original integrity. We can think of Herodotus' *Persian Wars*' ethnologic approach, Augustine's *City of God*'s intriguing eschatological vision, Gibbon's *Decline and Fall of the Roman Empire*'s deep reflection on rising and decadence beyond its particular case study, Michelet's *History of France*'s praise of the people as a historical actor, Burckhardt's *Civilization of the Renaissance*'s permanent model of inquiry of the rules governing the beauty, Braudel's *Mediterranean*'s structural synchronization of the three durations, and Hayden White's *Metahistory*'s interpretative keys for historical texts considered as liteary artifacts. They provide glimpses of the structure of historical consciousness, models of historical writing, places of reflection on the great historical questions, and, by implication, 'makes them worthy of study and reflection long after their scholarship has become outmoded and their arguments have been consigned to the status of commonplaces of the culture moments of composition'.[52]

The canon, analysed in Chapter 3, is the most complex of the five concepts examined in this book. In theory, it represents the consensual enshrinement of particular texts through history. But, in practice, the problem lies in the verification categorization or classification of this consensus. Traditionally,

---

[52] Hayden V. White, *The Content of the Form* (Baltimore: Johns Hopkins University, 1987), 180.

because of the effects of biblical studies, we have considered that a canon is closed, and that there cannot be additions or deletions. But, unlike the biblical narratives and the establishment of the canon by the authority of the Church, the historical texts do not have a higher authority capable of generating a closed list of canonical books. This makes the approach to the canon in historical texts more complex, but also more fascinating.

Unlike a classic, a canonical work is not a model: it comes from a golden age that cannot be recaptured but still endures. Yet, as postcolonial thinkers such as Mukherjee have argued, 'canonicity implies a formation of a corpus, the congealing of the "literary art of Memory", ... the making up of a list of books requisite for a literary education, and the formation of an exclusive club, however painstakingly contested the rules of inclusion (and exclusion) may be'.[53] So, the canon has also practical functions which make it susceptible to criticism and change. Thus, even if the notion of canon and the classic are closely related, the latter may not be reduced to the former, because the classic is primarily a singular act of literature, while the canon is a kind of 'aristocracy of texts' which may change depending on historical circumstances and consensual agreement.[54]

The task of constructing a canon has already been done for Western literature by critics such as Harold Bloom,

---

[53] Mukherjee, *What is a Classic?*, 31. The phrase 'the literary art of Memory', in Harold Bloom, *The Western Canon* (New York: Harcourt Brace, 1994), 17.

[54] Mukherjee, *What is a Classic?*, 31. The phrase 'an aristocracy of texts', in John Gillory, 'The Ideology of Canon-Formation: T. S. Eliot and Cleanth Brooks', *Critical Inquiry* 10 (1983): 173–178, here 175.

a task whose results have been approved by many but, arguably, rejected by many others. Yet it has not been done for history – the discussion about its eventual convenience has not yet occurred. From the 1970s onwards, postmodernism and postcolonial criticism have reactivated the disapproval of the canon. Its academic and pedagogical usefulness remains challenged by historians who have generally been sceptical of its critical value, its role as an instrument of hierarchization, and its standard of quality. Both the justification for the existence of the canon *in* history – which affects its content and function – and the criteria for the selection of an alleged canon *of* history – which affects its form and is concretized in a list – have been questioned.

Assuming these disagreements, but also in the obvious interest of this concept, Chapter 3 examines the place of the canon in history, arguing its relevance in history and historiography: what it says about the problems of permanence and change, its remission to a lost golden age, its formation, key turning points, convenience, usefulness, and the desirability of its existence itself. This leads to questions such as: what determines the systematic inclusion and exclusion of texts in bibliographical lists or in the indexes of the histories of historiographies? Why do the major canonical works usually imply a break with the past but, paradoxically, remain there when later works enter the list?

In my past–present approach to the canon, I conceive it as an imprint in the present of a common experience in the past, rather than as an ideological imposition in the present taking advantage of a common experience in the past. As a consequence, the question is not so much the existence of the canon, because whenever one canon loses its status, another arrives to replace it. We tend to think that what we defend in the present is the 'best', but historians know that 'the best' in the past can be surpassed – and, in fact, it is always surpassed – by something 'even better' in the future. So, it is not so much a question of challenging the presence of the canon – which is an obvious historical and rhetorical reality – but what kind of canon serves any given time, seen in ethical and moral terms.

In this chapter I also approach the question of what distinguishes the classic from the canon. It refers to their different potential for formalization – more abstract in the classic and more visible in the canon. I argue that this 'something structured and clublike' which characterizes the canon is a concept applicable to history, without necessarily contradicting my own idea, which I develop in this chapter, of seeing canonicity as something more liquid and protean than it is usually thought. In addition, I try to develop an idea that seems to be crucial to the thesis argued in this book: that the canon conveys continuity and discontinuity, emergence and permanence, simultaneously.

The fourth chapter of the book discusses the question of the plurality of historical genres, as well as the inductive verification that many of the classics in historiography have been pioneers in the use of some particular historical genre. This diversity shows that history is a more complex rhetorical activity than the nineteenth-century founders of this academic discipline imagined. The study of the genres chosen by historians is a privileged site for the analysis of the relationship between content and form in the historical operation, between permanence and change in history/historiography.

I argue that the shifting nature of historians' genre choices may be defined as historicist. This allows me to challenge the formal stability of the historical narratives, alleged by those who try to reduce the practice of history to a scientific operation. The examination of the variety of genres in which history is being represented immediately leads to important issues affecting historiography – especially those related to the generation of the canon in historiography – and, in general, the transmission of knowledge. The study of the multiplicity of genres practised by historians through history helps to understand the relationship between content and form, between the message and the medium, but at the same time its necessary distinction.

Though the genre is one of the key concepts of literary criticism, it has rarely been used in and applied to historical discourse. Nevertheless, it constitutes an ideal inductive platform to explore how a permanent content may survive in the enormous diversity of the genres in which history has been transmitted through history.

Finally, the analysis of the genres allows us to explore the concept of 'nature' – that is, the possibility of permanent surviving principles beyond the variety of specific historical contexts and multiples forms of representation, something immediately verified in the classic and the canon. The plurality of genres deployed by historians demonstrates that genres had no formal 'natures', which is to say, inherent substances or elements in historiography. But we need systems of practical classifications – open systems – subject to the mixture, change, and displacement according to the exigencies of different social and cultural situations. Yet, as Hayden White has argued, 'although genres had no natures, they most definitely had *histories*. This meant, among other things, that the best way to study the forms and contents of any mode of cultural expression, and the ways in which forms and contents were fused in any given moment of a society's evolution, was *historically*.'[55]

In the end, genres emphasize the changing forms of literature and history – but they do not give clues about the possibility of permanent principles in its content.

In the final part of the book, I engage the question of genealogy, understood as a locus of encounter between continuity and discontinuity. Unlike the classic or the canon, concepts which are more closely linked to the tradition of literary criticism, genealogy also has deep philosophical implications. It therefore has both a rhetorical and an experiential dimension. The two facets of genealogy – the continuity of the narrative 'genesis' and the discontinuity of the philosophical 'logos' – reflect this duality. So the analysis of genealogy, in its double dimension, continues the inquiry of the preceding chapters into the dynamics of the classics and canon. My discussion on genealogy – and my decision to include it in this book – is based on the conviction that 'genealogy' has been for much of the past an ally of the concepts of the classical and the canon. I argue that its function as *nemesis* of the classic and the canon has drawn attention only recently, in its Foucauldian dimension. For this reason, its analysis demands the same historicist – and *genealogical* – approach I propose

---

[55] Hayden White, 'Reflections on "Gendre" in the Discourses of History', *New Literary History* 40, 4 (2009): 867–877, here 868. Emphasis in the original.

with the concept of 'historical genres' in Chapter 4: this chapter therefore begins with genealogies as practised by the early Greek historians and ends with the resemantisation of the concept proposed by Foucault.

Genealogy has become a key concept in humanities, a centre of convergence of the problems associated with the continued interaction between permanence and change in history – and historiography. This chapter explores the modern development of genealogies after Nietzsche's alleged foundational statement and its Foucauldian reception, which emphasizes that there are no continuities in history but episodic emergencies. But it also seeks to connect these new modern and postmodern formulations of the genealogy with the others provided from Greek historiography to nineteenth-century national histories, which say much more about continuities, permanencies, and traditions than about discontinuities, ruptures, and emergences. I emphasise the polysemy of the concept of genealogy – the intriguing question of how one signifier (*signifiant*) can have encompassed such diverse meanings-signified (*signifié*) throughout history – and try to locate what has remained and what has changed in this long trajectory.

With the analysis of genealogy, the secondary sources move from literary criticism to philosophy. Modern philosophers such as Nietzsche and Foucault have used it as a key concept for discontinuity, change, and subversion. My interest – and my concern – in introducing this concept in my book lies in the fact that the specific meaning of genealogy may have shifted as it has circulated in modern and postmodern philosophical academic discourse. For this reason,

I posit that a historicist analysis of the concept may clarify the content that has been assigned to it in each period, and complete my approach to the concepts of the classic and the canon.

This would also elude the misunderstandings that, even among specialists in history and philosophy, have derived from the complex relationship between content and form – between meaning and signifier – that the notion of genealogy has carried over time. I argue that, from its first explicit use as a historical genre by early Greek historiography to the national history developed in nineteenth-century Europe, the emphasis of genealogy lay on the etymological sense marked by the first half of the term – a genetic one: *genesis* and pedigree. In contrast, in Late Modernity, from the genealogy of the spirit devised by Hegel to its moral application in Nietzsche and discursive approach in Foucault, the concept has pivoted towards the meaning suggested by the second half of the term, etymologically considered – a philosophical one: *logos*. Through this historicist approach to genealogy, we obtain some clues regarding the dynamics of permanence and change in history and historiography, especially those related to the most visible face of the discontinuities caused by subversion. In the end, a closer look at these aspects of genealogy allows for a better understanding of the dynamics of permanence and change associated with the concepts of the classical and the canon.

Among the five related concepts analysed in this book, I argue that we should engage durability first, to gain an understanding of what a classic in history is and how a canon should be constructed (or not), and then to the concepts of genre and genealogy – both clearly sharing some varieties of permanence and change. Some historical works might certainly fall under these five categories at the same time, but this is compatible with the fact they deserve diverse approaches, examinations, definitions, and analyses of internal rules because they respond to very different epistemic and rhetorical realities: durability is primarily related to temporal validation, while classic is about what is new and old in history, the canon requires external verification by critical observation and consensual agreement, the genre is constructed by audiences and critics, and genealogy implies the ambivalence of the *genesis* (sense of continuity) and the *logos* (emphasis on disruption).

The conclusions of the volume summarize some of the key ideas developed in the five chapters and launches some hypotheses about the main questions addressed in the book on the dialectics between permanence and change, between continuities and discontinuities in history. For too long, historians have usually left the analysis of the historical classical in the hands of literary critics and literary authors. Some decades ago, Thomas Mann captured this universalism in the narratives of some of the Greco–Roman historians: 'Anyone who has studied [Thucydides'] *Peloponnesian War* and Cicero's speeches and letters can be said to know enough about politics once and for all.'[56] This book attempts to fill this gap in the historiography not only by pointing out the *event* of the

---

[56] 'Wer den Peloponnesischen Krieg und Ciceros Reden und Briefe studiert hat, von dem kann man sagen, dass er im Politischen ein fur allemal genug Weiss', in Thomas Mann, *Altes und Neues. Kleine Prosa aud füng Jahrzehnten* (Frankfurt: S. Fischer, 1953), 373.

existence of the classical among historical narratives, but also by critically *interpreting* it. The dual historical–historiographical dimension of this project reflects my own itinerary, in which I have combined historical research of the medieval period with historiographical speculation, as materialized in the main questions which I will try to answer in the next pages.

1

The Conditions for Durability

My work has been composed,
not for the applause of today's hearing,
but as a possession for all time.

Thucydides, Histories

Only strong personalities can endure history;
the weak are extinguished by it.

Friedrich Nietzsche, The Use and Abuse of History

When we think in terms of the durability of historical texts, some works such as Herodotus' *Persian Wars*, Thucydides' *Peloponnesian War*, Edward Gibbon's *Decline and Fall of the Roman Empire*, Jules Michelet's *History of the French Revolution*, or Jacob Burckhardt's *The Civilization of the Renaissance in Italy*, among many others, immediately come to mind.[1] These works and models of that complex operation that we call history still play a part, in one way or another, in our cultural and historiographical landscape. They are not – and probably will never be – as well known as their counterparts in literature, such as Homer's *Iliad*, Dante's *Divine Comedy*, Cervantes' *Quixote*, Shakespeare's plays, and Dostoevsky's novels. Yet historians accept them as durable texts, part of a canon of history, whose reading enriches us as

---

[1] Earlier versions of portions of this chapter appeared as 'Writing Beyond Time: The Durability of Historical Texts', *History and Theory* 56 (2018): 50–70.

44

historians and as citizens. We could disagree on the details of the specific list of works that deserve to be called durable (this would otherwise be the task of building a hierarchy based on the concept of a canon, which is dealt with in Chapter 3) but, in any case, the fact of its duration is too evident to require a theoretical justification. Yet what does require a justification is *why* these and other historical texts have demonstrated durability, what conditions of creation and reception enabled this longevity, and what practical lessons we could learn from this fact.

The problem lies in finding the optimal cultural context within which this discussion might happen. Though Nietzsche might be considered one of the foundational figures of postmodernism, he would probably not be happy today with the ephemeral character of current historiographical trends, if we consider the epigraph of this chapter. In the last fifty years, historians have experienced a good number of *turns*, witnessed the succession of many *new* histories, and promoted the emergence of many *de-* and *post-* tendencies. In the context of rapidly developing theories and the shifting epistemic panorama, historians are compelled to seek labels that might define these new movements, which even include reiterative formulas such as 'new-new' histories or 'post-post' structuralisms and modernisms.[2] Consequently, historians appear to be experiencing difficulties in locating or identifying

[2] Ignacio Olábarri, '"New" New History: A Longue Durée Structure', *History and Theory* 34 (1995): 1–29; see also the chapter 'Postmodernity as the Age of Dominant Change: Poststructuralist Postmodernist', in Ernst Breisach (ed.), *On the Future of History* (Chicago: The University of Chicago Press, 2003), 57–166.

an 'enduring' history, within a shifting theoretical context and rapid generational transitions.

In this historiographical age of the ever-changing, to acknowledge that certain historical texts might be said to have achieved permanence might appear, at first, a subversive move. But I argue in this book that it is a necessary move in a fast-moving and fluctuating world. We have to try to overcome our natural overemphasis on the importance of our own time, a tendency usually called presentism. As has been argued by François Hartog, presentism has now replaced medieval traditionalism, early modern antiquarianism, and nineteenth-century futurism: 'While the past had dominated the old regime of historicity, and the future had taken on the leading role under the new regime, during the present regime only the present remained.'[3]

This *presentist* spirit moved T. S. Eliot to reflect on the condition of the classic in a lecture in 1944, when the last reverberations of the British Empire conditioned his perspective, leading him to reject any form of 'provincialism'.[4] We should be able to establish a firm balance between the past and the present, the enduring and the transient, since durable texts 'possess intrinsic qualities that endure, but possess also an openness to accommodation which keeps them alive under

[3] Hartog, *Chronos*, ix. See also, Hartog, *Régimes d'historicité*, 209. On the different perceptions of time, in accordance with the spirit of each epoch, see Gabrielle M. Spiegel, 'In the Mirror's Eye: The Writing of Medieval History in America', in A. Molho and G. R. Wood (eds.), *Imagined Histories: American Historians Interpret the Past* (Princeton, NJ: Princeton University Press, 1998), 238–262.

[4] See Eliot, 'What Is a Classic?', 53–71.

endlessly varying dispositions', as Frank Kermode suggests.[5]
We should also reflect on what is permanent in history, since,
paradoxically, it is the only way to discern what is really *new*
in history, as opposed to an adjustment or as a result of the
evolution of a paradigm, borrowing Thomas Kuhn's concept.
As Peter Burke explains, 'like scientific revolutions, historical
revolutions are constantly being discovered these days, and
our conceptual currency is in serious danger of debasement'.[6]
Inflation may function as a temporary therapy but it does not
provide stability and permanence.

Thus, surrounded as we are by the exaltation of innovation over tradition, I will examine in this chapter the conditions
that might be considered necessary for historical writing to
achieve durability and discuss what practical lessons we might
obtain from this inquiry. The dual historical-historiographical
dimension of the concept of durability explains the two main
questions which I will try to examine. First, we perceive the
fact that there are some historical texts that are quite simple
and durable, so that we may also inductively analyse how
they function, and what qualities might have contributed to
making them that way. I will approach this question with the
help of some concepts from literary criticism and philosophy:
chronotope, the effect of contemporaneity, temporalization,
and timelessness. Second, since the very concept of durability

[5] Kermode, *The Classic*, 43–44. See also Kenneth Burke, *Permanence and Change: An Anatomy of Purpose* (Indianapolis, IN: Bobbs-Merrill, 1965).
[6] Peter Burke, 'Ranke the Revolutionary', in Georg G. Iggers and James M. Powell (eds.), *Leopold von Ranke and the Shaping of the Historical Discipline* (Syracuse, NY: Syracuse University Press, 1990), 36–44, here 37.

has historical-temporal connotations, we can wonder whether there *should* be works that have such power, which leads me to delve into the double dimension of the 'historical past' and the 'practical past' recently emphasized by some theorists. This second question has evident normative implications, which I will try to approach at the end of the chapter, justifying why I argue that the reading and examination of these durable texts should be promoted among historians and may serve as landmarks of historical training.

Chronotope

Literary critics such as T. S. Eliot, J. M. Coetzee, and Frank Kermode, among others, agree on the ability of certain authors to create lasting works, privileging Virgil as the model of durability and classicism. To be sure, transpositions between literary criticism and historical criticism require caveats, since the experience of the durability of literary texts differs from that of historical texts, which are often more subject to the consequences of time. Leopold von Ranke gestures directly to this point when he states that 'while accomplished poetical creations are immortal, even outstanding historical works become outdated'.[7] In addition, Aristotle's conviction regarding the prominence of the universalism of literature over the particularism of history lies in the fact that creative writing transcends the requirement of the referentiality of historical

---

[7] Leopold von Ranke in a review of Enrico Caterino Davila's *History of the French Civil Wars*, quoted in Rudolf Vierhaus, 'Historiography between Science and Art' in *Leopold von Ranke*, 61–69, here 62.

narrations. James Joyce once said of his *Ulysses* that, 'I've put in so many enigmas and puzzles that it will keep the professors busy for centuries over what I meant, and that's the only way of ensuring one's immortality.'[8] His strategy may function for a novel but would be untenable in an historical narrative.

Notwithstanding this distinction between the durability of historical and literary writing, certain literary concepts may help elucidate the problem. Durability leads directly to the notion of coordination of space/time, embodied in Mikhail Bakhtin's concept of chronotope, 'the intrinsic connections of temporal ('chronos') and spatial ('topos') relationship that are artistically expressed in literature'.[9] Bakhtin refers here to the ability of literature to create a coherent sense of coordination between space and time, and narrate in accordance with it. He offers in his analysis some characteristic developments of narrative chronotopes, such as the genres of biography and autobiography, medieval chivalric romance, and other examples of global novels such as those by Cervantes, Rabelais, or Dostoevsky.[10] All these genres have evident parallelisms with history and, as

---

[8] Richard Ellmann, *James Joyce* (Oxford: Oxford University Press, 1959), 535.

[9] Mikhail Bakhtin, 'Forms of Time and of the Chronotope in the Novel: Notes Toward a Historical Poetics', in Mikhail Bakhtin (ed.), *The Dialogic Imagination* (Austin: University of Texas Press, 1981), 84.

[10] Bakhtin, 'Forms of time', 111. For the application of this concept to historiography see Hayden White, 'The Nineteenth-Century as Chronotope', in Hayden White (ed.), *The Fiction of Narrative* (Baltimore, MD: The Johns Hopkins University Press, 2010), 237–246 and Fredric Jameson, *The Political Unconscious* (Ithaca, NY: Cornell University Press, 1981), 210–213.

Bakhtin explains, with 'some general characteristics of the methods used to express time in these works'.[11] For instance, *Don Quixote* reveals the parodied hybridization of the 'alien, miraculous world' – chronotope of medieval chivalric romances – with the 'high road winding through one's native land' – chronotope of the picaresque novel contemporary to Cervantes. Bakhtin shows that chronotopes are organizing centres for the fundamental narrative events of a novel and, analogically, of historical works.

When one considers Bakhtin's chronotope as a condition of durability, some historical texts come to mind, ones that have opted for long duration and synchronization between the narrated past and the lived present. This way, they can create that particular sense of coordination between space and time, and between the remote past and the present. Jacob Burckhardt's *The Civilization of the Renaissance in Italy* (1860), for instance, synchronizes several spaces and periods such as 'Classic Antiquity', 'Carolingian Renaissance', 'Twelfth-Century Renaissance', and 'Italian Early Modern Renaissance'. He projects all of them to the present of the readers, who may apply the discussion to their own culture. Burckhardt achieves in his text what Bakhtin described as the ability of 'literary artistic chronotope' of fusing 'spatial and temporal indicators … into one carefully thought-out concrete whole. Time, as it were, *thickens*, takes on flesh, becomes artistically visible; likewise, space becomes charged and responsive to the movements of time, plot, and history. This intersection of axes and fusion of indicators characterizes the

---

[11] Bakhtin, 'Forms of Time', 146.

artistic chronotope.'[12] Thanks to this, and beyond its apparent anachronism, its generalizations, and that most of its content has been critically surpassed by the work of later Renaissance scholars, *The Civilization of the Renaissance* has achieved a durability that has been highlighted by Benjamin Nelson among many others: '[R]arely has a historical work had so persistent an influence.'[13]

Another example comes from one of the founders of the French historical schools of the Annales. In his ambitious long-term analysis (*longue-durée*) of the feudal society of eleventh- to fourteenth-century Europe, published in 1938, Marc Bloch connected the specific problems of medieval society with modern and contemporary social challenges. After hundreds of pages of a detailed examination of how feudal societies functioned, he described feudalism as a 'type of society' with an 'essential element' – that is, a concept that goes beyond time itself, and also serves modern societies.[14] His short but enlightening chapter 'The Persistence of European Feudalism', at the end of his book, illustrates how detailed research into a particular historical topic may open broad perspectives that contemporary readers might apply to their particular political and social experiences.[15] Indeed, I argue that Bloch's control of the chronotope ('the intrinsic connections

---

[12] Bakhtin, 'Forms of Time', 84. Emphasis in the original.

[13] Benjamin Nelson, 'Introduction', in Jacob Burckhardt (ed.), *The Civilization of the Renaissance in Italy* (New York: Harper, 1958), 3–19, here 4.

[14] Marc Bloch, *Feudal Society. Vol. 2. Social Classes and Political Organization* (Chicago: The University of Chicago Press, 1968), 442.

[15] Bloch, *Feudal*, 448–452.

THE CONDITIONS FOR DURABILITY

of temporal and spatial relationship') and his synchrony (his ability of making the past and the present harmonious) made his *Feudal Society* worthy of durable and continuing historical and sociological interest.

Fernand Braudel's *La Méditerranée et le monde méditerranéen a l'époque de Philippe II* (1949) is another key example of how the effective deployment of chronotope supports the durability of historical texts. At first, Braudel aimed to analyse a relatively short time period, from 1550 to 1660, of the evolution of the Mediterranean. Yet, in order to understand the whole picture, he examined the three big spatial structures – geology formations, physical geography, and human landscapes – and three great temporal synchronic rhythms – short, middle, and long duration.[16] Braudel's historical analysis provides a holistic historical picture that has inspired the work of historians for decades, as well as professionals in other social sciences such as geography and sociology. The astonishing amount of continuing scholarly work on the Mediterranean as a whole might stem from the broad perspective that Braudel proposed.[17]

In Burckhardt's *Renaissance*, Bloch's *Feudal Society*, Braudel's *Mediterranean*, and other durable historical texts, the chronotope functions as a combination of temporal, spatial, and sociocultural categories that replace one-dimensional concepts of periods. This explains why Hayden White argues

---

[16] Fernand Braudel, *La Méditerrané et le monde méditerranéen à l'èpoque de Philippe II* (Paris: Colin, 1966).

[17] Jaume Aurell, 'Autobiographical Texts as Historiographical Sources: Rereading Fernand Braudel and Annie Kriegel', *Biography* 29 (2006): 425–445.

that, 'for historical studies, the idea of the chronotope has advantages over the notion of the period in a number of ways [since it] demands a greater degree of specificity and of referential concreteness than does the notion of the "period"'.[18] Chronotopes enable these historians to construct 'strategies of containment' and 'modes of exclusion', to borrow Jameson's phrases, which allows them to create generalizations and conceptualizations such as 'the spirit of the age' (Burckhardt), 'the dominant structures of hegemony' (Braudel) and 'modes of production' (Bloch).[19] These conceptualizations permit readers to make deductions, establish interrelations and inferences, and mark continuities and discontinuities to create a general picture and imagine analogies and parallelism with their own cultures.

Yet, at this point, the difference between historical and literary accounts re-emerges and helps us understand Ranke's remark – or, better, Ranke's complaint – regarding the contrast between the immortality of certain literary narratives and the ephemeral existence of even the most outstanding historical texts: 'while accomplished poetical creations are immortal, even outstanding historical works become outdated'.[20] We might argue that literature generally contains semantic and rhetorical elements that transcend temporal and spatial structures *external* to the text, while historical accounts are inevitably subject to them. As Reinhart Koselleck puts it, 'that a "history" pre-exists extra-linguistically ... sets limits to [its]

---

[18] White, 'The Nineteenth-Century', 242.
[19] Jameson, *The Political Unconscious*, 213.
[20] Quoted in Vierhaus, 'Historiography', 62.

representational potential', so that 'only temporal structures, that is, those internal to and demonstrable in related events, can articulate the material factors proper to this [historical] domain of inquiry'.[21] The constrained epistemic nature of history may explain why durability is more difficult to achieve in historical than in literary texts but does not make it entirely impossible.

Effect of Contemporaneity

Koselleck adds one crucial condition to those of the space/time and past/present coordination for the achievement of durability. He distinguishes between chronological and historical time, reflecting respectively the natural and human dimensions of time.[22] Chronological time follows the rhythm of nature. It depends on the fixed and predictable cadence of external coordinates, as experienced by people in traditional societies.[23] Historical time is, however, produced by human actions, and has human and cultural implications, making it unpredictable. This chronological/historical dualism allows the contemporaneity of two events even if they belong to different chronological moments: as anthropologists such as Edward

---

[21] Koselleck, *Futures Past*, 105 and 94.
[22] See especially his epigraph 'Development of and Understanding of Specifically Historical Time', in Reinhart Koselleck (ed.), *The Practice of Conceptual History* (Stanford, CA: Stanford University Press, 2002), 118–123.
[23] Jacques Le Goff, 'Au Moyen Âge: temps de l'Église et temps du marchand', *Annales. Economies, Sociétés, Civilisations*, 15 (1960): 417–433.

E. Evans-Pritchard and Clifford Geertz have demonstrated, we can find synchronies between the cultures of two tribes located in very different spaces or times.[24] Koselleck concludes that both natural and historical times belong to the conditions of historical temporalities, but the former never subsumes the latter: '[H]istorical temporalities follow a sequence different from the temporal rhythms given in nature.'[25]

This disruptive and asynchronic relationship between natural and historical time helps us understand the connection between synchronicity and diachronicity that some historical texts achieve. Since some historians are able to combine both kinds of levels of time (diachronicity and synchronicity) through narrative and emplotment, their readers perceive the contemporary relevance of their writings. Writing within this diachronic–synchronic frame, even if the historians deal with the remote past, readers may find analogies with their present because of the effect of the historical time deployed in the texts. Thus, historians who are able to create durable works establish their writings on the solid foundations of that 'supportive ground of the process in which the present is rooted', which is, in turn, based on the equidistance and dialectic between remoteness and distancing, as Gadamer and Ricoeur have posited.[26]

---

[24] Two fascinating examples developed by anthropologists of this reality are: Edward E. Evans-Pritchard, *The Nuer* (Oxford: Clarendon Press, 1940) (on the contemporaneity of different space coordinates) and Clifford Geertz, 'Ritual and Social Change: A Javanese Example', *American Anthropologist* 59 (1957): 32–54 (on the contemporaneity of different temporal coordinates).

[25] Koselleck, *Futures Past*, 96.

[26] Gadamer, *Truth and Method*, 297; Ricoeur, *Time and Narrative*, III: 220.

Gabrielle M. Spiegel's thoughts in her *The Past as Text* convey this ability of some historical texts to make us reflect on the present as we learn about the past:

> It is only by appreciating how deeply this attitude of piety towards the past ran in medieval society that we can begin to understand the use made of history. It is a question not of the mindless repetition of tradition, nor of an inability to innovate or create, but of a compelling necessity to find in the past the means to explain and legitimize every deviation from tradition. In such a society, as Joseph Reese Strayer remarked, 'every deliberate modification of an existing type of activity must be based on a study of individual precedents. Every plan for the future is dependent on a pattern which has been found in the past.' The eternal relevance of the past for the present made it a mode of experiencing the reality of contemporary political life, and the examples the past offered had an explanatory force in articulating the true and correct nature of present forms of political action. The overall tendency of the chronicles of Saint-Denis was to assimilate past and present into a continuous stream of tradition and to see in this very continuity a form of legitimation.[27]

Spiegel deals with the burden of tradition in medieval societies, but we keep examining the meaning of innovation in our time, wondering if we could learn something about the difference. She also describes the aspiration of medieval historiography – more specifically, of the thirteenth-century

---

[27] Spiegel, *The Past as Text*, 85. The quote of Joseph Reese Strayer in Jacques Barzun et al. (eds.), *The Interpretation of History* (Princeton: Princeton University Press, 1943), 10.

French historical text *Grandes Chroniques de France* – to 'assimilate past and present', precisely the quality I propose as a requisite for durability in historical texts. The medieval texts analysed by Spiegel confirm François Hartog's intuition, developed in his *Chronos*, on the texture of the present, always 'omnipresent, inevitable, ineluctable'.[28] Hartog draws on the warning of Paul Valéry, who argues that history is not so much about the questions of the past as about the eternal novelty and originality of the present: it *serves* 'to not prevent seeing the present original'.[29] In early modernity, the clergyman H. H. Milman, one of the first reviewers of *Decline and Fall*, appreciated Gibbon's architectonic feat in 'bridging the abyss between ancient and modern times, and connecting the two worlds of history'.[30]

In the twentieth century, Ernst Kantorowicz's *The King's Two Bodies* (1957) achieves this effect of contemporaneity by signalling the congruency of medieval Europe with contemporary political and juridical issues. Robert E. Lerner signals this connection between the text's historical content and its readers' current context as the key to its durability:

> Without treating the longer-term reception at any length, it may yet be noted that the book became much more popular twenty years after its appearance than it was when it first appeared and then kept up the new pace. ...

[28] François Hartog, *Chronos: L'Occident aux prises avec le Temps* (Paris: Gallimard, 2020), 11.

[29] Paul Valéry, *Cahiers II* (Paris: Gallimard, 1974), 1490.

[30] H. H. Milman, quoted by Patricia B. Craddock, *Edward Gibbon, Luminous Historian, 1772–1794* (Baltimore, MD: The Johns Hopkins University Press, 1989), 355.

The shift to cultural history in the later twentieth century made it clear that Kantorowicz's work had much of importance to say about the rites and representations of power.[31]

Current intellectual, social, and political debates such as power, body, rites, and representation emerge from the book's reading by new generations of readers. Learning about the transformations of the doctrine of the king's two bodies and the arcane mysteries of medieval political theology sets us thinking about our own current social and political problems and makes William Chester Jordan conclude that this 'remains a wonderfully exciting and constantly rewarding book'.[32] One then wonders how this can be possible in a book with such dense prose and hundreds of almost detective-like notes. The only explanation is that the historical interest in Kantorowicz's project overcomes any problems with his heavy prose.

Another explanation of the durability of *Two Bodies*, beyond its academic value, may lie in our continuing interest in the text's focus. The problem of the transferences between the temporal and the spiritual, between the political and the religious, conveyed by the metaphor 'political theology' of the subtitle, is a permanent problem, not a circumstantial one. The metaphor of the 'two bodies' makes the general dilemma of the transferences between the spiritual and the temporal

---

[31] Robert E. Lerner, *Ernst Kantorowicz: A Life* (Princeton, NJ: Princeton University Press, 2017), 356–357.

[32] William Chester Jordan, 'Preface', in Ernst Kantorowicz (ed.), *The King's Two Bodies* (Princeton, NJ: Princeton University Press, 1997), ix–xv, here xv.

more specific and gives the book its necessary foundation, but it does not lessen the universal analogy used by the author. The duality of the king's bodies emerged from the fact that every ecclesiastic was a 'mystical body' or a 'body politic'. Accordingly, the king, too, was, or had, a body politic which 'never died'. Kantorowicz concludes that 'Notwithstanding, therefore, some similarities with disconnected pagan concepts, *the king's two bodies* is an offshoot of Christian theological thought and consequently stands as a landmark of Christian political theology.'[33]

The efficacy of Kantorowicz's use of metaphors helps us understand the numerous labels and catchphrases associated with the book sixty years after its publication: 'postmodernism', 'new historicism', 'text archaeology', 'history of the body', and 'Foucauldian interest in power and the body'.[34] Yet one can imagine Kantorowicz's bewilderment, had he overcome his proverbial 'anti-eternity complex' and could hear today these labels on his work. For good and for bad, enduring historical works survive their authors, and most of the time have different lives than those imagined by their writers.

Another example of this assimilation of past/present or the *effect of contemporaneity* – I use this phrase to distinguish this peculiar quality with the presentism, that is, the reduction of the past to the present – comes from Natalie Zemon Davis's masterpiece of narrative history *The Return of Martin Guerre* (1983). At some point in her narration, she *imagines* Bertrande's feelings when facing the difficulties due

---

[33] Kantorowicz, *King's Two Bodies*, 506. Emphasis in the original.
[34] These labels are quoted and documented by Lerner, *Kantorowicz*, 357.

to the disappearance of her husband Martin Guerre, in a small village in sixteenth-century France:

> When urged by her relatives to separate from Martin, she firmly refused. Here we come to certain character traits of Bertrande de Rols, which she was already displaying in her sixteenth year: a concern for her reputation as a woman, a stubborn independence, and a shrewd realism about how she could maneuver within the constraints placed upon one of her sex. Her refusal to have her marriage dissolved, which might well have been followed by another marriage at her parents' behest freed her temporarily from certain wifely duties. It gave her a chance to have a girlhood with Martin's younger sisters, with whom she got on well. And she could get credit for her virtue.[35]

Davis's portrait of Bertrand contests the supposed submission of women in medieval and early modern societies generally depicted by historians. We certainly perceive the hypothetical language, as Davis uses the conditional form when inferring feelings or thoughts. But we are also compelled by the logical conjectures of her historical methodology and coherent narrative. Yet what most impressed me the first time I read the book – apart from Davis's digressions on Bertrande's psychology – is that I found myself thinking at two chronological levels simultaneously. The first, and the most obvious, involved trying to imagine the life of a peasant woman in a society as traditional as sixteenth-century France. The second, though implicit, was the projection of twentieth-century feminism into Bertrand's thoughts. Davis

---

[35] Natalie Zemon Davis, *The Return of Martin Guerre* (Cambridge, MA: Harvard University Press, 1983), 28.

established key connections between Bertrande's thoughts with the concerns of twentieth-century women forging a key *chronotopic* connection through the effect of contemporaneity.[36]

Grandes Chroniques de France, Kantorowicz's *King's Two Bodies*, and Davis's *Martin Guerre*'s enduring significance arguably arises from the critical insights they provide to the present, rather than their visions of the past. This justifies Max Weber's claim that the 'authority of the eternal yesterday' structures the permanent present.[37] The present conveyed by certain durable historical works may become 'the inaugural force of a history that is yet to be made', as Ricoeur puts it.[38] Here, we arrive at Nietzsche's idea of the 'strength of the present', which provides us with the 'inspiring consolation of hope', and turns 'disadvantages' into the 'advantages' of history.[39] Koselleck defines this process as 'the contemporaneity of noncontemporaneous'.[40] Martin Heidegger, in turn, moved from the notion of 'temporality' to that of 'temporalization' to convey that *making-present* that some durable historical works attain.[41] Finally, Ricoeur locates this level of

---

[36] Natalie Zemon Davis, 'On the Lame', *American Historical Review*, 93 (1988), 572–603.

[37] Max Weber, 'Politics as a Vocation', in *From Max Weber: Essays in Sociology* (New York: Oxford University Press, 1946), 77–128, here 77.

[38] Ricoeur, *Time and Narrative*, III: 240.

[39] Friedrich Nietzsche, *On the Advantage and Disadvantage of History for Life* (Indianapolis, IN: Hackett, 1980), 63.

[40] Koselleck, *Futures Past*, 95.

[41] Ricoeur, *Time and Narrative*, III: 255. Koselleck's use of the term *temporalization* is analogous to that of Heidegger, but he specifically uses it to strengthen his theories on the distinction between chronological and historical time (Koselleck, *The Practice of Conceptual History*, 121).

making-present 'on the side of historical consciousness', and argues that it constitutes 'the force of the present'.[42]

Temporalization

Heidegger's process of temporalization is historiographically verified, for instance, in the moral teachings that we obtain from historical narrations, irrespective of the period or the events they describe. Durable historical works convey the fact that, although historical circumstances change, passions are timeless. The ways in which Herodotus, Thucydides, Polybius, and Plutarch formulate the effects of their characters' motives and conduct continue to compel readers. As a consequence, we tend to identify with Herodotus' praise of Athens, and in some sense tend to project our own civilization, whatever it is, in those words:

> For there is not anywhere in the world a large enough
> quantity of gold, nor a country so exceptional in its
> beauty and fertility, that we would accept it in return for
> medizing and enslaving Greece. Many and great are the
> things that would prevent us from so doing, even should
> we wish to. First and most important are the statues
> and temples of our gods, which have been burned and
> demolished: on this account we are compelled to exact
> retribution to the great degree, rather than make terms
> with the one who carried out such actions. Next, there
> is the fact of our Greek identity: our sharing the same
> blood and the same language, and having temples of the

---

[42] Ricoeur, *Time and Narrative*, III: 256.

gods and sacrifices in common, and shared customs. It would not be good for the Athenians to become traitors of all of this.[43]

Polybius applies the same praise to the Romans but the historical form, by analogizing the past with the present, remains:

> But the Romans have subjected to their rule not portions, but nearly the whole of the world and possess an empire which is not only immeasurably greater than any which preceded it, but need not fear rivalry in the future. In the course of this work it will become more clearly intelligible by what steps this power was acquired, and it will also be seen how many and how great advantages accrue to the student from the systematic treatment of history.[44]

Perhaps our tendency to consider Greek and Roman civilizations as the epitome of the classic and their identification with the peak of universal culture has been in part shaped by the effect of these durable historical texts.

From a political point of view, the relationship between natural and historical time that Koselleck posits invites a comparison of revolutions, wars, and different legal constitutions at a certain level of abstraction or typology: '[B]esides such diachronic structures for events, there are

---

[43] Herodotus, *Histories*, 8: 144, quoted in Emily Baragwanath, *Motivation and Narrative in Herodotus* (Oxford: Oxford University Press, 2008), 161.

[44] Polybius, *The Histories*, trans. W. R. Paton (Cambridge, MA: Harvard University Press, 1998), 333 (Book II: 37), 7, Book I: 2.

also longer-term structures that are more familiar today.'[45] Braudel's *Méditerranée* also managed to synchronize very diverse geographical, social, economic, and political temporal structures. Braudel's structural approach to history is based both on the natural-chronological diachronicity of events and on the human-historical synchronicity of structures, beyond the different strata of time in which they may be located. He uses the synchronic and the diachronic procedures simultaneously, 'favouring synchrony when he describes, and diachrony when he narrates', as historians generally do – or try to do.[46] He created a new type of plot, which 'unite[s] structures, cycles, and events by joining together heterogeneous temporalities and contradictory chronicles'.[47] That is why he privileged long over short duration, structures over conjunctures, and permanence over change, making him a durable historian:

> In the historical explanation such as I see it, at my own risk, it is always the long duration that ends up winning. Negative of a crowd of events, of all those that it does not manage to drag into its own current and that it mercilessly dismisses, it certainly limits the freedom of men and the part of chance itself. I am a 'structuralist' by temperament, little solicited by the events, and only half by the conjuncture, this grouping of events of the same sign.[48]

---

[45] Koselleck, *Futures Past*, 106–107.
[46] Koselleck, *Futures Past*, 217.
[47] Ricoeur, *Time*, 1: 216.
[48] Fernand Braudel, *La Méditerranée et le monde méditerranéen à l'époque de Philippe II* (Paris: Colin, 1966), II: 520.

As cultural agents, historians establish a written tradition, which involves a peculiar but unique co-existence of past and present, 'insofar as present consciousness has the possibility of a free access to everything handed down in writing'.[49] Thus, historical texts facilitate the co-existence of the past and the present, as the classic images of the contemporaneity of historical texts (Benedetto Croce), the history as exile (Siegfried Kracauer), or history as re-enactment (Robin G. Collingwood) remind us.[50] As Gadamer concludes, 'a written tradition is not a fragment of a past world, but has already raised itself beyond this into the sphere of the meaning that it expresses'.[51] Or, as he explains in hermeneutical terms, 'only the part of the past that is not past offers the possibility of historical knowledge'.[52]

Yet, my point is that not all historical texts can bring the past into the present through the different forms of contemporaneity, re-enactment, or classicism. Indeed,

---

[49] Gadamer, *Truth and Method*, 390.

[50] On the contemporaneity of historical texts by Benedetto Croce, see Nicola Conati, 'History as Contemporary History in the Thinking of Benedetto Croce', *Open Journal of Philosophy* 5 (2015): 54–61; on history as exile by Siegfried Kracauer, see Gertrud Koch, '"Not Yet Accepted Anywhere": Exile, Memory, and Image in Kracauer's Conception of History', *New German Critique* 54 (1991): 95–109; on history as re-enactment by Robin G. Collingwood, see William H. Dray, *History as Re-Enactment: R. G. Collingwood's Idea of History* (Oxford: Clarendon Press, 1995) and Joseph M. Levine, *Re-Enacting the Past: Essays on the Evolution of Modern English Historiography* (Aldershot: Ashgate, 2004).

[51] Gadamer, *Truth and Method*, 391.

[52] Gadamer, *Truth and Method*, 289.

most historical texts are written, experienced by readers, acknowledged by critics, or simply judged by the passage of time, as transient archaeological artefacts rather than lived contemporary creations. So, the process of temporalization suggested by Heidegger is only attained by certain privileged historical texts that have attained durability. They function as dynamic and living documents rather than inert primary sources.

Establishing these rhetorical connections between the past and the present in their historical texts is not easy for historians. The assumption of the 'effect of contemporaneity' implies the creation of a new kind of literary authority, universality, and originality. Historians writing durable works manage to develop a set of techniques and assumptions that make possible new approaches to a given subject, a new genre, a new methodology, and new theoretical assumptions. Some of them have made explicit this intuition to their readers from the beginning of their narration. Thucydides openly acknowledges that he writes 'not for the applause of today's hearing, but as a possession for all time'.[53] Polybius defines himself as a historian different from the 'former historians, dealing with the history of one nation, such as Greece of Persia' since he has 'undertaken to describe the events occurring in all known parts of the world'.[54] Eusebius' task of writing about a Christian emperor presented new problems in the past, called for new solutions in the present, and left the

---

[53] Thucydides, *Histories*, I: 22, 4, quoted in Lowell Edmunds, *Chance and Intelligence in Thucydides* (Cambridge: Harvard University Press, 1975), 150.

[54] Polybius, *The Histories*, 333 (Book II: 37).

original charm of his political biography intact.[55] Even if the historical data and most of his interpretations are currently outdated, Edward Gibbon remains 'the first of the historians of the Roman Empire', and a continuing source of inspiration for anyone trying to understand not only Roman political and social structures but also the rules governing the never-ending dialectic between rising and decadence, permanence, and change.[56] Leopold von Ranke and Jacob Burckhardt viewed history as uniquely important in making readers look beyond the course of events and see the decisive role that values play in human development.[57] Johan Huizinga's *The Waning of the Middle Ages* anticipated some of the most relevant twentieth-century historiographical tendencies – the *Annales* School of the 1930s, the post-1945 American school of symbolic anthropology headed by Victor Turner and Clifford Geertz, the cultural history associated with the Russians Mikhail Bakhtin and Aaron Gourevitch, and the narrative history practised by Natalie Zemon Davis, among many others.[58] These durable books also illustrate Thomas Kuhn's idea of the essential tension between tradition and innovation proper of the best scientific and academic creations. They established a tension between convergent and

[55] Averil Cameron and Stuart G. Hall, 'Introduction', in *Eusebius: Life of Constantine* (Oxford: Clarendon, 1999), 27.

[56] Roy Porter, *Edward Gibbon: Making History* (London: Weidenfeld, 1988), 164.

[57] Felix Gilbert, *History: Politics or Culture? Reflections on Ranke and Burckhardt* (Princeton: Princeton University Press, 1990), 103–4.

[58] Norman F. Cantor, *Inventing the Middle Ages* (New York: Morrow, 1991), 381.

divergent thinking because they were firmly rooted in contemporary scientific tradition and produced a new one.[59]

Thus, historians generating durable works simultaneously represent stability and provoke rupture. They are breakthroughs in historical writing, as they usually lead readers to re-think and re-make history.[60] Yet they also acquire the obligations of primogeniture in a lineage. They may or may not have followers and disciples – actually, most of them have not really established a 'school' *per se*, as shown in the case of Jacob Burckhardt, Johan Huizinga, and Ernst Kantorowicz, which shows that a certain degree of unconventionality is required for becoming perennial. Yet what remains in collective memory – in this particular case, professional historians' collective memory – are those first works, rather than their contemporaries or successors.

Nietzsche's and Foucault's concept of genealogy, which I discuss in greater depth in Chapter 5, may help us to understand this apparent contradictory ambivalence of historians as agents of rupture with the past, continuity in the present, and durability for the future.[61] Once pioneering historians establish a new subject, genre, methodological, or theoretical paradigm, historians of historiography construct a genealogy that exalts particular links in the chain, constituted

[59] Thomas S. Kuhn, 'The Essential Tension: Tradition and Innovation in Scientific Research', in Thomas S. Kuhn (ed.), *The Essential Tension* (Chicago: The University of Chicago Press, 1977), 225–239, here 226.

[60] Averil Cameron, 'Eusebius of Cesarea and the Rethinking of History', in E. Gabba (ed.), *Tria Corda: Scritti in onore di Arnaldo Momigliano* (Como: Edizioni New Press, 1983), 71–88.

[61] Foucault, 'Nietzsche', 139–164.

basically for those durable historians and historical works to which I have referred in the preceding paragraphs. They combine 'historical time', since durable works always live in the present and we can find synchronies beyond the different periods in which those works have been created, and 'chronological time', when they are objects of the history of historiography and one can establish a coherent diachronic narrative in their accounts 'from Herodotus to the present'.

Timelessness

The particular effect of contemporaneity of durable historical works, and its simultaneous negotiation with tradition and innovation, leads us to another marker of the durability of historical writings: timelessness. Enduring works focus on the past, but they also deal in one way or another with the present and are open to the future. This is clear from the beginning of Western historical practice since Greek historians directed their *Histories* not only to the past and to the present, but also towards future readers. Herodotus deals with the past but added comments on the present. When he states that his account will cover both small and large cities equally, he mentions the evolution of the measure of these cities 'since the majority of cities that in earlier times were important have become small, and those that were important in my time were formerly small'.[62] His examination of the history of small as

---

[62] Herodotus, *Histories*, I: 5, 4, quoted in C. Dewald, 'Wanton Kings, Pickled Heroes, and Gnomic Founding Fathers: Strategies of Meaning at the End of Herodotus' Histories', in D. Roberts, F. Dunn, and D. P.

well as large cities also demonstrates his belief that significance lies at both the micro- and macro-levels. In addition, Herodotus' open ending invites future interpretations.

Herodotus' natural transition from the past to the present and the future renders a simultaneously diachronic and synchronous approach. This has made Herodotus' work a site of interpretation in itself, as François Hartog has done with his *Le miroir d'Hérodote*.[63] Herodotus considers the result of every action and event, so that,

> This decision is significant in inviting us to recognize that the meaning of his text is not to be bounded *diachronically* by the limits of his authorial intentions. And the same appears to be true also on a *synchronous* level, for Herodotus foregrounds the fact that history is contested territory: that different interpretations and explanations of historical events and personalities arise from the perspectives of different individuals or groups.[64]

In their polyphonic symphony, and blending temporal perspectives, historians authoring enduring works construct texts that open a multiplicity of perspectives for

Fowler (eds.), *Classical Closure: Reading the End in Greek and Latin Literature* (Princeton: Princeton University Press, 1997), 62–82.

[63] François Hartog, *Le miroir d'Hérodote: Essai sur la représentation de l'autre* (Paris: Gallimard, 1980).

[64] Baragwanath, *Motivation*, 2. On Herodotus, see also C. W. Fornara, *Herodotus. An Interpretative Essay* (Oxford: Oxford University Press, 1971); F. S. Naiden, 'The Prospective Imperfect in Herodotus', *Harvard Studies in Classical Philology* 99 (1999): 135–149; E. J. Bakker, 'The Making of History: Herodotus' Histories Apodexis', in E. J. Bakker, I. J. F. de Jong, and H. Van Wees (eds.), *Brill's Companion to Herodotus* (Leiden: Brill, 2002), 3–32.

readers. They explain their protagonists' thoughts and motivations as they initiate a polyphonic dialogue between the author, the characters of the story, and the readers: '[H]istory arises from a conversation between the historian and historical agents, other scholars and the consumers of history.'[65] History becomes intermingled in the actors' and author's minds, an idea that Collingwood modelled in his 'history as re-enactment'.[66]

Durable historical works arguably link the past with the present, encouraging the audience's imagination yet – crucially for my argumentation – without falling into reductive presentism. This complex rhetorical operation, which I call the 'effect of contemporaneity' to distinguish it from presentism, was first practised by historians of antiquity. Jonas Grethlein has noted that Thucydides restored 'the presentness to the past'.[67] Historical works endure when they serve methodological purposes and provide tools for understanding the present without damaging the integrity of the past. Indeed, Lours E. Lord notes of Thucydides what might clearly describe this form of durability: 'In his conception of what is required of a writer of history he [Thucydides] is nearer to the twentieth century AD than he is to the fifth BC.'[68]

---

[65] Marnie Hughes-Warrington, *Fifty Key Thinkers on History* (London: Routledge, 2000), 55–56.

[66] Dray, *History as Re-Enactment.*

[67] Jonas Grethlein, 'The Presence of the Past in Thucydides', in A. Tsakmakis and M. Tamiolaki (eds.), *Thucydides between History and Literature* (Boston: De Gruyter, 2013), 91–118.

[68] Lours E. Lord, *Thucydides and the World War* (Cambridge: Harvard University Press, 1945), 216.

Thus, the value of durable historical texts can also be attributed to this contemporaneity, as we can appreciate in the works of modern historians such as Marc Bloch, Fernand Braudel, Edward Thompson, and Ernst Kantorowicz. They show that historiographical durability is mainly about the form rather than the content. Thucydides' *History* draws readers into its distinctive worldview because of its kinship to the contemporary language and structure of classical tragedy rather than the beauty of his prose.[69] Indeed, it has been argued that some durable historical texts have analogies with their counterparts in literature because of the similarities in genre: Herodotus' *Histories* with Homer's epics, Thucydides' and Jean Froissart's chronicles with Sophocles' tragedies, and Jules Michelet, Carlo Ginzburg and Natalie Zemon Davis with the modern novel.[70] The analogy with literary genres endows some historical texts with that universality that led Aristotle to claim the superiority of literature over history. Not by chance does Hayden White's *Metahistory* (an enduring work itself) reflect Frye's categorization of genres that shaped his concept of 'modes of emplotment'.[71]

Using the effect of contemporaneity, enduring historical works raise questions 'that can and must be asked over and over again and, in so doing, implicate the one who asks – that is, it must perform tragic temporality. Moreover,

---

[69] Darien Shanske, *Thucydides and the Philosophical Origins of History* (Cambridge: Cambridge University Press, 2007).

[70] F. W. Walbank, 'History and Tragedy', in J. Marincola (ed.), *Greek and Roman Historiography* (Oxford: Oxford University Press, 2011), 389–412.

[71] White, *Metahistory*, 7–11.

the seriousness of these questions demands that they not be stilled with facile answers.'[72] This elevates enduring historical narratives to the universal rather than the particular. Michelet's works, for example, are governed by the universality of principles such as justice, freedom, patriotism, hope for the future, and a cosmopolitan ideal.[73] Bryan Palmer notes that one of the strengths of Thompson's book on the formation of the English working class was his move beyond the particularities of specific experiences to a full comprehension of the world in motion.[74] Michelet's and Thompson's references to the present and projection to the future make their work timeless. This frame helps us understand the entry in Ranke's diary, probably from 1816–1817:

> One might assume that the difference between poetry and philosophy originates from the fact that poetry strives to represent the infinite by the finite, while the aim of philosophy is to explain the finite by the infinite. The intermediate link would be an ideal historian which depicts the infinite in the finite and traces it as it is manifest as an idea and on the whole, and would bring it before our eyes and mind.[75]

To summarize my arguments, to move into the practical and propositive part of this chapter, I posit that

---

[72] Shanske, *Thucydides*, 152–3.

[73] Oscar A. Haac, *Les principes inspirateurs de Michelet* (New Haven: Yale University Press, 1951).

[74] Bryan D. Palmer, *The Making of E. P. Thompson* (Toronto: New Hogtown, 1981), 73.

[75] Quoted in Rudolf Vierhaus, 'Historiography between Science and Art', in *Leopold von Ranke*, 61–69, here 67.

the durability of historical texts is thus guaranteed by their ability to connect the past with the present to overcome temporality, to make available the past that historians are accurately narrating in the present of the audience's imagination. This involves rhetorically attaining the presentness of the past without losing the conviction of the inviolable integrity of the pastness of the past. Until this point, I have tried to show the ability of certain durable historical texts to pull the past into the present. But, *how* have they attained this effect of contemporaneity? What can we learn from this process?

Historical Past and Practical Past

The philosopher Michael Oakeshott describes the intellectual and rhetorical process of bringing the past into the present in these terms: 'The past is a consequence of understanding the present world in a particular manner;' 'The past, in whatever manner it appears, is a certain sort of reading of the present;' 'The activity of the historian is pre-eminently that of understanding present events – the things that are before him – as evidence for past happenings.'[76] The Spanish novelist Carmen Martín Gaite wrote in 1979 that: 'The meaning we attributed to things we look at them is what covertly prompts memory to pick them out for later.'[77] Though philosophers and poets have

---

[76] Michael J. Oakeshott, *Rationalism in Politics* (Indianapolis: Liberty Fund, 1991), 161, 164, and 165.

[77] 'El sentido que se atribuye a las cosas al mirarlas es lo que incita oscuramente a la memoria a seleccionarlas para luego', in Carmen Martín Gaite (ed.), *Cuadernos de todo* (Barcelona: Areté, 2002), 385.

conveyed this reality, historians understand the difficulty of gaining contemporaneity in historical writing without falling into presentism or anachronism, since this operation involves rhetorically achieving the presentness of the past, to maintain readerly attention. Historians must respect the pastness of the past while recognizing the presentism of the written past: 'In resisting the present, the historian demonstrates his true love of the past, a past that is all the more "adorable" because it is untainted by the present and the practical.'[78] Yet historians have always tried to keep this balance between the past and the present. Some of them, authors of enduring works, have attained this equilibrium, so that they have shown that the rhetorical operation of pulling the past into the present is, at least, possible.

In his article 'The Activity of Being an Historian', Oakeshott notes three modes of experience corresponding to three modes of approaching the past, which govern our attitudes towards the past: the scientific, the practical, and the contemplative.[79] These three different ways of perceiving the present are projected in three different ways of viewing the past. Each of these conveys the three transcendentals of reality defined by philosophers: the scientific/epistemic refers to the truth as the practical/professional would refer to goodness and the contemplative/poetic to beauty. Truth (search for the reality of the past: the content of history), goodness (pedagogic, ethical, and political function; history as a school of moral action: the uses of history), and beauty (aesthetics,

---

[78] Gertrude Himmelfarb, *The New History and the Old* (London: Harvard University Press), 174.

[79] Oakeshott, *Rationalism in Politics*, 151–183.

style, method: the form of history) are the three categories engaged by historians.[80]

The practical attitude – proper to politicians, social scientists, and other professionals – understands the past in relation to the present. It seeks in the past the origins of whatever appears in the present. The past is used to improve the moral orientation of professions in order to obtain benefits for them or for society. It tends to presentism. The contemplative attitude, proper to artists and poets, appears in its purest form in the historical novel, where the past becomes a storehouse of images. It has a strong aesthetic component. It tends to antiquarianism – its relative noun 'antiquarian' refers to a dealer who negotiates with nice old objects. Finally, the scientific attitude considers the past a 'foreign country' (David Lowenthal), and tries to establish distance from it. Its approach involves understanding it by subsuming individual events and characters under general laws, so that the past it deals with is a timeless world, one made up not of factual events, but of hypothetical situations. It seeks historical accuracy and referentiality. It should tend to an adequate equidistance between antiquarianism and presentism.

I posit that enduring historical works are those which have attained this balance between the practical, the contemplative, and the scientific attitude, negotiating with real events of the past rather than fictional or imaginative. Certainly, there are historical works whose

[80] See Herschel Baker, *The Race of Time: Three Lectures on Renaissance Historiography* (Toronto: University of Toronto Press, 1967) and the three parts of this volume: 'The Truth of History', 'The Use of History', and 'The Form of History', which reflects the triple dimension I describe in the text.

scientific dimension exceeds the contemplative or practical, as in the case of Leopold von Ranke, Marc Bloch, and Ernst Kantorowicz. Others stand out for their aesthetic and narrative power, such as the works of Jules Michelet, Johan Huizinga, Georges Duby, and Natalie Zemon Davis. Still, others are remarkable for their practicality, especially those related to cultural, gender, postcolonial, and subaltern studies such as Edward Said and Yuval Noah Harari. But all of them achieve an adequate balance between the three dimensions so that they cannot be criticized for their excessive presentism, their lack of aesthetics, or their inaccuracy.

Reshaping Oakeshott's arguments, some historians have recently retrieved the distinction between the practical and the historical past. His original impulse was to distinguish professional history from other practical uses of the past, mainly to justify actions and beliefs in the present.[81] Hayden White has recently stressed the danger that professionals of history might become irrelevant to society, which seeks answers for present concerns in the past.[82] His theories echo those put forward decades earlier by Gertrude Himmelfarb, who argued that historians have perpetually oscillated between the historical and the practical past:

> the historical enterprise is in one sense exceedingly modest, aspiring to no large visions of enduring truths,

---

[81] Michael Oakeshott, *On History and Other Essays* (Indianapolis: Liberty Fund, 1999), 38–48.

[82] Hayden White, *The Practical Past* (Evanston: Northwestern University Press, 2014). See also Jonas Ahlskog, 'Michael Oakeshott and Hayden White on the Practical and the Historical Past', *Rethinking History*, 20 (2016), 1–20.

producing only a kaleidoscope of changing pictures. In other sense, however, it is enormously ambitious, for it requires the historian to resist the overwhelming tendency of all time, and of the present time most especially. In resisting the present, the historian demonstrates his true love of the past, a past that is all the more 'adorable' because it is untainted by the present and the practical.[83]

Durable historical works have attained this balance between the historical and the practical past so graphically illustrated by Himmelfarb's paradox of the 'modest-ambitious' historian. This paradox, which lies at the heart of the historical operation, has been highlighted by Carlo Ginzburg: 'The quantitative and anti-anthropocentric approach of the sciences of nature from Galileo onwards has placed human sciences in an unpleasant dilemma: they must either adopt a weak scientific standard so as to be able to attain significant results, or adopt a strong scientific standard to attain results of no great importance.'[84]

When historians face the dilemma described by Himmelfarb and Ginzburg, the cognitive and epistemic dimension, bound with the content of historical narrations, should be 'non-negotiable', since the 'irreducible otherness of the past', to use Spiegel's phrase, must be preserved by historians.[85] Thus, this conviction of the otherness of the past

---

[83] Himmelfarb, *The New History*, 174.

[84] Carlo Ginzburg, 'Roots of a Scientific Paradigm', *Theory and Society*, 7 (1979): 273–288, here 276.

[85] Gabrielle M. Spiegel, 'The Task of the Historian', *American Historical Review* 114 (2009): 1–15, here 1.

compatible with the presentism of the written past, and its consequent balance between the historical and practical past, is what makes the historical operation complex and explains the existence of very few durable historical works. Even among these few works, the balance between the historical and the practical is not always perfect, as we find some works which succeed more specifically in one of the two modes of approaching the past.

Actually, in some of the historical works described in this chapter as 'durable', we perceive the difficulty of achieving a perfect balance between the historical and the practical past. Thompson's *The Making of the English Working Class* functions as a clear example of the practical mode, with his political and ideological engagement, his shaping of the 'history from below', and his personal commitment to Marxism. Davis, in her *The Return of Martin Guerre,* is another prototype of the practical mode in her dialogic operation between a sixteenth-century rural woman of sixteenth-century France (the past) and the theories around twentieth-century women (the present) but, in this case, there is general agreement among critics about the beauty of her narrative. Conversely, Huizinga's *The Waning of the Middle Ages*, Braudel's *Mediterranean*, and Kantorowicz's *The Two King's Bodies* are prototypical instances of contemplative, analytic, and interpretative engagement with the past, though they do not succeed in the practical.

Yet, even within this imbalance between the historical and the practical representations of the past, these works have achieved enough balance to be durable – as they manifestly are. Huizinga's *The Waning* has been defined as a

'unique book [that] should be read today', and the scope of
the subjects treated (heroism, love, death, religion, symbolism, art) may easily apply to all times via analogy, beyond the
specific period the author is dealing with.[86] More than fifty
years after its publication, Braudel's *Mediterranean* remains
'a document, not a monument', and the extraordinary interest in it probably lies in the ideal of a Mediterranean united
beyond countries, races, ages, and religions, as with his concern with geography and environment.[87] Kantorowicz, the
scholar who did not wish to have any kind of funeral because
of his 'anti-eternity complex', has achieved durability with
his historical work.[88] *The King's Two Bodies'* main virtue has
been summarized with the word 'remain'.[89] The endurance
of such a dense project may be explained by Kantorowicz's
clever use of metaphors 'as a supporting element, not only
of language, but of reality itself'.[90] Both phrases of the title –
The King's Two Bodies and *Political Theology* – are metaphors
themselves. They provide the book with a multi-disciplinary
frame which makes it readable from different perspectives,
and a sense of analogy between the past narrated by the
historian and the reader's present: 'The construction of the

[86] The quote is from Cantor, *Inventing*, 381.
[87] The quote is from John A. Marino, 'Introduction', in John A. Marino
(ed.), *Early Modern History and the Social Sciences: Testing Limits
of Braudel's Mediterranean* (University Park: Pennsylvania State
University Press, 2002), xviii.
[88] The phrase 'anti-eternity' is used, documented, and justified by
Kantorowicz's main biographer: Lerner, *Ernst Kantorowicz*, 387.
[89] William C. Jordan, 'Preface (1997)', in Ernst Kantorowicz (ed.), *The
Two King's Bodies*, xiv.
[90] Ottavia Niccoli, 'Images of Society', in *Early Modern History*, 101–122.

metaphor works by means of a linguistic movement through fluctuating meanings borrowed from several domains, without any necessary recourse to its political substance, to its referent.'[91]

In the end, all these historical works have the virtue of durability beyond their different graduation of *practicality* or *historicalness*. They have achieved a sufficient quantity of serious research on the past (scientific mode with truth), intensive reflection on the present (practical mode with moral implications), and rhetorical presentation (contemplative mode with aesthetic accomplishment). They have respected the inviolable pastness of the past (contemplative and scientific mode) but, at the same time, they have been aware of the inescapable presentism of the written past (practical mode).

The End of Durability?

In his *The Fiction of Narrative*, Hayden White regrets that the lack of narrativization of history has led historians to lose the discipline's rhetorical and ethical dimension. Yet,

> very few of the great classics of historiography were undertaken out of disinterested motives, and most of them have been undertaken as a search, not so much for the truth of the past as, rather, a search for what the truth *means* for living people. Although the mode of history's presentation of the past is dramatistic – laying

---

[91] Alain Boureau, *Kantorowicz: Stories of a Historian* (Baltimore: The Johns Hopkins University Press, 2001), 98.

out a spectacle of the great events and conflicts of times past – it has always sought to contribute to the question that Kant defined as the soul of ethics: What should I (we) do?[92]

Historians have always tried to answer the questions that lie at the heart of knowledge and wisdom: 'What should we know?,' 'what should we do?' Knowledge and ethics require (or should be complemented by) imagination, aesthetics, and art in order to attain contemplation. Thus, ethics and aesthetics join epistemic to construct those durable works of historiography.

White adds that 'modern scientific historiography has diminished the role of the imagination in the construction of a past that might be useful for helping living people to make that move'.[93] I wonder if, in an age of scientific innovation, which privileges schematic papers over comprehensive monographs, and short messages via social media over articulated rationalizations, we will cease to create any durable historical works. Some historians have considered the traditional ways of expressing themselves in the academy to be insufficient. They are thus turning to non-conventional ways of writing histories, such as the use of new digital platforms and diverse forms of life writing, simply to say things that they feel they cannot say within the framework of academia. Thus, using these new genres and platforms, historians try to deliberately break the rules of the game with conventional (and in some sense arbitrary) boundaries that keep historians and

---

[92] White, *The Fiction of Narrative*, xi.
[93] White, *The Fiction of Narrative*, xi.

other scholars from sharing things they know and searching for new paths to durability.

Certainly, we should welcome these news forms of history, since academic historical production requires, proportionally, an academic reading, able to reproduce the specific operations produced by it.[94] Yet history cannot be assimilated to science or literature, at the risk of losing that unifying 'concept of history', argued by Koselleck, which distinguishes its narrations from other non-historical or ahistorical accounts.

To be sure, history will never have those universally-known celebrities of scientists such as Galileo, Newton, or Einstein; philosophers such as Aristotle, Plato, Augustine, Kant, Hegel, Nietzsche, or Heidegger; artists such as Phidias, Giotto, Botticelli, Michelangelo, Caravaggio, Van Gogh, or Picasso; and writers such as Virgil, Dante, Cervantes, or Shakespeare. We can all recite these names by heart. But ask people about the most outstanding historians ever and most people might have difficulty thinking of more than one or two, if at all. This should be, I think, our condition, since I believe the text (the historical account) matters more than the author, and the object of the study (the past) more than the historian. That is why in literature a classic may be in some sense a synonym for celebrity or popularity while in history a classic should be a synonym for durability. Durability is thus the value within which history and literature meet: '[J]ust as with the starry skies, the unreachable literary and historical epic past continues to delight us as sources of admiration and knowledge of otherwise inaccessible things, and as a dim but

---

[94] Pierre Bourdieu, *Homo Academicus* (Paris: Minuit, 1984), 35.

significant and enduring source of light, which will still be there for us once every other source has extinguished.'[95]

To confirm these thoughts on the condition of historians, Spiegel has argued that being a historian lives in the writing, not in the posthumous life of a text. Yet, the reality of the short-lived importance of some historians and of their historical texts is compatible with that other reality of those historical texts which have surpassed time. They have actually survived the facts they have narrated.[96] They deserve to be kept, at least for instructive purposes. Thomas Kuhn once complained that, 'science students [were not] encouraged to read the historical classics of their fields – works in which they might discover other ways of regarding the problems discussed in their textbooks, but in which they would also meet problems, concepts, and standards of solution that their future professions have long since discarded and replaced'.[97]

Aware of the difficulties of explaining the durability of historical texts, my aim in this first chapter has been, at least, to put this question on the agenda of historians and, more specifically, of theorists and critics of history. Approaching problems like this may help us to discern, in Hayden White's words, 'what is the use of criticism and

---

[95] Dimitri Nikulin, 'Establishing the Laws of History. Or, Why Tolstoy Is Not Homer', *Graduate Faculty Philosophical Journal* 37, 2 (2016): 1–18, here 15.

[96] On Huizinga, Cantor, *Inventing*, 381; on Braudel: Hans Kellner, *Language and Historical Representation* (Madison: University of Wisconsin Press, 1989), 187; on Kantorowicz: Jordan, 'Preface', xv.

[97] Kuhn, *The Essential Tension*, 229.

especially meta-criticism in a field of study like history', which leads him to the conclusion that

> it is imperative to have cadres of scholars and intellectuals who specialize in what might be called the social import of fields of creative production like literature and the rest of the arts. Not in order to regulate them, but to provide opinion on the nature and consequences of their products. Thus, [Frank] Kermode concluded, literary critics and theorists do the *serious* reading for community.[98]

As Hans Kellner put it, the operation of criticism on historical writings 'is crucial – who reads histories, and who writes them'.[99] Thus, following the universal aspiration to *le dur désir de durer* – what one critic has poetically defined as 'the harsh contrivance of spirit against death, the hope to over-reach time by force of creation'[100] – it would be unfortunate to lose that magical place, inhabited by those historical per-durable works, imagined by Georges Duby when he was re-reading Braudel's *Mediterranean*: 'I have the feeling that the book's riches are inexhaustible, like one of those palaces that one finds on the coast of Amalfi, palaces through which one can wander endlessly along porticoed galleries nobly arrayed in terraces overlooking the sea.'[101]

---

[98] Hayden White, 'Foreword', in K. Pihlainen (ed.), *The Work of History: Constructivism and a Politics of the Past* (New York: Routledge, 2017), ix–xii, here x–xi.

[99] Hans Kellner, 'Comment on Aurell's paper', 5 (manuscript presented at the Conference 'Writing as Historical Practice', Vanderbilt University, Nashville, TN, 18–19 May 2017).

[100] Steiner, *Language and Silence*, 21.

[101] Georges Duby, *History Continues* (Chicago: The University of Chicago Press, 1994), 85–86.

To be sure, durable historical works are those audible voices among the many implicit appropriations that we historians do in our work, as conveyed by Peter Burke's metaphor: 'Fortunately, a few voices remain audible, among them the deep bass of Braudel.'[102] Let us try to keep those voices alive, and create new worlds like those imagined by Braudel and Duby.

---

[102] Peter Burke, 'Civilizations and Frontiers. Anthropology of the Early Modern Mediterranean', in John A. Marino (ed.), *Early Modern History and the Social Sciences* (University Park: Pennsylvania State University Press, 2002), 123–141, here 141.

2

The Dynamics of the Classic

> Gibbon ranks with Thucydides and Tacitus,
> and is perhaps the clearest example that
> brilliance of style and accuracy of statement
> are perfectly compatible in an historian.
>
> J. B. Bury, *Introduction to Gibbon*

The question of durability implies a temporal condition, which makes the philosophical questions of time discussed in the previous chapter highly relevant.[1] Having examined those issues allows us to enter with greater guarantees to the concept of the classic, more complex and comprehensive. The classic encompasses other qualities of much greater scope, such as aesthetic and literary, in addition to the temporal, and requires the contribution of literary critics in addition to philosophers.

This chapter focuses on some specific features of the historical classic, offering a series of reflections to expand a debate on this complex topic. Based on some examples of the Western historiographical tradition, I discuss to what extent historians should engage the concept of the classic, as has been done for literary and artworks. I will argue that it is possible to identify a category of the classic text in historical writing. Because of their narrative condition, historical texts

---

[1] Earlier versions of portions of this chapter appeared as 'What is a Classic in History?', *Journal of Philosophy of History* 16 (2022): 54–91.

share some of the features assigned to literary texts such as durability, timelessness, universal meaningfulness, resistance to historical criticism, susceptibility to multiple interpretations, and ability to function as models. Yet, since historical texts do not construct imaginary worlds but try to achieve some realities external to the text, they also have to attain some specific features according to this referential content such as the surplus of meaning, historical use of metaphors, effect of contemporaneity, and a certain appropriation of 'literariness'.

It is true that historians have tended to shy away from reflection on the category of historical classics because they focus on changes rather than continuities in the past. But some of them use this category as a given. The critic Horace Walpole exclaimed, 'Lo! A truly classic work has appeared', after reading the first volume of Gibbon's *Decline and Fall* in 1776.[2] John Clive describes 'the sense that [Gibbon's] *The Decline and Fall* was a classic that was two hundred years young, one that had barely begun its majestic and assured journey into immortality' as he advises us to 'turn to the modern as well as the older classics of historical writing' and wonders 'what today's historians can learn about the rhetoric of history from the classical historians of *modern* times'.[3] Jack Hexter acknowledges some qualities 'that make it [Braudel's *Mediterranean*] a classic'.[4] In his book on style in history, Peter Gay describes

[2] Porter, *Edward Gibbon*, 2.
[3] Clive, *Not by Fact Alone*, 52, 306 and 298.
[4] Hexter, *On Historians*, 119.

THE DYNAMICS OF THE CLASSIC

history as 'a progressive discipline and a timeless house of classics'.[5] Gregory Crane calls Thucydides' *History* 'a classic of realist analysis'.[6] Hayden White informs readers of his *Metahistory* that he privileges 'the great historians' classics' and 'historians and philosophers of distinctively classic achievement' and that 'the recognized classics of Western historiography always add something else'.[7] Peter Brown appreciates 'how *Mahomet et Charlemagne* is the sort of classic that can render itself unnecessary'.[8] John Burrow makes reference to Robin G. Collingwood's 'classic book *The Idea of History*'.[9] Peter Burke argues that 'another classic example of historical analysis comes from the *History of Italy* written by Machiavelli's younger contemporary, Francesco Guicciardini'.[10] Anna Green and Kathleen Troup propose to do some readings 'from the classic, such as the extract from *The Making of the English Working Class*, to the recent, such as Henrietta Whiteman's work'.[11]

[5] Gay, *Style in History*, 216.

[6] Gregory Crane, *Thucydides and the Ancient Simplicity: The Limits of Political Realism* (Berkeley: University of California Press, 1998), 4.

[7] Hayden White, 'The Historical Text as Literary Artefact', in R. H. Canary and H. Kozicki (eds.), *The Writing of History: Literary Form and Historical Understanding* (Madison: University of Wisconsin Press, 1978), 59; White, *Metahistory*, 4 and White, 'An Old Question Raised Again: Is Historiography Art or Science?', *Rethinking History* 4, 3 (2000): 391–406, here 395.

[8] Brown, *Society*, 73.

[9] Burrow, *A History of Histories*, xiv.

[10] Burke, *Renaissance Sense*, 81.

[11] Anna Green and Kathleen Troup, *The Houses of History: A Critical Reader in Twentieth-Century History and Theory* (Manchester: Manchester University Press, 1999), vii–viii.

J. B. Bury conveys a somewhat more elaborate reasoning for Gibbon's classical status, making his name the metonymy for his *Decline and Fall*:

> Gibbon is one of those few writers who hold as high a place in the history of literature as in the roll of great historians. … But the fact that his work, composed more than a hundred years ago, is still successful with the general circle of educated people, and has not gone the way of Hume and Robertson, whom we laud as 'classics' and leave on the cold shelves, is due to the singularly happy union of the historian and the man of letters. Gibbon thus ranks with Thucydides and Tacitus, and is perhaps the clearest example that brilliance of style and accuracy of statement—in Livy's case conspicuously divorced—are perfectly compatible in an historian.[12]

These critics of historiography have instinctively used the concept of classic to refer to certain singular historical works and their ability to function as models of historical writing. Nevertheless, none of them have explicitly defined the term, nor engaged its theoretical and practical considerations. Setting aside their reluctance, and based on some examples of Western historiographical tradition, I will discuss in this chapter the extent to which historians should engage the concept of the classic and the benefits this rhetorical exercise can have for history as a practice and as a discipline. If one assumes that the historical text is not only a referential account but also a

---

[12] J. B. Bury, 'Introduction', in E. Gibbon (ed.), *The History of the Decline and Fall of the Roman Empire*, Vol. 1, ed. J. B. Bury (Cambridge: Cambridge University Press, 2015, originally 1896), xxxi.

narrative in prose analogous to a literary text, then the concept of the classic becomes one of the keys to understanding the historical text – and may improve our understanding not only of historiography but also of history itself.

In this rhetorical exercise, my approach is analytic rather than normative. The construction of a canon emerging from the classics, of what Roland Barthes once defined as a text 'that is read in class' may be a more or less convenient task, but is not my objective here. Although I will use examples of specific works of history of the Western tradition to illustrate or justify my point, my approach to the classic in history does not involve cataloguing a canon of texts – if this is possible at all. Rather, I aim to reflect on the rules that govern the epistemic, ethical, and aesthetic qualities in those historical works which we perceive as classics of our discipline or in our area of specialization.

Endurance is the first quality of a classic highlighted by most of the authors. Kermode puts it simply but effectively: 'A classic is a book that is read a long time after it was written.'[13] Since we have seen in the previous chapter the conditions that make it possible for historical work to become enduring, I can now focus on other qualities, especially those referring to temporality and referentiality, two specific essential features of historical writings.

Between Authorship and Criticism

I start from the assumption that history and literature share their narrative form, but they differ in the content – and in the intention

---

[13] Kermode, The *Classic*, 117.

of the author. Based on this difference, my initial hypothesis is that the great realistic narratives of the past have been able to introduce a certain *literary* into their historical texts through figurative language, but – crucially – without losing their *historical* condition. Yet, this surplus of literary has not substantially damaged their referentiality – the integrity of the past.

These enduring historical works contrast with those others which, as Nietzsche puts it, have provided a perfectly truthful account of a series of past events that nonetheless contained not one iota of a specifically historical understanding of them.[14] The literary dimension of historical narratives has been confirmed because of the failure of the nineteenth- and twentieth-century professional historians' ideal of making historical studies a science. To validate this, a clear 'return of narrative' has been promoted by historians from the 1970s, along with its subsequent 'material' and 'anti-narrativist' turn.[15]

---

[14] This is the 'antiquarian history' which Nietzsche described in his essay 'On the Utility and Liability of History for Life', in K. Ansell Pearson and D. Large (eds.), *The Nietzsche Reader* (Malden: Blackwell publishing, 2006), 124–141.

[15] Lawrence Stone, 'The Revival of Narrative: Reflections on a New Old History', *Past and Present* 85 (1979): 3–25. Since 2000, the new narrative has been enriched – and, in some sense, replaced by – new realistic concepts such as presence (Hans U. Gumbrecht, *Production of Presence: What Meaning Cannot Convey* (Stanford: Stanford University Press, 2004)), experience (Martin Jay, *Songs of Experience: Moderns American and European Variations of a Universal Theme* (Berkeley: California University Press, 2005)), the sublime (Ankersmit, *Sublime Historical Experience*), materiality (Daniel Miller (ed.), *Materiality* (Durham: 2006) and Kalle Pihlainen, 'The Possibilities of "Materiality" in Writing and Reading History', *Historia da Historiografia* 12 (2019): 7–81), and representationalism (Kuukkanen, *Postnarrativist Philosophy*).

Without denying the historicist revolution's epistemic benefits, historians have recognized that any historical interpretation of the events of the past requires a literary as well as a scientific approach. Previous attempts to reduce history to science have produced no more than 'boring and shallow historiographic ad hoc interpretations of theories that could be relevant only for one facet of history'.[16] The acknowledgement of this literary dimension of historical texts leads to the recognition of the literarity achieved by classics in history:

> Historiography adds something to a merely factual account of the past. This something added may be a pseudo-scientific explanation of why events happened as they did, but the recognized classics of Western historiography – which is what we are discussing – always add something else. And I think that it is 'literarity' which they add, for which the great modern novelists provide between models than the pseudo-scientists of society.[17]

The first problem historical works with this surplus of literarity has to confront is the multiplicity of interpretations it enables. Kermode unequivocally believes that 'without the co-operation of the reader's imagination [the classic] can hardly exist at all, except for readers so naïve as to be contented with what, as a simple tale, must seem ill-told'.[18] This leads him to conclude that a classic's survival depends on 'a more or less continuous chorus of voices asserting the value

---

[16] Tucker, *Our Knowledge of the Past*, 211.
[17] White, 'An Old Question', 395.
[18] Kermode, *The Classic*, 114.

of the classic'.[19] Kermode uses Barthes's phrase, 'l'oeuvre pro-pose, l'homme dispose' ('the work proposes, man disposes') to confirm his position. The multiplicity of critical readings must certainly result from the work's 'constitutive ambiguity', an expression that Barthes borrows from Roman Jakobson.[20]

Ultimately, these critics draw attention to the con-structed nature of the text, wherein readers' opinions influence the book's status. I, however, argue that the consoli-dation of a classic is not simply a process based on consensus or on reception, but that there are previous conditions of a particular work of history that make it a classic, allowing it to be perceived by readers as such. Clearly, the approach of these critics helps clarify that the two dimensions of the clas-sic – the text itself and the model of the classic constructed by the critics – support each other, even if the former has life in itself and the latter has it only in relation to the former. Yet, the interdependence between the text and its representation opens the hermeneutical (and greatly paradoxical) dilemma that the more open to interpretation a text is, the more classic it may become.

This *interpretive paradox* may function in litera-ture, but it is particularly problematic in history since one assumes that historical texts, which aim towards a scien-tific standard of accuracy, should be as unambiguous as possible. Jonathan Culler rightly pointed to this paradox some decades ago when he argued that philosophy and sci-ence always 'aimed at putting an end to writing' in their

---

[19] Kermode, *The Classic*, 117.
[20] Roland Barthes, quoted in Kermode, *The Classic*, 137.

epistemological cloak.[21] But literary critics would never say this for literature, and *most* historians, like this author, would never say this for history.

From the mid-nineteenth century, history was viewed as a scientific operation in which rigorous access to primary sources with a systematic application of certain methodological rules would guarantee an accurate representation of the past. In their highly programmatic and influential textbook *Introduction aux études historiques* (1898), Charles-Victor Langlois and Charles Seignobos banned figurative language for historiographic writing, assuming the long positivist and historicist traditions accumulated during the nineteenth century.[22] This orientation was even increased by the three historiographic dominant paradigms of post-war: Marxism, structuralism, and quantitativism. If we take this epistemic principle, based on the categories of experimental and social sciences, as an absolute truth, historical texts would never fall under the systematic concept of classic provided by philosophers, or under the historical categories of the archaic, the classic, or the baroque provided by literary scholars and art historians. There could be no classics in history or science

---

[21] Jonathan Culler, *On Deconstruction: Theory and Criticism after Structuralism* (London: Routledge, 1983), 90. Although I cannot enter this debate in detail, it is important to note that at least some philosophers of science such as Max Black and Mary Hesse have certainly recognized some 'literary' elements in the sciences (Ankersmit, *History and Tropology*, 9).

[22] Philippe Carrard, *History as a Kind of Writing: Textual Strategies in Contemporary French Historiography* (Chicago: The University of Chicago Press, 2017), 2–8 and 167.

following these paradigms because, as Kermode argues, in the context of the stability and timeless character of the classics, 'discrepancies between the model and observational data [would] require too many new rules – epicycles, *translationes* – for the model itself to remain credible; a new model is required'.[23] This has been confirmed by the ephemeral validity of many scientific theories and experimentations verified in the past. And it shows that any form of historical writing may never attain the status of a classic *only* because of its scientific value or its historical data, no matter how valuable or original.

Yet, when we read or analyse historical works like Polybius' *Histories*, Jean Froissart's *Chronicles*, Edward Gibbon's *Decline and Fall of the Roman Empire*, Jules Michelet's *History of France*, and, more recently, Fernand Braudel's *Mediterranean*, Edward Thompson's *The Making of the English Working Class*, Carlo Ginzburg's *The Cheese and the Worms*, Natalie Zemon Davis's *The Return of Martin Guerre*, and Robert A. Rosenstone's *Mirror in the Shrine*, we perceive that these works are, and have been, susceptible to multiple interpretations. We may then apply Culler's conclusion to historical writing: 'paradoxically, the more powerful and authoritative an interpretation, the more writing it generates'.[24] One single historical text should invite and support varieties of interpretations. In fact, one of the key features of a classical text is that it has received diverse interpretations in the past and keeps providing the basis for re-readings in the present and models for the future.

---

[23] Kermode, *The Classic*, 117.
[24] Culler, *On Deconstruction*, 90.

Numerous scholars of history deal with particular topics and publish countless books and *papers* – an ephemeral genre in itself. Only very few of these texts pass the test of time. One realizes that one of the signposts of durability, and what makes them classics, is precisely their ability to generate ongoing historiographical debates. Yet the plurality of interpretations inspired by one single classic text leads to the problem of the *difficulty* of approaching them. In his essay 'On Difficulty', George Steiner describes issues related to reading classic texts, since all of them manifest a key openness, an ability to be interpreted in many different ways.[25] Thus, historical writing has to overcome not only the test of time to turn into a classic but also the fact that, as Steiner argues, the criterion of validating works as classic itself changes with time, depending on particular contexts: '[O]ur alternances of judgment are neither axiomatic nor of lasting validity.'[26]

Nevertheless, beyond this idea that scholarly consensus or general agreement by the audience may help to *create* some classic texts, Gadamer privileges the autonomous existence of the text over the consensual agreement. Even if he does not deny the influence of the latter to provide classics with a special legitimacy, Gadamer argues that

> It is not at all the case, as the historical mode of thought would have us believe, that the value judgment which accords something the status of a classic was in fact

[25] George Steiner, 'On Difficulty', in George Steiner (ed.), *On Difficulty and Other Essays* (Oxford: Oxford University Press, 1978), 18–47.
[26] George Steiner, 'Humane Literacy', in George Steiner (ed.), *Language and Silence* (London: Faber and Faber, 1985), 21–29, here 26.

destroyed by historical reflection and its criticism of all teleological construals of the process of history. Rather, through this criticism the value judgment implicit in the concept of the classical acquires a new, special legitimacy.[27]

At first, the eternal present of the classic makes it resistant to historical criticism, since 'it precedes all historical reflection and continues in it'.[28] But, in the end, the judgement of the critic on the classic would add something to its legitimization, instead of building an essential part of its creation.

Figurative Language

Kermode's intuitions on the classics' openness to multiple interpretations, Steiner's emphasis on the difficulty of the critical approach to the classics, and Gadamer's conviction of the legitimizing function of criticism for classics are reflections that, admittedly, could apply both to the classics of literature and the classics of history – with the above-mentioned exception of the necessity for historical writing to avoid ambiguity. More specific to the classic in history is its particular use of metaphorical language, a necessary condition to becoming a classic as argued by Ricoeur's and Danto's highlighting of the resemblance of metaphor to intentional historiographical contexts.[29]

---

[27] Gadamer, *Truth and Method*, 287.

[28] Gadamer, *Truth and Method*, 287.

[29] Ricoeur, *Time and Narrative*, I: 161–163; Ricoeur, *The Rule of Metaphor*, 216–256 (Study 7: 'Metaphor and Reference.'); and Arthur C. Danto, *The Transfiguration of the Commonplace* (Cambridge: Harvard University Press, 1983), 187–189. See also Jacques Derrida, 'White Mythology: Metaphor in the Text of Philosophy', in Jacques Derrida (ed.), *Margins*

Some theorists of history have actually highlighted the relevance (and convenience) of the metaphorical dimension of historical texts. Frank Ankersmit has argued that 'the best history is the most metaphorical one because it offers the finest "belvedere", the broadest panorama of insight'.[30] Assuming that 'the contract between historian and reader has changed' in order to satisfy our desire for presence and to make history matter, Kalle Pihlainen argues for the rejection of interpretive and narrative closure in historical texts, at least to the same extent readers of literary narratives do.[31] Decisively, White's *metahistorical* concept reflects this metaphorical structure of historical discourse, not only because his theory of the tropes achieved a rapprochement between history and literature (because both have in common the use of figurative language), but also because of his belief in the analogy between the historical

of Philosophy (Brighton, 1986), 228; Ankersmit, *History and Tropology*, 12–13; and Mark Johnson (ed.), *Philosophical Perspectives on Metaphor* (Minneapolis: University of Minnesota Press, 1981).

[30] Ankersmit, *History and Tropology*, 41 and Hans Kellner, 'The Return of Rhetoric', in Nancy Partner and Sarah Foot (eds.), *The Sage Handbook of Historical Theory* (Los Angeles: Sage, 2013), 148–161, here, 157.

[31] Kalle Pihlainen, *The Work of History: Constructivism and a Politics of the Past* (London: Routledge, 2017), 85 and 105. For the concept of 'closure' (that is, the idea that all various textual means for meaning-creation come to focus in one preferred interpretation) see Michael Riffaterre, 'Syllepsis', *Critical Inquiry* 6 (1980): 625–638 and Michael Riffaterre, 'Interpretation and Undecidability', *New Literary History* 12 (1981): 227–242. For the application of this concept in literature, see Frank Kermode, *The Art of Telling* (Cambridge University Press, 1972), 61, 67–68, and 72.

text and reality itself.[32] Thus, the historical operation consists of translating a text of the past into a narrative text in the present. This 'translation procedure' leads historians to use literary tropes (metaphor, metonymy, synecdoche, or irony) in their historical narratives. Yet, crucially for my argument, this use of figurative language does not necessarily lessen the historicity of their texts. As Philippe Carrard has argued,

> Rhetoricians, linguists, and philosophers of language have long debated whether figurative language as such provides information, or whether it is essentially decorative and reducible to its paraphrase in literal language. The consensus is that figurative language does indeed have informational value: a figurative utterance is always significant, whether it is the creative, 'live' metaphor of the poet, the functional analogy of the scholar or … the 'dead' tropes we use in everyday communication. The figures on which New Historians rely certainly tell us something fundamental about these historians' endeavors.[33]

---

[32] To be sure, White's position is not particularly original on this specific point, since Wilhelm Dilthey had argued a century earlier that 'it is not just that sources are texts, but historical reality itself is a text that has to be understood' (Gadamer, *Truth and Method*, 198).

[33] Carrard, Poetics of the *New History*, 208. For confirming his idea of 'consensus', Carrard quotes Ricoeur, *The Rule of Metaphor*, Samuel R. Levin, *The Semantics of Metaphor* (Baltimore: Johns Hopkins University Press, 1977); Earl R. MacCormac, *A Cognitive Theory of Metaphor* (Cambridge: MIT Press, 1990); Andrew Ortony, *Metaphor and Thought* (Cambridge: Cambridge University Press, 1993); Mark Johnson (ed.), *Philosophical Perspectives on Metaphor* (Ann Arbor: UMI, 1981); and Wolf Paprotté and René Driven (eds.), *The Ubiquity of Metaphor* (Amsterdam: J. Benjamins, 1985).

Applying this idea to my argument regarding the classics in history, and arguing that this use of the metaphor is different from what literary authors do, I believe that the more skilfully historians use these tropes (especially the metaphor), the greater their possibilities of achieving classic status. The metaphor in historical writing is a powerful epistemological tool – for instance, it allows for the capture of a whole epoch with one image. Metaphor in historical texts, as described by the history critics I quote in this section such as Ankersmit, Pihlainen, White, Carrard, and LaCapra does not make the historical text a classic in the sense that literary critics such as Ricoeur and philosophers such as Gadamer have in mind. The metaphors that historians use to describe, for instance, the Middle Ages, are not ones that speak to us as metaphors we can apply to our own age. But it greatly enriches the content of the historical narrative (as a part of the 'surplus of meaning' I am assigning to the classics of history), because it helps us to understand a past era from the present. From this perspective, too, the classic in history is different from the classic in literature: the use of figurative language serves very diverse ends.

It is highly symptomatic, for instance, that most of the historical works considered classics use a metaphor in their title or made it play a central role in their argument. Examples of this include 'The Cheese and the Worms' (Carlo Ginzburg), 'The Triumph of Purgatory' (Jacques Le Goff), 'Death Untamed' (Philippe Ariès), and 'Rembrandt's eyes' (Simon Schama) to quote some examples from the twentieth century. Others, particularly the historians of the Annales school, are masters of using metaphors to state their heuristic objectives and define the key concepts of their arguments:

> Braudel, in his introduction to *L'Identité de la France*, relies on a metaphor borrowed from the field of natural phenomena to familiarize new readers with his idea of research conducted in the long time-span: his project is to describe the 'tides' and 'floods' coming from the past of France, and to follow how they 'flow into the present as rivers flow into the sea'. Braudel, then, sketches the central question of the 'identity' of France with geological metaphors of the same type: this identity is the result of what the past has left in 'successive layers', just as the 'powerful strata' of the earth's crust originate in the deposits of 'marine sediments'. If France has an identity, it should thus be regarded as a 'residue', an 'amalgam', the outcome of 'additions' and 'mixtures'.[34]

The section 'Commentaire' in Georges Duby's *Le Dimanche de Bouvines* (1973) contains numerous metaphoric phrases:

> War in the thirteenth century was thus a 'hunting party', whose distinctiveness lay in the fact that 'venerers' appeared less interested in killing the 'stag' than in taking it alive, to collect a ransom and recover their expenses. Likewise, Duby describes a battle as a 'liturgy', a 'ceremony', and even a 'sacrament'. But he also views it as a 'game', where kings showed up 'flanked with pawns, knights, and rooks, as in chess', and where the participants' main concern was to play 'well' and 'fair' as much as to gain victory.[35]

[34] Carrard, *Poetics of the New History*, 201–202.
[35] Carrard, *Poetics of the New History*, 203.

Carrard explains that figurative language helps Braudel and Duby function as scholars who approach big questions like 'What used to happen?', 'How do people behave?' or 'What were things like?' In those cases, metaphors supply handy answers, illuminating for contemporary readers the medieval and early modern codes, rules, conventions, and attitudes. A medievalist like myself might question the legitimacy of characterizing medieval culture as a kind of permanent festival, as some of Duby's metaphors seem to imply. But I empathize – as an author, theorist, and reader of history myself – with the effectiveness of metaphors to improve the historical understanding of the past.

Thus, metaphor rather than mimesis produces historical texts with that 'surplus of meaning' I assign to the classics in history. This 'surplus of meaning' related with the metaphoric use of the language in historical writings contributes decisively to answer how a work bond to its own time and place – its Bourdieuian 'habitus' – also speaks beyond it. As Ankersmit argues, historical texts that use metaphorical language become more mimetic of the reality of the past, as mimetic and archaeological historical texts tend to impoverish it: 'the *making* or *poetic* function of narrative [is more realistic than] the *matching* function that has always been so dear to the mimetic epistemology of positivism'.[36] Ultimately, the ability of metaphor to multiply meanings ('metaphors always show us something in

---

[36] Dominick LaCapra, *Rethinking Intellectual History* (Ithaca: Cornell University Press, 1983), 76, paraphrased by Ankersmit, *History and Tropology*, 66. Emphasis in the original.

terms of something else')[37] opens historical texts to multiple interpretations:

> It is this mediative function that permits us to speak of a historical narrative as an extended metaphor. As a symbolic structure, the historical narrative does not *reproduce* the events it describes; it tells us in what direction to think about the events and changes our thought about the events with different emotional valences. This historical narrative does not *image* the things it indicates; it *calls to mind* images of the things it indicates, in the same way that the metaphor does.[38]

As the *fin-de-siècle* impressionistic picture aimed to distinguish itself from a photograph without losing its referentiality, historians who use metaphorical language do not aim to 'close' their representation of the past. Rather, they operate by 'replacing mimetic meaning [by] extended metaphor'.[39] The naïve realism which identifies a historical account of the past with a picture is replaced by the belief that historical narrative is a complex linguistic code – one that adequately reflects in its turn the complexity of the past itself. To use another image, the historical use of the metaphor would function as an opaque text, as its mimetic language would function just as a transparent glass, as Ankersmit has argued:

---

[37] Ankersmit, *History and Tropology*, 65.

[38] Hayden V. White, 'Historical Text as Literary Artifact', in *Tropics of Discourse* (Baltimore: The Johns Hopkins University Press, 1978), 91 (emphasis in the original).

[39] White, 'Historical Text', 91 and Kalle Pihlainen, 'The Moral of the Historical Story: Textual Differences in Fact and Fiction', *New Literary History* 33 (2002): 39–60, here 45.

The historian's language is not a transparent, passive medium *through* which we can see the past, as we do perceive what is written in a letter through the glass paperweight lying on top of it. ... The historian's language does not strive to make itself invisible like the glass paperweight of the epistemological model, but it wishes to take on the same solidity and opacity as a thing. ... Metaphor and the historical narrative have the density and opacity we ordinarily associate only with things or objects; in a way, they *are* things.[40]

The analogy between the opacity of a text and the transparency of glass clarifies the difference between the openness of the classic and the *closed* nature of the science mentioned above, since, in Ankersmit's words, 'the transparency view of language is better suited to the sciences that have come into existence since the seventeenth century'.[41] Ankersmit's analogy seems to me very useful, not only to understand the difference between history and science ('for [scientists] metaphor is a perversion of scientific rigor and clarity')[42] but also to highlight the function of the metaphor in historical texts, generally considered. In addition, from the point of view of the development of historical writing, it alerts us to the naivety of the epistemological presupposition that the historian's language is merely a *mirror* of the past as posited in some radical applications by positivisms and historicisms.

[40] Ankersmit, *History and Tropology*, 65 (emphasis in the original).
[41] Ankersmit, *History and Tropology*, 66. He quotes Foucault, *The Order of Things*, 34–46.
[42] Ankersmit, *History and Tropology*, 215.

White illustrates these ideas through an interpretation of *The Education of Henry Adams*, itself a classic. He differentiates the first part of Adams' autobiography, which works as 'document' of intellectual history – 'so beloved by diplomatic historians for its observations of the diplomatic scene and by those with a conventional notion of what a "narrative" should be' – from the second part, which functions as 'classic text', 'with its metahistorical speculations and tone of pessimism (which offends those who have a conventional notion of what a proper "autobiography" should be)'.[43] White bases his distinction on the dialectic between 'documentary' and 'classic' texts, echoing Nietzsche's distinction between 'archaeological' and 'critical' history. The former encloses the richness of the past in a document, while the last serves as a tool for further understanding and interpretation of the world – past and present:

> The classic text seems to command our attention because it not only contains ideas and insights about 'the human condition' in general but provides an interpretative model by which to carry further our investigations in our own time or, indeed, any time. In reality, however, the classic text, the master text, intrigues us, not because (or not only because) its meaning-content is universally valid or authoritative … but because it gives us insight

---

[43] See also, Hayden White, 'The Context in the Text: Method and Ideology in Intellectual History', in *The Content of the Form*, 185–213, here 212. Similar ideas in White, 'Method and Ideology in Intellectual History', in Dominick LaCapra and Steven L. Kaplan (eds.), *Modern European Intellectual History: Reappraisals and Perspectives* (Ithaca: Cornell University Press, 1982), 280–310.

into a process that is universal and definitive of human species-being in general, *the process of meaning production.*[44]

White concludes that the condition of the historical classic would come from its ability to reveal a high degree of complexity in the meaning-production process – this process becoming the text's own subject matter, its own ideological content.[45] Consequently, a classic such as *The Education of Henry Adams* becomes valuable because of its 'meaning production rather than with the meaning produced, with processes of the text rather than with the text as product'.[46] In the end, the apparent 'flaws' of the classic texts – those ambiguities, duplicities, hesitancies, thematic obsessions, and persuasive irony subtly created by Adams in his autobiography, or what Pihlainen describes as 'offenses against expected or "objective" ways of presentation'[47] – is what makes it a classic work: 'an example of self-conscious and self-celebrating creativity, poiesis'.[48]

Surplus of Meaning

My own reflection on the classics in history has actually been moved by my concern with the increasing divorce between scholars of history and general audiences. Certainly, as

[44] White, 'The Context in the Text', 211 (emphasis added).
[45] Pihlainen, 'The Moral', 43.
[46] White, 'The Context in the Text', 212.
[47] Pihlainen, 'The Moral', 47.
[48] White, 'The Context in the Text', 212.

Pihlainen rightly notes, the referentiality that historians have to observe brings limitations to their narrative, so that 'historical narratives generally [produce] less compelling metaphors and literary fiction [produces] more compelling metaphors'.[49] Nevertheless, even considering the epistemic limitations proper to referential language, I argue that historians should be more aware of the challenges in using metaphorical language.

All these arguments lead me to claim that the metaphorical dimension of history creates certain surplus of meaning which reveals the complexity of the past. 'Surplus of meaning' is a critical concept, originally applied to literature, especially the realist novel in the style of Jane Austen, which points to the way that some works are about very specific characters in plausible locales. They render their narrative in representational detail that keeps the plot firmly situated in its context. Nonetheless, they 'speak' to themes and questions far bigger than their literal subject matter, although the author never raises these issues directly or explicitly. This is the correlative power of classic histories: beyond the concrete stories they tell and the specific contexts they represent, they make readers think about large questions of social life, power, individuality, and life in time.

I argue that, at this point, classical historical works would act as their literary peers. In his essay 'Metaphor and Symbol', Paul Ricoeur opposes the functioning of signification in works of literature to its role in scientific works, whose significations are to be taken literally rather than figuratively.

[49] Pihlainen, 'The Moral', 43.

To achieve literality, works of literature receive their signification from a 'surplus of meaning', which is what expands
their formal richness to an expressed content. The key question, then, is 'whether the surplus of meaning characteristic
of literary works is a part of their signification or if it must be
understood as an external factor'.[50] Ricoeur concludes that it
may be part of their signification, and finds the answer in the
inexhaustible capacity of metaphor to endow literary narratives with this surplus of meaning.

To achieve the surplus of meaning, history writing
must then find a balance between literal and figurative language and meaning. Both are equally necessary, but the ability of historical texts to endure is granted by their figurative
rather than literal meaning. Literal and symbolic signification
are mutually dependent, since they require one another. This
is especially relevant in the historical operation, in which the
literal sense becomes indispensable. For this reason, historical writing is particularly sensitive to the need for balance
between the one and the other. If the literal prevails, history
becomes insipid. If the symbolic becomes hegemonic, the historical narrative becomes empty of content. Classical historical works teach us that it is possible to maintain this balance,
so they also function as paradigms and models.

Put in historiographical terms, Georges Duby's treatment of the 'three orders of feudal society' is applicable to
many other analogous realities of social stratification in other
historical periods. Edward Gibbon's analysis of the 'decline' of
the Roman Empire means much more than when we simply

---

[50] Ricoeur, *Interpretation Theory*, 45.

treat the concept of 'decline' abstractly. Fernand Braudel's approach to 'Mediterranean space and time' tells us much about how we should generally perceive the relations between time and space in history. Kantorowicz's image of 'the king's two bodies', applied in principle only to the Middle Ages, is capable of illuminating the entire field of relations between the temporal and the spiritual, no matter in what time and space. All these *historical* metaphors take on a figurative meaning that places the text on an abstract plane capable of reaching universal realities, without losing its necessary contextual limits.

I prefer not to give negative examples, but it is obvious that many historical monographs that do not pass the threshold of literality remain mere reiterations of the primary sources on which they have been based. Their readers may wonder whether it would not have been preferable to produce a catalogue of primary sources, to make them available to future researchers, rather than just a literal reiteration of them. Conversely, thanks to the figurative treatment of Duby's *Three Orders*, Gibbon's *Decline and Fall*, Braudel's *Mediterranean* and Kantorowicz's *Two Bodies*, the specific themes of these classical historians go far beyond what they can tell us about history. Not all historians have such sublime literary qualities, but we should at least try to achieve a minimum of literary creativity in our work. This would allow us to reach a wider audience and also to achieve a language that is paradoxically more properly historical because it allows for more analogous comparisons with the past. As Ricoeur concludes, a symbol contains more meaning than the literality itself, so that 'this surplus of meaning is the residue of the literal interpretation'.[51] This is why I have argued elsewhere that theoretical and literary training is so essential in the education of young history students.[52]

Perhaps this ability to create multiple meanings is what White found in those historians he chose as exemplars of classics in his *Metahistory*, such as Jules Michelet, Leopold von Ranke, Alexis de Tocqueville, and Jacob Burckhardt. Indeed, he identifies one of the keys of becoming a classic in the ability of some historical texts to imitate narrative fiction when they

> provide glimpses of the deep structure of historical consciousness and, by implication, of both historical reflection and historical discourse. This resemblance between historical narrative and fictional narrative, which is a function of their shared interest in the mystery of time, would account, I surmise, for the appeal of those great classics of historical narrative – from Herodotus's *Persian Wars* through Augustine's *City of God*, Gibbon's *Decline and Fall of the Roman Empire*, Michelet's *History of France*, and Burckhardt's *Civilization of the Renaissance in Italy* down to, yes even Spengler's *Decline of the West* – that makes them worthy of study and reflection long after their scholarship has become outmoded and their arguments have been consigned to the status of commonplaces of the culture moments of composition.[53]

---

[51] Ricoeur, *Interpretation*, 55.

[52] Jaume Aurell, 'Rethinking History's Essential Tension: Between Theoretical Reflection and Practical Experimentation', *Rethinking History* 22 (2018): 439–458.

[53] White, *The Content of the Form*, 180. Similar sentence in White, *Tropics of Discourse*, 58.

The metaphorical dimension of the classic in history makes them 'open books', susceptible to re-interpretation and aesthetic fascination, rather than closed artefacts which inspire merely scientific persuasiveness, archaeological interest, or contemplative fascination. They help us 'move away from institutional history and toward popular forms'.[54] They open up a vision of the past that inspires more study in the present and projects towards the future. They prove that understanding the past is a complex cognitive operation, full of ethical and rhetorical implications. They alert us to take the task of history critics and theorists of history more seriously. They are revisited again and again because they are interpretative rather than simply explanations, analyses, or descriptions. Trevor-Roper argues that Braudel's *The Mediterranean* 'as with many classics, it is difficult to define [in] its peculiar quality. A classic, by definition, breaks through the accepted standards of its time, by which it must at first be judged'.[55] As Ankersmit explains,

> The great books in the field of history of historiography, the works of Ranke, de Tocqueville, Burckhardt, Huizinga, Meinecke or Braudel, do not put an end to a historical debate, do not give us the feeling that we now finally know how things actually were in the past and that clarity has ultimately been achieved. On the contrary: these books have proved to be the most powerful

[54] Kalle Pihlainen, 'The Work of Hayden White II: Defamiliarizing Narrative', in *The SAGE*, 119–135, here 132.
[55] H. R. Trevor-Roper, 'Fernand Braudel, the *Annales*, and the Mediterranean', *The Journal of Modern History* 44, 4 (1972): 468–479, here 472.

stimulators of the production of *more* writing – their effect thus to estrange us from the past, instead of placing it upon a kind of pedestal in a historiographical museum so that we can inspect it from all possible perspectives.[56]

The proliferation of historical interpretation generated by those texts we consider classics also shows that they are able to combine the originality that lies at the basis of our readerly admiration with the difference enabled by their multiple interpretations. Thus, Derrida's concept of *différance* helps to explain the category of the classic, since the theory that 'texts may differ from themselves' may apply to the classics of history, because it explains why classics are open to multiple interpretations. Yet, in my view, we should emphasize that using metaphorical language in history does not imply (or should not imply) diminishing referentiality. Rather, it may approach realities of the past that would otherwise be difficult to recreate literally or mimetically. I am not only referring to those realities defined as 'longue durée' by Braudel or 'metahistorical' by White but to most of the *data* related to intellectual and cultural history, the history of concepts or ideas, and reflections on great anthropological notions such as destiny or temporality that have long fascinated philosophers of history. The durability of Gibbon's reflections on the decline of the Roman Empire illustrates this point:

> Every great historical narrative is an allegory of temporality. Thus, long after its scholarship has been

[56] Frank R. Ankersmit, 'The Dilemma of Contemporary Anglo-Saxon Philosophy of History', *History and Theory* 25 (1986): 1–27, here 25 (emphasis in the original).

superseded and its arguments exploded as prejudices of the cultural moment of its production (as in Gibbon's contention that the fall of Rome was caused by the solvent effects of Christianity on pagan manly virtues), the classic historical narrative continues to fascinate as the product of a universal human need to reflect on the insoluble mystery of time.[57]

This 'allegory of temporality' argued by White is exactly what Augustine and Burckhardt convey through their sublimation of a specific historical reality – the decadence of Rome and the rising of the Renaissance, respectively – into the hidden action of timeless spiritual forces. In the preface of his *City of God*, Augustine declares that

> Most glorious is and will be the City of God, both in this fleeting age of ours, wherein she lives by faith, a stranger among infidels, and in the days when she shall be established in her eternal home. Now she waits for it with patience, 'until righteousness returns to judgement'; then she shall possess it with preeminence in final victory and perfect peace. In this work, on which I embark in payment of my promise to you, O dearest son Marcellinus, it is my purpose to defend the City of God against those who esteem their own gods above her Founder. The work is great and difficult, but God is my helper.[58]

Burckhardt uses the same majestic style, the same moral appeal to the reader, in the portico of his *Renaissance*:

[57] White, *The Content of the Form*, 181.
[58] Augustine, *City of God* (Cambridge: Harvard University Press, 2014), 11.

'To each eye, perhaps, the outlines of a given civilization present a different picture; and in treating of a civilization which is the mother of our own, and whose influence is still at work among us, it is unavoidable that individual judgment and feeling should tell every moment both on the writer and on the reader.'[59]

Aesthetic Sublimation

Evidently, the more metaphorical, allegorical, and figurative the language the historians use, the more pleasing the text might be. This aesthetic dimension is a vital element in the creation of a classic in literature or in art, as well as in the writing of history. Some historical works achieve a certain aesthetic standard, even if their historical styles are completely different: Michelet as romance, Burckhardt as satire, Huizinga as modernism, Braudel as total-scientific history, Duby as essay, and Davis as narrative, among others. Yet the quality of their historical prose and ability to follow a coherent thesis in the midst of abundant historical data are common to all and give them a place in the pantheon of the classics of history.

François Furet praises Michelet's *French Revolution* as 'the cornerstone of all revolutionary historiography'.[60] Yet Michelet did not use conventional historical prose but, rather, the technique of a literary romance to describe the epic of the

[59] Jacob Burckhardt, *The Civilization of the Renaissance in Italy* (New York: Harper, 1958), 21.
[60] François Furet, *Revolutionary France, 1770–1880* (Oxford: Blackwell, 1995), 571.

French people's struggle against tyranny and injustice. His prose seems to give the past new life:

> From the priest to the king, from the Inquisition to the Bastille, the road is straight, but long. Holy, holy Revolution, how slowly dost thou come! – I, who have been waiting for thee for a thousand years in the furrows of the middle ages, – what! Must I wait still longer? – Oh! How slowly time passes! Oh! How I have counted the hours! – Wilt thou never arrive? … And as thou art Justice, thou wilt support me in this book, where my path has been marked out by the emotions of my heart and not by private interest, nor by any thought of this sublunar world. Thou wilt be just towards me, and I will be so towards all. For whom then have I written this, but for thee, Eternal Justice?[61]

Michelet's passion draws in the reader from the first paragraph, and validates Furet's assertion that this, too, is a 'literary monument'.[62] Burckhardt published his master-piece just two decades after Michelet's *French Revolution*, in a satiric, rather than romantic style. It responds to a very different political – the pre-unified Germany rather than the post-revolutionary France – and historiographical context, at the margins of classic German historicism instead of at the core of French romantic historiography. Karl Löwith credits Burckhardt for liberating history from myth and from the abstractions of the philosophy of history.[63] But Hayden White

---

[61] Jules Michelet, *History of the French Revolution* (Chicago: University of Chicago Press, 1967), 78 and 80.

[62] Furet, *Revolutionary*, 571.

[63] Karl Löwith, *Meaning in History: The Theological Implications of the Philosophy of History* (Chicago: University of Chicago Press, 1949), 26.

adds that while Burckhardt liberated history from the myths of Michelet's romance, Ranke's comedy, and Tocqueville's tragedy,

> [h]e consigned it to the care of another, the *mythos* of Satire, in which historical knowledge is definitively separated from any relevance to the social and cultural problems of its own time and place. In Satire, history becomes a 'work of art', but the concept of art which is presupposed in this formula is a purely 'contemplative' one – Sisyphean rather than Promethean, passive rather than active, resigned rather than heroically turned to the illumination of current human life.[64]

Burckhardt's emphatic rhetorical style, prone to exaggerations and idealizations, reflects this, especially in his approach to Italian pre-renaissance poetry:

> If we were to collect the pearls from the courtly and knightly poetry of all the countries of the West during the two preceding centuries we should have a mass of wonderful divinations and single pictures of the inward life, which at first would seem to rival the poetry of the Italians. Leaving lyrical poetry out of account, Godfrey of Strasburg gives us, in *Tristram and Isolt*, a representation of human passion, some features of which are immortal. But these pearls lie scattered in the ocean of artificial convention, and they are altogether something very different from a complete objective picture of the inward man and his spiritual wealth.[65]

---

[64] White, *Metahistory*, 233.
[65] Burckhardt, *The Civilization of the Renaissance*, 305.

Michelet and Burckhardt make a different approach to the Revolution since the former idealizes it while the latter demonizes it. But both use metaphors to increase the dramatic and aesthetic effect of their narrations. In contrast with Michelet's 'cycles of nature', Burckhardt's metaphors are 'wave' and 'metastasis' which express the notion of constant change and the lack of continuity between the impulses.

Already in the twentieth century, Huizinga uses a very different rhetorical method in his *Waning of the Middle Ages*, since he shifts between a historicist's deployment of massive amounts of data and narrative prose. His style appears shaped by the dominant impressionist and modernist mood in art and literature. As Norman F. Cantor explains, historians of the 1920s and 1930s, 'encountered the formidable challenge of writing non-narrative history, a new mode of analytical history that reflected the method of close reading of a segment of past society and avoided the longitudinal projection of narrative histories that covered long-term developments, which was the fashionable mode of the nineteenth century.'[66]

These historians would take a certain moment in time or a specific topic and render hundreds of detailed impressions of aspects of the culture, religion, art, or politics without abandoning their aim to capture the whole picture, in parallel with impressionist painters. In this context, Huizinga's *Waning* establishes an equilibrium between the analytical monographic approach that follows strict academic rules of the historical discipline and the need to appeal to a

---

[66] Norman F. Cantor, *The American Century: Varieties of Culture in Modern Times* (New York: Harper, 1997), 142.

non-specialist audience, which his fellow historians could judge as non-referential generalizations:

> To the world when it was half a thousand years younger, the outlines of all things seemed more clearly marked than to us. The contrast between suffering and joy, between adversity and happiness, appeared more striking. All experience had yet to the minds of men the directness and absoluteness of the pleasure and pain of child-life. Every event, every action, was still embodied in expressive and solemn forms, which raised them to the dignity of a ritual. For it was not merely the great facts of birth, marriage and death, which, by the sacredness of the sacrament, were raised to the rank of mysteries; incidents of less importance, like a journey, a task, a visit, were equally attended by a thousand formalities: benedictions, ceremonies, formulae.[67]

Historical prose drastically shifted from narrative to analytical from Huizinga's *Waning* to Braudel's *Mediterranean*. This masterpiece has been 'universally acknowledged as one of the most significant works of the discipline of history in the twentieth century' and it is 'remembered above all for its innovative approach to historical time and narrative'.[68] Even if its author explicitly aimed to emphasize the book's objectivity, it is full of metaphors, especially personifications. This seems ironic, since Braudel is considered one of the most scientifically-oriented historians ever

---

[67] Johan Huizinga, *The Waning of the Middle Ages* (New York: Doubleday Anchor Books, 1954), 9.

[68] Howard Caygill, 'Braudel's Prison Notebooks', *History Workshop Journal* 57 (2004): 151–160, here 152.

and explicitly argued against using metaphors in historical discourse. But he remains 'the uncontested master in personification', as Carrard demonstrates, especially when he applies metaphors to the geological and geographical phenomena he analyses for his long-durée study.[69]

In addition, Braudel does not hesitate to reveal his emotional involvement with his subject – a movement supposedly forbidden for those 'scientific historians' – as he opens his *Mediterranean* with the sentence 'J'ai passionnément aimé la Méditerranée' ('I have passionately loved the Mediterranean').[70] H. Stuart Hughes argues that the tone of *The Mediterranean* is 'subject to disconcerting shifts, oscillating erratically between the statistical and the poetic' as 'romantic flights of prose' alternate with 'merciless quantification'.[71] The result of all these apparent contradictions is a book full of historiographical nerve which still fascinates historians coming from different intellectual, cultural, methodological, and theoretical traditions.

During the 1980s, Duby replaced Braudel as the generational leader of the Annales School, as he shifted from scientific language to essayistic analysis and from structuralism to mentalités. But he kept the use of historical metaphors and

---

[69] Carrard, *Poetics of the New History*, 205. On the use of the metaphor among other French historians, see Carrard's epigraph 'The Return of Figurative Language', 198–217.

[70] Braudel, *La Méditerranée et le monde méditerranéen à l'époque de Philippe II* (Paris: Armand Colin, 1990), I: 10. On Braudel's emotional empathy with his own historical work see Aurell, 'Autobiographical Texts', 425–445.

[71] H. Stuart Hughes, 'The Historians and the Social Order', in *The Obstructed Path: French Social Thought in the Years of Desperation (1930–1960)* (New York: Harper, 1966), 19–64 here 59.

the narrative of the succession of changes within a social system, as his *The Three Orders: Feudal Society Imagined* shows. In his study of a tripartite construct of the hierarchical medieval French society – people who pray, people who fight, people who work – Duby deploys the same allegory of temporality we noted in other classics:

> Ideology, we are aware, is not a reflection of real life, but a project for acting on it. If this action is to have any likelihood of success, the disparity between the imaginary representation and the 'realities' of life should not be too great. This being the case, and supposing that the ideological discourse does not go unnoticed, new attitudes may then crystallize, changing the way men look upon the society to which they belong. To observe the system in which the model of the three 'orders' is embodied as it comes to light in France, to attempt to follow its course through success and misfortune from 1025 to 1225, is to confront one of the central questions now facing the sciences of man: the question of the relationship between the material and the mental in the evolution of societies.[72]

Natalie Zemon Davis, in turn, shifted from the analysis of the impersonal systems to the narrative of personal actors. But the rhetorical effect of her classic historical prose emulates that of her predecessors. She literally revives Bertrande, the peasant who was accused of adultery because of the confusion between her husband, Martin Guerre (who had left the town years earlier), and another man who pretended

---

[72] Georges Duby, *The Three Orders. Feudal Society Imagined* (Chicago: The University of Chicago Press, 1982), 8–9.

to be Martin Guerre and whom she accepted as her husband. Davis's historical imagination enters Bertrande's mind and tries to understand her thoughts just before the crucial trial which might condemn her to death. The twentieth-century historian seems to project her struggle in favour of women's rights into the sixteenth-century historical actor:

> For Bertrande, who knew the truth, there were yet other consequences of the lie. She had tried to fashion her life as best she could, using all the leeway and imagination she had as a woman. But she was also proud of the honor and her virtue and was, as she would say later in court, God-fearing. She wanted to live as a mother and family woman at the center of village society. She wanted her son to inherit. Would God punish them because of the lie? And if their marriage were only an invention, was she a shameful adulteress in her mother's eyes and in those of the other village women? And would her daughter Bernarde be stained, since it was said that a child conceived in adultery was marked with the sins of its parents? She loved her new Martin, but he had tricked her once; might he after all not trick her again? And what if the other Martin Guerre came back?[73]

Contemporary Relevance of the Past

The historical classic manages to avoid ambiguity in spite of its many interpretations, to foreground referentiality, to preserve the duality of the event and its representations, and to use

---

[73] Davis, *The Return of Martin Guerre*, 60–61.

historical metaphorical language. In addition, it links ancient authority – one consolidated by the perspective of time and materialized in tradition – and a modern perspective, one that interprets the past as the present requires. Eusebius and Frederic Jackson Turner are, for instance, masters at creating this effect. Eusebius aims to bring back the noble spirit of the origins of Christianity to his own times:

> The succession of the holy apostles along with an account of the times extending from our Saviour to our own day; the magnitude and significance of the deeds said to have been accomplished throughout the ecclesiastical narrative, how many governed and presided over these affairs with distinction in the most famous communities; how many of each generation served as ambassadors of the Divine Logos, either in unwritten form or through written compositions; (…) I shall begin from nowhere else than the beginning of the divine economy relating to our Saviour and Lord Jesus, God's Christ.[74]

Turner's long article on the 'American Frontier' models how generalizations, projections, and simplifications may turn an essay into a classic of history, starting with his ability to feel the readers' identification with the heroic past period – again, the noble spirit of the origins – he studies:

> Up to our own day American history has been in a large degree the history of the colonization of the Great West. The existence of an area of free land, its

---

[74] Eusebius of Caesarea, *The History of the Church* (Oakland: University of California Press, 2019), 39, Book 1, Chapter 1.

continuous recession, and the advance of American settlement westward, explain American development. Behind institutions, behind constitutional forms and modifications, lie the vital forces that call these organs into life and shape them to meet changing conditions. The peculiarity of American institutions is the fact that they have been compelled to adapt themselves to the changes of an expanding people – to the changes involved in crossing a continent, in winning a wilderness, and in developing at each area of this progress out of the primitive economic and political conditions of the frontier into the complexity of city life.[75]

This meeting between the past and the present creates a text about the past's contemporary relevance. But how might a historical text show contemporary relevance? I argue this happens through a serious anthropological project, as a historical classic conveys that deep human reality, pointed out by Frye, 'that shows us that time itself has a shape and a significance in life, and that life itself is not just one clock-tick after another, as it was to the despairing Macbeth'.[76]

In classifying 'the Classics of Nineteenth-Century Historiography' – that is, Jules Michelet, Leopold von Ranke, Alexis de Tocqueville, and Jacob Burckhardt – White defines

---

[75] Frederick Jackson Turner, 'The Significance of the Frontier in American History', delivered at the 1893 meeting of the *American Historical Association* in Chicago, published in *Annual Report of the American Historical Association* (1893): 197–227, here 197.

[76] Northrop Frye, 'Convocation Address: McGill University', in R. D. Denham (ed.), *Northrop Frye on Literature and Society, 1936–1989* (Toronto: University of Toronto Press, 2002), 337–339, here 338.

them as works that 'comprehend the past in ways that illuminated contemporary problems'.[77] This contemporaneity fixes the classics in the past they illuminate and in the present they engage, and projects them to the future. To the point where the classics fall under the category of the 'practical past', I argue that its classical condition is precisely what saves them from the reductionism of an eventual practicality because its timelessness protects them from simplistic presentism that damages the integrity of the past.

What we appreciate in Eusebius' panegyric history, Gibbon's secularized history, Michelet's patriotic history, Ranke's scientific history, Croce's historicist history, Thompson's Marxist history, and Davis's feminist history is not their ideological commitment. These claims may actually lead them to historical reductionism or manipulation: Eusebius' exaltation of Constantine, Gibbon's struggle against clericalism, Michelet's sublimation of France, Ranke's resistance against history as art, Croce's anti-essentialism, Thompson's exaltation of the working class, and Davis's projection of late twentieth-century female vindication onto her historical sixteenth-century historical characters. Rather, we keep reading them because of the creative ways they engage the past, perceive their present, and project to the future. Their approach rejects turning history into mere antiquarianism by consistently making connections to the present or into mere monumentalism by having a practical purpose beyond their care for aestheticism. They recount events of the studied past and link them with the problems and needs of the

---

[77] White, *Metahistory*, 140.

experienced present, thus emphasizing the relevance of historical engagement today. It can be argued that this is precisely the essence of historiography. But, clearly, only a few historical works have been able to achieve this essence, while others grasp some part of it.

While this contemporariness renders these historical classics scientifically vulnerable because of their tendency to ideology, it also makes the critics more indulgent with their possible heuristic and analytic weakness. After examining Jacob Burckhardt's *The Civilization of the Renaissance in Italy*, Benjamin Nelson and Charles Trinkaus argue that 'despite his oversights and errors, his deep cultural and moral commitments, his book exhibits a reality that subsequent scholarship, however reluctantly, has been compelled to affirm'.[78] Jouni-Matti Kuukkanen observes this same paradox for philosophers: 'Perhaps we can divide philosophers into two kinds. There are those who are very systematic and rigorous but who do not seem to open that many new paths for others to follow. Then there are those who are creating and opening new unexpected routes but may lack rigour and be somewhat unsystematic in their work.'[79]

Kuukkanen's duality occurs often in the history of historiography. History classics belong to the second group. Donald Kelley explains that 'the paradigms established by these two devotees of the muse of history [Herodotus and

---

[78] Benjamin Nelson and Charles Trinkaus, 'Introduction', in Jacob Burckhardt (ed.), *The Civilization of the Renaissance*, 3–19, here 4.

[79] Jouni-Matti Kuukkanen, *Meaning Changes: A Study of Thomas Kuhn's Philosophy* (Saarbrücken: VDM Verlag Müller, 2008), 232. On this idea, applied to historiography, see Peter Brown, 'In Gibbon's Shade', in *Society*, 49–62.

Thucydides] have persisted, in a complex and kaleidoscopic way, for almost twenty-five centuries'[80] – from Herodotus' cultural (anthropological, theological) to Thucydides political (power, agency, military) history. Peter Gay states that Chapter 3 of Macaulay's *History of England* 'with all its failings, permitted social history to become a serious discipline'.[81] Peter Brown argues that 'like all great books, [Gibbon's] *Decline and Fall of the Roman Empire* raises themes that stretch far deeper and far wider than a conventional interpretation of this title leads us to expect'.[82] Alan Boureau assigns to Ernst Kantorowicz's *King's Two Bodies* the foundational historical field of political theology.[83] Peter Burke argues that Marc Bloch's *Royal Touch* 'was a pioneer contribution to what was later called the history of "mentalities"'.[84] Burke also explains that Fernand Braudel's *Mediterranean* 'has permanently enlarged the possibilities of the genre in which it was written' and Hug Trevor-Roper argues that 'this work was at once recognized as a historical classic, although, as with many classics, it is difficult to define its peculiar quality'.[85] William Sewell refers to E. P. Thompson's *The Making of the English Working Class* as 'the obligatory starting point for any contemporary discussion of the history of working-class formation. [It] effectively set the agenda for an entire generation

---

[80] Kelley, *Faces of History*, 2–5.
[81] Gay, *Style*, 117.
[82] Brown, *Society*, 56.
[83] Boureau, *Kantorowicz*, 1–2.
[84] Peter Burke, *The French Historical Revolution: The Annales School, 1929–2014* (Cambridge: Polity, 2015), 20.
[85] Burke, *The French*, 48 and Trevor-Roper, 'Fernand Braudel', 472.

of labour historians'.[86] Le Roy Ladurie's *Montaillou* is, for Burke, 'an early example of what came to be called "micro-history". The author studied the world in a grain of sand or, in his own metaphor, the ocean through a drop of liquid.'[87] I have assigned elsewhere to Carolyn Steedman's *Landscape for a Good Woman* the foundation of a new way to understand social history, one that uses autobiography to find new ways to understand its logics.[88]

All these historians have been remembered, and have entered the canon constructed by some of the most followed historians of historiography (Burrow, Burke, Kelley, Iggers, and Breisach among them) not because of their use of the sources, methodology, or accuracy, but because of their ability to forge new paths and open up new oceans in historiography, such as social history (Macaulay), history of mentalities (Bloch), Marxism (Thompson), structuralism (Braudel), and new narrative history (Le Roy). Kuukkanen's point on the history of philosophy and science may thus apply to historiography, comes particularly close to the concept of classic, and connects with the Western myth of the forerunner – St. John the Baptist.[89] Vico's *New Science* is particularly paradigmatic of this intellectual phenomenon:

---

[86] William H. Sewell, Jr., 'How Classes Are Made: Critical Reflections on E. P. Thompson's Theory of Working-Class Formation', in H. J. Kaye and K. McClelland (eds.), *E. P. Thompson: Critical Perspectives* (Cambridge: Polity, 1990), 50–77, here 50.

[87] Burke, *The French*, 95–96.

[88] Jaume Aurell, *Theoretical Perspectives on Historians' Autobiographies* (London: Routledge, 2017), 178–187.

[89] Peter Burke, *Vico* (Oxford: Oxford University Press, 1985), 8.

The *New Science* remains well worth studying, partly because it is a great imaginative achievement, like the poems of Homer and Dante, and partly because it is a seminal work, in the sense that it has again and again shown its capacity to sow fruitful seeds in the imaginations of its readers. Vico's remarkable gift for seeing unsuspected connections has not lost its power to stimulate and to inspire.[90]

The Fruits of the Unconventionality

Gossman has described 'Kuukkanen's paradox', noting that some of the great works of history have turned into *bad* histories from the point of view of the critique: 'Because [Michelet] was such a "bad" historian by certain standards, he helped to transform historiography and continue to inspire the most innovative historians, from Lucien Febvre to Fernand Braudel'[91] – there must be certain 'un-orthodoxy' and 'non-conventionality' among the historians able to create a classic work of history. Peter Brown conveys the same idea for Gibbon:

> It may well be that it is those aspects which make Gibbon appear to be most alien to the sympathies of modern scholars that he has remained most relevant: for behind his dismissal of much of the evidence and many of the phenomena that have come to interest us, there lies a theory of the relation between the ideas and society of a large empire which still merits our careful attention.[92]

[90] Burke, *Vico*, 95.
[91] Gossman, *Between History and Literature*, 200.
[92] Brown, *Society and the Holy*, 25.

In their search for new paths and abandonment of disciplinary orthodoxy, classic historical works usually show a remarkable determination to challenge established theoretical and disciplinary standards – at the risk of losing their contemporaries' critical appreciation. These historians have not been disciplined by the conventions of the field so much as they radicalized the discipline itself.[93] They maintain a balance between traditions and the freshness of the contemporary moment. This form of working at the 'cutting edge of the profession', which Lawrence Stone admired in some of the new narrativist historians of the 1970s, was defined by Thomas Kuhn as the necessary 'essential tension' between tradition and innovation that made science progress.[94]

Writers of historical classics usually value a certain amount of non-conventional work at the margins of scholarly norms, even as they attend to established disciplinary traditions. I am thinking of texts like Marc Bloch's *Royal Touch*, E. P. Thompson's *The Making of the English Working Class*, or Natalie Zemon Davis's *The Return of Martin Guerre* – milestones in the renovation of twentieth-century historiography: Annales, Marxism, and new narrativism. Their critical content and rejection of the conventional theories and practices – Bloch's foundation of the history of collective mentalities, Thompson's approach to *history from below*, and Davis's rupture with the post-war scientific paradigms – shapes a

---

[93] On the concepts of 'disciplination' and 'domestication' of history, see Hayden V. White, 'The Politics of Historical Representation: Discipline and De-Sublimation', *The Content of the Form* (Baltimore, MD: Johns Hopkins University, 1987), 58–82, here 61.

[94] Stone, 'The Revival', 10 and Kuhn, 'The Essential Tension', 226–239.

good part of the 'surplus of meaning' which I argue is one of the marks of classic historical texts. This leads us to recognize the ethical power of classic historical narratives, one that rocks the boat of established practices. As Ankersmit points out, academic disciplines 'have always demonstrated an anarchistic resistance to the monopolization of metaphor by epistemology – and the writing of history is the best example in point'.[95] Historians have usually been particularly attached to this resistance, often at the price of denigrating those who have subsequently proven to be classic authors, who have had to pay a very high price for their daring to tread new paths in historiography.

The Essential Tension

In the end, classics 'serve as paradigms of a distinctively modern historical consciousness'.[96] The operation of examining the classic implies understanding not merely the past world to which the classic belongs and the past to which the classic refers, but recognizing the enduring present naturally involved in the classic that makes it attractive to us as a model, that is, the present world permanently attached to the classic. Thus, a historical text is of particular interest to the reader when it is able to refer to the present. As Gadamer explains,

> In the human sciences we cannot speak of an object of research in the same sense as in the natural sciences, where research penetrates more and more deeply into nature.

[95] Ankersmit, *History and Tropology*, 215.
[96] White, *Metahistory*, 141.

Rather, in the human sciences the particular research
questions concerning tradition that we are interested in
pursuing are motivated in a special way by the present and
its interests. The theme and object of research are actually
constituted by the motivation of the inquiry.[97]

Gadamer connects with the essential tension into
which the classic in history always falls: between history and
literature, between science and art, and between the past and
the present, between tradition and innovation. This last section is devoted to discerning the extent to which this tension
shapes our understanding, not only of the concept of the classic in history, but also of history's disciplinary status itself.

Science is progressive while 'poetry does not improve
or progress with the times; it produces classics and continues to rewrite its classics with the same mental attitudes.'[98]
Gadamer emphasizes the progressive structure of natural sciences and Frye highlights the timeless condition of poetry. But,
what about the eternal and paradoxical hybrid genre of history,
always fighting to find its way between art and science, between
poetry and nature? Applying these ideas to the specificity of
historical operation, Peter Gay has described this dialectic play
which has dominated the entire history of historiography from
its disciplinary foundations, and its implications for the classics:

> The dual nature of history – at once science and art –
> emerges even more strikingly in the related paradox
> that history is at the same time a progressive discipline

---

[97] Gadamer, *Truth and Method*, 284.
[98] Frye, 'Tradition and Change in the Theory of Criticism', in *Northrop Frye on Literature*, 243–254 (here 248).

and a timeless treasure house of classics. Nowadays the historian will not begin his studies of ancient Rome with Gibbon or Mommsen; they are no longer the last word. Yet *The Decline and Fall of the Roman Empire* and the *Römische Geschichte* are imperishable masterpieces which no amount of fresh facts or revisionist interpretations will eject from the pantheon. What makes them immortal is more than their sheer literary merit, great though that is. Their view of the past embodies truths that have been confirmed by other historians and have become a permanent cultural possession. These books, and others like them, are like exquisitely drawn if somewhat old-fashioned maps: delightful to consult, a model to later mapmakers, and still useful for showing others the way.[99]

While working on this book, I had in mind the difference between some classics in literature such as texts by Virgil, Dante, Cervantes, Shakespeare, Goethe, and Proust, with their corresponding classics in historiography such as those written by Herodotus, Thucydides, Eusebius, Guicciardini, Michelet, Ranke, Burckhardt, Bloch, Braudel, or Duby. The former may achieve and, in fact, have achieved a wide general audience. The latter have been usually confined to a scholarly or to, at most, a learned readership. Aristotle's notion of the difference between poetics and history, quoted earlier, serves us at this point: The historian tells what happened, while the other tells what can happen: 'for poetry deals with universals, history with particulars.'[100]

---

[99] Gay, *Style*, 215–216.
[100] Aristotle, *Poetics*, 83 (Chapter 9).

Certainly, the notion that 'history tends to express the particular', as writers of history experience day after day, has full implications for our inquiry of historical texts as classics. What we assess as historical classics lies in their aim to overcome particularism and to reach universalism, even if they have to deal with thousands of particular data. Yet this universalism in history is only possible when historians effectively deploy literariness in their texts. As J. G. A. Pocock puts it, 'if we ask the question "what made Gibbon a great historian?" the possibility arises that the adjective "great" lies more in the province of the student of literature than in that of the historian of speech acts and discourse generally.'[101] This operation certainly has to do with the utopian but stimulating French structuralist historians' aspiration to construct 'total history', leaving Braudel's *Mediterranée* as its incomplete but still inspiring model of exhaustive explanation.[102] It also connects to queries for a holistic explanation based on some principles of the philosophical or social scientific theories dominant in history, as we have admired in Jacob Burckhardt's *Civilization of the Renaissance*, Alexis de Tocqueville's *Democracy in America*, and Thompson's *The Making of the English Working Class*.[103] It is connected with the adoption of some 'organizational principles (that) are uniformly typological', as White found in Ernst Cassirer's 'modes of thought,' Huizinga's 'forms of thoughts and expression,' and A. J. Lovejoy's 'unit-ideas.'[104] It fits well

---

[101] Pocock, *Barbarism and Religion. Volume Six. Triumph in the West* (Cambridge: Cambridge University Press, 2015), 9.

[102] Aurell, 'Autobiographical Texts', 425–445.

[103] White, *The Fiction of Narrative*, 233–234.

[104] White, *The Fiction of Narrative*, 86.

with this tendency to define a whole period with one image, such as Huizinga's 'Waning of the Middle Ages' or Henri-Inrénée Marrou's *antiquite tardive* ('late antiquity').

We clearly face here the dilemma exposed by Carlo Ginzburg, in his statement, already quoted in Chapter 1: 'The quantitative and anti-anthropocentric approach of the sciences of nature from Galileo onwards has placed human sciences in an unpleasant dilemma: they must either adopt a weak scientific standard so as to be able to attain significant results, or adopt a strong scientific standard to attain results of no great importance.'[105]

Classical historical works have clearly tended towards the first equation of Ginzburg's dilemma. Using narrative and metaphorical language, they have adapted the standards of literature to attain significant results in historical standards, even at the cost of *appearing* less scientific. Without denying the beauty of the historical prose of some of the historical works intuitively considered classics, such as monographs by Gibbon, Michelet, Burckhardt, Huizinga, Bloch, Braudel, and Duby, their brilliant verbal style or persuasive rhetorical eloquence cannot be dissociated from their validity as simple historical explanations. All of this has to do with, but is not reduced to, the concept of 'style in history' analysed by Peter Gay, who follows J. B. Bury's belief that 'history is almost a science and more than a science' and emphasizes 'the tense yet productive coexistence of engagement and detachment that differentiates [the historian] from the novelist on one side and the physicist

---

[105] Ginzburg, 'Roots of a Scientific Paradigm', 276.

on the other'.[106] He concludes: 'Historical narration without analysis is trivial, historical analysis without narration is incomplete.'[107] Or as White's formula based on Aristotle's insight, explains: '[H]istory without poetry is inert, just as poetry without history is vapid.'[108]

Ultimately, the timelessness of historical classics is founded on their ability to ask about the meaning of life rather than focus on a mere description of the events in the past, as necessary as they are in any historical account. This meaning may hardly be resolved by pure reason since it often takes the form of an enigma. Rather,

> it can be grasped in all its complexity and
> multilayeredness in symbolic thought and given a real,
> if only provisional, comprehensibility in those true
> allegories of temporality that we call narrative stories.
> Their truth resides not only in their fidelity to the facts
> of given individual or collective lives but also, and most
> importantly, in their faithfulness to that vision of human
> life informing the poetic genre of tragedy.[109]

Here White supports Ricoeur's conviction that the meaning of history resides in its resemblance to the drama of the human project to endow life with meaning, which is carried out in the awareness of the corrosive power of time.[110] My tentative conclusion for this chapter suggests that this

---

[106] Gay, *Style*, 215.
[107] Gay, *Style*, 189.
[108] White, *The Fiction of Narrative*, xi.
[109] White, *The Content of the Form*, 181.
[110] Ricoeur, *Time and Narrative*, I: 32.

enduring interest in some historical works lies in their ability to adopt some literary qualities, especially those related to the narration. This immunizes them from the operation of historiographical renewal that usually appears in each generation, and which consists of discarding the *old* history in the face of the *new* history. We keep reading these classic historical works because we appreciate in them some permanent qualities that are beyond the wages of historical scholarship.

3

The Inescapability of the Canon

> [Thucydides'] narratives seemed to me
> admirable and worthy of imitation.
>> Dionysius of Halicarnassus, *Critical Essays*

The canon had been long considered valid as a mechanism of classification and essential for education.[1] The humanities and social sciences had shown a deep taxonomic tendency since the consolidation of their respective academic disciplines in the eighteenth century. This was the case of the famous *canon* created by David Ruhnken in his influential introduction to the edition of the works of the Roman orator Rutilius Lupus *Critical History of the Greek Orators* as early as the mid-eighteenth century.[2] History, literature, and art were not only creative but also scholarly activities, and therefore needed to order and classify their knowledge in some way.

This principle of the canon in scholarship, created by the academic pioneers of the eighteenth century, was still alive in the mid-twentieth century. Because of contextualist and historicist movements in literary criticism and art history, the canon was not only acknowledged de facto, but its usefulness as a critical tool became a topic of reflection. Its existence and

---

[1] Earlier versions of portions of this chapter appeared as 'The Canon in History', *Rethinking History* 26, 4 (2022): 439–465.

[2] Rudolph Pfeiffer, *History of Classical Scholarship. From the Beginnings to the End of the Hellenistic Ages* (Oxford: Cambridge University Press, 1968), 207.

usefulness were defended by some literary and art critics, canon-ical themselves, such as Erich Auerbach and Ernst Gombrich.[3] In a lecture delivered at the Sheldonian Theatre, Oxford, on 22 November 1973, Gombrich expressed his conviction regarding

> the real role [that] the canon plays in any culture. It offers points of reference, standards of excellence which we cannot level down without losing direction. Which particular peaks, or which individual achievements we select for this role may be a matter of choice, but we could not make such a choice if there really were no peaks but only shifting dunes.[4]

At the same time, he made it clear that 'the canon is not the same as a ranking order'.[5]

Nevertheless, the idea of a canon (the operation of making visible the classic), has lost public favour in the last decades. In 1989, John Clive lamented the decline of the canon as a critical and educational tool, pointing to the fact that the course *The Great Historians*, which had long been popular in American universities, was disappearing from the curriculum: 'We marvel at the true originality of these few historians of genius who, regardless of later corrections and emendations, will continue to delight and instruct the amateur, and fill with envy as well as inspire the professional historian.'[6]

---

[3] Auerbach, *Mimesis* and Ernst H. Gombrich, *The Story of Art* (London: Phaidon, 1950).

[4] Ernst H. Gombrich, *Ideals & Idols: Essays on Values in History and in Art* (London: Phaidon, 1979), 163.

[5] Gombrich, *Ideals & Idols*, 171.

[6] Clive, *Not by Fact Alone*, 17.

The next generation of literary critics, Frank Kermode and Edward Said among them, were more sceptical of the category and usefulness of the canon but, as Jan Gorak explains, 'Kermode and Said show the impossibility of expelling [the canon] completely from any ambitious and responsive critical system.'[7] This new generation of scholars mistrusted the critical fragility of a concept that, as Frye explains, tends to reductionism and ideologization: 'Every deliberately constructed hierarchy of values in literature ... is based on a concealed social moral, or intellectual analogy.'[8]

From the 1970s onwards, postmodernism and postcolonial criticism recovered some of the postulates of modernism and reactivated disapproval of the canon mainly for three reasons.[9] First, the establishment of a canon would represent or privilege particular ethnic, national, linguistic, cultural, or ideological values, which might antagonize the natural diversity observable in reality, leading to a form of discrimination. Second, the canon necessarily refers to certain ahistorical and essentialist realities, given that its construction presupposes the existence of certain epistemological, ethical, and aesthetic rules that would remain unaltered over time. And third, a canon implies normativity, something always difficult to accept.[10]

The aversion of social minorities, feminism, and postcolonial criticism to the hegemonic, essentialist, and

[7] Jan Gorak, *The Making of the Modern Canon* (London: Athlone, 1991), 7.
[8] Frye, *Anatomy of Criticism*, 23.
[9] Gorak, *The Making of the Modern Canon*, 77.
[10] Mike Fleming, *The Literary Canon: Implications for the Teaching of Language as Subject* (online, accessed 1 January 2022).

normative dimension of the canon became most apparent through the reactions to the publication of Harold Bloom's *The Western Canon* in 1994.[11] Bloom's book generated the most intense debate, to this day, around the idea of the possibility of constructing a literary canon. Said's (1978) and Mukherjee's (2014) anti-imperial and post-colonialist denunciations and other critics' similar racial and gender claims have been diversely but progressively assimilated by Western critique in recent decades.[12] The creation, consolidation, and global spread of postcolonial, ethnic, and gender studies have challenged established cultural, intellectual, and academic stereotypes and conventions resulting from Eurocentric perspectives.

Today, the interpretation of the canon itself, however, varies greatly. It oscillates between the more traditional conception – updated a few decades ago by Harold Bloom – in which the canons are artistic resources of inspiration created by thinkers that are simply there *and* artists who sought Foucault's contextualist definition, for whom the canons would simply be institutional constructions of prime importance created for the preservation of power.[13]

---

[11] Harold Bloom, *The Western Canon* (London: Macmillan, 1994). See John Guillory, *Cultural Capital: The Problem of Literary Canon Formation* (Chicago: The University of Chicago Press, 1993), 15–19.

[12] Edward W. Said, *Orientalism* (New York: Pantheon Books, 1978) and Mukherjee, *What Is a Classic?*

[13] Elihu Katz, Tamar Liebes, Avril Orioff, and John D. Peters, 'Introduction', in Elihu Katz, Tamar Liebes, Avril Orioff, and John D. Peters (eds.), *Canonic Texts in Media Research* (Cambridge: Polity. 2003) 3–4.

From the examples quoted, there is no doubt that the question of the canon has aroused much more interest in literary and art criticism than in historiography. Both the justification for the existence of the canon *in* history – which affects its content and function – and the criteria for the selection of an alleged canon *of* history – which affects the form and is articulated in a list – have seemed irrelevant to historians. In fact, we find no academic literature devoted to the study of the canon in history, while hundreds of publications engage canons in literature, art, and biblical studies.[14] However, certain historians appear systematically in all the lists quoted by history critics, from the catalogues elaborated by Dionysius of Halicarnassus and Lucian of Samosata in antiquity to the histories of historiographies by Benedetto Croce (1917) and Robin G. Collingwood (1946) in the twentieth century and the global approaches by Daniel Woolf (2012) and Georg Iggers, Edward Wang, and Supriya Mukherjee (2017), at the beginning of the new millennium.[15]

Arguing its relevance in historiography, and its connection with the related concept of the classic, this chapter examines the place of the canon in history: its formation, key turning points, convenience, usefulness, and the desirability

[14] For the canon in literature: Lee Morrissey (ed.), *Debating the Canon: A Reader from Addison to Nafisi* (New York: Palgrave Macmillan, 2005); for art: Paul Crowther, *Defining Art, Creating the Canon: Artistic Value in an Era of Doubt* (Oxford: Clarendon, 2007); for biblical studies: Lee M. McDonald and James A. Sanders (eds.), *The Canon Debate* (Peabody: Hendrickson, 2002).

[15] Croce, *Theory and History*; Collingwood, *The Idea of History*; Woolf, *A Global History of History*; Iggers, Wang, and Mukherjee, *A Global History*.

of its existence itself. This leads to questions such as: what determines the systematic inclusion and exclusion of texts in bibliographical lists or in the indexes of the histories of historiographies? Why do the major canonical works usually imply a break with the past but, paradoxically, remain there when later works enter the list? Why are some historical works systematically quoted in the histories of historiography? What are the epistemological conditions that make this possible?

In the first part of the chapter ('Constructions'), I examine the six main turning points in the formation of the canon in history: the late Greco-Roman period, when the first catalogues of canonical books in Western historiography were generated; some academic pioneers of the eighteenth century; the interwar period in the twentieth century, which combined the traditional canon with the influence of the first professionalization of the historical discipline; the inclusion in the canon of narrative history during the 1970s, as opposed to the analytical–professional methodology dominant in the previous century; the expansion of postcolonial theories, with its consequent re-evaluation of the source of canonicity; and, finally, the globalization of the historiographical canon, from the beginning of the twenty-first century. The second part of the chapter ('Canonizing') examines three case studies of the canon in history – its origins, spread, shifts, consolidation, and use in academic discourse. The third part ('Resistances') explores the rejection of the canon among historians, describes some of its manifestations and reflects on its motivations. The fourth part ('Paradoxes') details the main characteristics of the historical canon, points out the differences among other canons such as the literary and artistic, and explores the peculiar combination of art and science that every historical operation entails, which explains most of the peculiarities of the historical canon. It also emphasizes the relevance of the concept of 'genealogy' to understand the dynamics of the notions of canon and classic, which ties in with the fifth chapter, dedicated to this concept. The conclusive section ('Inescapability') argues for the great paradox of the canon: the impossibility of conducting cultural and intellectual exchanges without it.

My inquiry into the dynamics of the canon in historiography does not aim to produce a list of the most read or cited historical books over time – a canon *of* history. For this, it would suffice to describe the canon through analytical research: the statistical analysis of the history books most cited by historians in their histories of historiographies, the most repeated in class bibliographies, and the most sold by booksellers. Rather, I am interested in exploring and defining the historical and literary circumstances that has led to the existence and deployment of the canon *in* history, its relevance, and its inescapability.

Constructions

Some Greek and Roman history critics of antiquity, particularly Dionysius of Halicarnassus and Lucian of Samosata, argued in favour of the canons' utility as a critical tool – including for the historical practice itself.[16] As Momigliano explains,

[16] Ivan Matijasic, *Shaping the Canons of Ancient Greek Historiography* (Berlin: De Gruyter, 2018); David L. Toye, 'Dionysius of Halicarnassus on the First Greek Historians', *The American Journal of Philology* 116 (1995): 279–302; G. M. A. Grube, 'Dionysius of Halicarnassus and Thucydides',

The Greek and Latin historians we consider great and exemplary were already considered great and exemplary by ancient readers. They owe their preservation to their reputation; though, of course, not all the historians who were reputable were preserved. The use of certain books in the schools and mere chance played their part in the transmission of texts. What I want to emphasize is that our judgement on the ancient historians of Greece and Rome is in substantial agreement with the ancient canons of judgement. Herodotus, Thucydides, Xenophon and Polybius were already the models for the Greek and Roman historians who were in a position to read them. Similarly, Sallust, Livy and Tacitus were exemplary for their Latin successors.[17]

For Dionysius of Halicarnassus – one of the pioneers of historical criticism – inquiring into the canon in history allowed historians to delve into the relationship between the content and the peculiar forms of expression of historical narratives. He not only theorizes about the canon *in* history, but he proposes perhaps the first canon *of* history: the list of

---

Phoenix 4 (1950): 95–110. See also George A. Kennedy, 'The Origin of the Concept of a Canon and Its Application to the Greek and Latin Classics', in J. Gorak (ed.), *Canon vs Culture* (New York: Garland, 2001).

[17] Momigliano, *Essays in Ancient and Modern*, 161. He adds that for the canon of the historians the main evidence is in Cicero, *De oratore*, II, 13, 55–58; Dionysius of Halicarnassus, *De imitation*, 3; Quintilianus, *Institutio Oratoria*, X, I, 73–75; Dio Chrysostomus, *Oratio*, XVIII, 9. On modern discussions, Pfeiffer, *History of Classical Scholarship*, 206, and Peter Burke, 'A Survey of the Popularity of Ancient Historians, 1450–1700', *History and Theory* 5 (1966): 135–152.

the most relevant historians who have preceded him. As he explains:

> Before I begin to write about Thucydides I propose to say a little about the other historians, both his predecessors and those who flourished during his lifetime. This will show both his purpose, in which he surpassed his predecessors, and his special talents. There were many early historians in many places before the Peloponnesian War, including Eugeon of Samos, Deiochus of Proconnesus, Eudemus of Paros, Democles of Phygele, Hecataeus of Miletus, Acusilaus of Argos, Charon of Lampsacus and Melesagoras of Chalcedon. Among those who were born not long before the Peloponnesian War and survived into Thucydides's own lifetime were Hellanicus of Lesbos, Damastes of Sigeum, Xenomedes of Chios, Xanthus of Lydia and many others.[18]

In addition, he notes three elements a canon involves, as he judges the work of Thucydides. First, he argues, contrary to what one might think, that the canon does not speak of permanence and continuity, but of change, innovation and discontinuity: 'Thus he [Thucydides] differed from the earlier historians firstly in the choice of his subject, ... and secondly by his exclusion of all legendary material and his refusal to make his history an instrument for deceiving and captivating the common people, as all his predecessors had done when they wrote stories like those of female monsters at Lamia.'[19]

Second, a work of the canon is worthy of imitation:

---

[18] Dionysius of Halicarnassus, *Critical Essays*, 1: 471–473.
[19] Dionysius of Halicarnassus, *Critical Essays*, 1: 477.

This and narratives like it seemed to me admirable
and worthy of imitation, and I was convinced that in
such passages as these we have perfect examples of the
historian's sublime eloquence, the beauty of his language,
his rhetorical brilliance and his other virtues. ... Reason
and instinct will combine in one voice; and these are the
two faculties with which we properly judge all works of
art.[20]

Third, Dionysius refers to the canon's normativity,
the element that has made it objectionable to our postmodern mentality: 'My own view would be that history should not
be written in an arid, unadorned and commonplace style: it
should contain an element of artistry; and yet it should not
be entirely artificial, but should be just a step removed from
everyday language.'[21]

Dionysius finally argues for the evaluative and narrative function of the canon, even if this might be unacceptable
for his readers and critics: 'I suspect that some readers of this
treatise will censure me for daring to express the view that
Thucydides [is] the greatest of the historians'.[22]

Two centuries after Dionysius, Lucian of Samosata's
How to Write History inaugurates the reflection of the writing of history itself and the way history *should* be canonically represented. The first section of his work enumerates
faults to be avoided when writing history. For example, in
the early chapters, he discusses what he considers the ruinous effect of flattery on the writing of history. He criticizes

[20] Dionysius of Halicarnassus, *Critical Essays*, 1: 543.
[21] Dionysius of Halicarnassus, *Critical Essays*, 1: 619.
[22] Dionysius of Halicarnassus, *Critical Essays*, 1: 465.

those who centre on praising their own generals and vilifying those of the enemies, rather than recounting the events as objectively as possible. His proposal evidences the influence of Herodotus and Thucydides, the most valued canonical authors. As Emily Greenwood argues, 'in [Lucian's] *True Stories*, Herodotus is the more obvious model for Lucian's project of telling an account of a journey made in the interests of *Sophia/theôria*, while Thucydides is an ironic interlocutor'.[23]

After the classical period, interest in the historiographical canon seems to wane. During the medieval and early modern periods, authorship is no longer so explicit, and certain authors' names serve as metonyms for their books. This explains the exclusion of these works in the popular making of the historiographical canon, with a few exceptions such as Bede's *Ecclesiastical History*, Anna Komnene's *Alexiad*, Gregory of Tours's *Historia Francorum*, Geoffrey of Monmouth's *History of the Kings of Britain*, William of Malmesbury's *Chronicle of the Kings of England*, Matthew Paris's *Chronica Majora*, Otto of Freising's *Deeds of Emperor Frederick*, or Jean Froissart's *Chronicles*. Other medieval chronicles, such as the crusader testimonies of Robert of Clari, Geoffroy of Villehardouin, Philip of Novara, and Jean of Joinville, were also very popular at the time – authentic *bestsellers* – but lost their presence in the canon due to the particularities of their subject and approach. A third group, the Catalan chronicles of Jaume I the Conqueror, Bernat

[23] Emily Greenwood, *Thucydides and the Shaping of History* (London: Duckworth, 2006), 113.

Desclot, Ramon Muntaner, and Peter IV the Ceremonious, did not pass the test of time because they were written in a beautiful but minority vernacular language. Yet their relevance and originality – with two unique autobiographies of kings among them – calls for greater attention from the historiographical community, as does the original autobiographical chronicle of the Holy Roman Emperor and Bohemian king Charles IV.[24] The quality and relevance of these works is compatible with the fact that they are not usually quoted among the historiographical canon. This brings us back to the issue of the fragility of the canon, and the desirability of avoiding reliance on presentist arguments when approaching the historical canon.

The same reflection can be applied to the chronicles of early modernity. Here the lack of specific works in the historical canon results from the process of metonymy mentioned in the previous paragraph. The celebrity of historians such as Giovanni Villani, Niccolò Machiavelli, or Francesco Guicciardini is well established. However, few would be able to cite their respective historical works: Villani's and Machiavelli's *History of Florence*, which initiated the influential genre of 'city history', and Guicciardini's *History of Italy*, which paved the way for a new style and genre in historiography with his use of government sources to support his arguments and his realistic historical analysis. These Italian authors cover the period from the fourteenth to the

---

[24] For these autobiographies of kings, see Aurell, *Authoring the Past*, chapters 2, 5, 7 and *Vita Caroli Quarti. Die Autobiographie Karls IV*, E. Hillenbrand (ed.) (Stuttgart: Fleischhauer & Spohn, 1979).

mid-sixteenth century. Most of the histories of historiography go then directly from Guicciardini, who died in 1540, to the great authors and works of the nineteenth century, such as Macaulay, Michelet, and Ranke, with only three intermediaries: Macaulay (seventeenth century), Gibbon (eighteenth century) and, of course, Giambattista Vico, but the latter only in the field of the philosophy of history.

Nevertheless, as Philip S. Hicks explains, during the sixteenth and seventieth centuries,

> a number of continental historians had gained acclaim as peers of the ancient historians – Machiavelli, Guicciardini, [Phillippe de] Commynes, [Juan de] Mariana, [Enrico Caterino] Davila, [Jacques Auguste] de Thou, [François Eudes de] Mézeray, [Pablo] Sarpi, and others. These 'neoclassical' [i.e. 'new classics' imitating the historiographical style of the 'ancient classics'] historians had written something Englishmen had failed to write: history in the grand manner, a majestic, authoritative narrative of political and military deeds often containing the character sketches, political maxims, and invented speeches for which the classical historians were famous. These celebrated neoclassical historians did not write histories of the classical period but did write in imitation of the classical historians.[25]

This was one of the factors that influenced that, after the medieval and early modern parenthesis, the second major period in the formation of a historiographical canon was the

---

[25] Philip S. Hicks, *Neoclassical History and English Culture: From Clarendon to Hume* (New York: St. Martin's Press, 1996), 1.

eighteenth century. I have already mentioned at the beginning of this chapter that the principle of the canon in scholarship was created by the academic pioneers of the eighteenth century such as David Ruhnken. There is contemporary evidence, for instance, that by the middle of the eighteenth century, English historians shared a canon of ancient historians worth imitating, such as Herodotus, Thucydides, Xenophon, Polybius, Sallust, Livy, and Tacitus.[26]

After the classicism and enlightenment, the third great moment in the formation of the historical canon happened during the first half of the twentieth century, in the context of the professionalization of the historical discipline. Benedetto Croce's *Theory and History of Historiography* (1917) and Robin G. Collingwood's *Idea of History* (1946) histories of historiography, became widely accepted in time, generating notable canonical consens and normative power. Both served as a sort of Vasari of history since they provided the canonical idea that historiography, like any literary practice, has practitioners who deserve more critical attention than others. These new histories of historiography emphasize the fact that historians such as Herodotus, Thucydides, Polybius, Eusebius, Augustine, Froissart, Guicciardini, Machiavelli, Edward Gibbon, or Jules Michelet had in common a new way of approaching their interpretation of the past that had reshaped the course of historiography, attracting the attention of other historians. This not only earned them celebrity but also

---

[26] Hicks, *Neoclassical History*, 1 and Momigliano, *Essays in Ancient*, 161. Both provide some contemporary evidences for this canon formation, such as Henry Felton, *A Dissertation on Reading the Classics, and Forming a Just Style* (Menston: Scholar, 1971 [1709]).

established them as authorities for future generations, despite the fact that many of the heuristic contents of their works had already been displaced by the next generations of historians.

In the second part of his text, which focuses on the history of historiography, Croce reveals his canonical purpose, combining a historical discussion with a critical approach:

> We possess many works relating to the history of historiography, both special, dealing with individual authors, and more or less general, dealing with groups of authors (histories of historiography confined to one people and to a definite period, or altogether 'universal' histories). Not only have we bibliographical works and works of erudition, but criticism, some of it excellent, especially in the case of German scientific literature, ever the most vigilant of all in not leaving unexplored any nook or cranny of the dominion of knowledge. It cannot, therefore, form part of my design to treat the theme from its foundations: but I propose to make a sort of appendix or critical annotation to the collection of books and essays that I have read upon the argument. I will not say that these are all, or even that they are all those of any importance, but they are certainly a considerable number.[27]

Like his classical predecessors, Dionysius and Lucian, Croce also makes canonical assessments, inferences, and comparisons: 'Machiavelli, for instance, (to use the same example) would there figure as an Italian patriot and defender of absolute power, while Vico (a much greater historian than

---

[27] Croce, *Theory and History of Historiography*, 165.

Machiavelli) would not be able to appear at all, or hardly at all, because his relation with the political life of his time was remote and general.'[28]

Writing two decades later, Collingwood not only based his history of historiography on Croce's theoretical and critical premises but also followed his canonical plot. Herodotus, for example, first distinguished between history and myth, verified 'the creation of scientific history', and gave history its foundation.[29] Collingwood privileges Herodotus, Thucydides, and Polybius among the Greek historians and Livy and Tacitus among the Romans. Then, during the period of the expansion of Christianity, he emphasizes Augustine and Eusebius of Caesarea. But, like everything else in the late antique and medieval period, these historians contributed nothing particularly original – a reductionist canonical idea in itself – as they merely continued the tradition of Hellenistic and Roman historiography, such that 'the method remains unchanged'.[30] Machiavelli stands out in the Renaissance, and he classifies Edward Gibbon as 'a typical Enlightenment historian'.[31] The transition towards scientific historiography – 'The Threshold of Scientific History' – with Ranke, Mommsen, or Maitland, as 'the masters of detail', allowed Collingwood to organize historical knowledge from a national perspective.[32] This new generation include a group of scholars that Collingwood associates with history but

[28] Croce, *Theory and History of Historiography*, 171.
[29] Collingwood, *Idea of History*, 17.
[30] Collingwood, *Idea of History*, 52.
[31] Collingwood, *Idea of History*, 79.
[32] Collingwood, *Idea of History*, 127.

some of them are philosophers of history: Francis H. Bradley, J. B. Bury, Michael J. Oakeshott, and Arnold J. Toynbee in England; Wilhelm Windelband, Heinrich Rickert, Georg Simmel, Wilhelm Dilthey, Eduard Meyer, and Oswald Spengler in Germany; and Felix Ravaisson's spiritualism, Jules Lachelier's idealism, and Henri Bergson's evolutionism in France.

With his progressive and historicist view of the development of historiography, Collingwood consolidated a clear canonical tendency in the twentieth century that would privilege English, German, and French historiographies over all others, which obviously left other European, not to mention American, Asian, and African historiographies in the margins. In his view, thus, the canon did not reside in Europe, but in the three most powerful nations at that time (Great Britain, Germany, and France). Indeed, the canon always reveals its most presentist face, which varies according to each contextual moment.

Despite its reductionist Eurocentricity, Croce and Collingwood's historiographical canons shaped the second half of the twentieth century. This was the golden age of the historical canon, with the consolidation of the sub-discipline of the history of historiography, the publications of many studies on the topic, and its academic validation in Western universities. Croce and Collingwood did not outline the criteria that led them to select certain historians and reject others, since they took for granted the straightforward rule that a canonical author is one who has been most read and cited because he/she is *there*. But, in fact, they fixed a first historiographic canon, well established just before (and after) the postcolonial critiques of the end of the century, as attested by works such as those of John Barker (1982), Ernst Breisach (1983), Donald R. Kelley (1998, 2003, 2006), John Burrow (2007), Georg G. Iggers (2012), and Richard Cohen's more popular audience oriented *Making History* (2022).[33] These synthetic works have become the basis of academic courses on the history of historiography that were increasingly taught at universities, which centred on Western historiography and basically followed the canon established by Croce and Collingwood.

A particularly intense paradigm shift in historiography, and therefore of new additions to the canon in the next phase, occurred in the 1970s. At the end of that decade, Lawrence Stone produced a well-known diagnosis of the 'new narrative' that had been imposed on historiography in those years, where he captured the continuity/discontinuity binary operation of the canon in history. At the beginning of his article, he states:

> Historians have always told stories. From Thucydides and Tacitus to Gibbon and Macaulay the composition of narrative in lively and elegant prose was always accounted their highest ambition. History was regarded as a branch of rhetoric. For the last fifty years, however, this story-telling function has fallen into ill repute among those who have regarded themselves as in the vanguard of the

---

[33] John Barker, *The Superhistorians: Makers of Our Past* (New York: Charles Scribner's Sons, 1982); Breisach, *Historiography*; Kelley, *Faces of History*; Kelley, *Fortunes of History*; Kelley, *Frontiers of History*; Burrow, *A History of Histories*; Iggers, *Historiography in the Twentieth Century*; Richard Cohen, *Making History: The Storytellers Who Shaped the Past* (London: Simon & Schuster, 2022).

profession, the practitioners of the so-called 'new history' of the post-Second-World-War era. In France story-telling was dismissed as 'l'histoire évènementielle'. Now, however, I detect evidence of an undercurrent which is sucking many prominent 'new historians' back again into some form of narrative.[34]

The new narrative history, expanded globally since the end of the twentieth century, consolidated certain canonical works, such as Emmanuel Le Roy Ladurie's *Montaillou* (1975), Carlo Ginzburg's *The Cheese and the Worms* (1976), Natalie Zemon Davis's *The Return of Martin Guerre* (1982), and Robert Darnton's *The Gat Great Massacre* (1984) as visible links of the chain. But, despite its greater epistemological ambition, which connected it with the classical tradition, it did not manage to overcome the Eurocentrism of the previous canons. This explains why, in recent decades, scholars from different disciplines practising postcolonial critiques have denounced the persistence of particular Western stereotypes which have dominated the historiography – and the critical interpretation of it – in the past. Ankhi Mukherjee criticizes the notion of canonicity by declaring that:

> it seems perverse to revisit troubled ideas of canonicity … in the era of cultural-economic globalization increasingly exhibiting symptoms of what Michel Foucault called 'the epoch of space,' a contestatory resituating of history on spatial rather than temporal axes … In the context of increasingly globalized structures of labor, trade, environment,

[34] Stone, '*The Revival of Narrative*', 3–24, here 3.

warfare, and knowledge, however, the question of the classic is [or should be] no longer bound to class imperatives, 'cognitive acquirement,' or the power-knowledge nexus of a colonial canon.[35]

Mukherjee here echoes Said, who had claimed several decades earlier that human sciences should provide the contemporary scholar 'with insights, methods, and ideas that could dispense with racial, ideological, and imperialist stereotypes of the sort provided during its historical ascendancy by Orientalism'.[36] Said and Mukherjee's anti-imperial and post-colonialist denunciations and other critics' racial and gender claims have been progressively assimilated by Western critique, such that they have challenged established cultural, intellectual, and academic stereotypes, conventions, and canons, resulting from Eurocentric perspectives. Consequently, contemporary approaches to the canon in history should consider that 'the invention of modern classics is sustained by a dynamic and variable conversation between the past and the present …, as that conversation goes from being specifically Western to being worldwide'.[37]

Postcolonial, ethnic, and feminist critiques have amplified the notion of the canon itself since they have highlighted the multiplicity of traditions that had previously been elided by hegemonic Western conceptions of history. But the application of these critiques to the interpretation of the

---

[35] Mukherjee, *What Is a Classic?*, 8. The quote is from Michel Foucault, 'Of Other Spaces', *Diacritics* 16 (1986): 22–27, here 22.
[36] Said, *Orientalism*, 328.
[37] Mukherjee, *What Is a Classic?*, 8.

canon in history should not distort the fact that the Western historiographical tradition was considered universal until the mid-twentieth century by writers and readers, as they provide a 'corrective to provincialism,' in T. S. Eliot's phrase. These recent critiques cannot change the historical circumstances surrounding the creation and reception of most of the canonical works I referred to in this book. Nevertheless, these new approaches have to be included not only as canonical themselves (I am thinking specifically of Said's *Orientalism* [1978], Mukherjee's *What is a Classic?* [2014], and Dipesh Chakrabarty's *Provincializing Europe* [2007]) but also because they serve as interpretative tools to how the historical canon functions.[38]

This postcolonial criticism has led to a greater globalization of historiography, and therefore to a geographical amplification of its canon. It has helped develop broader global histories of historiographies more open to other historiographical traditions. Yet, these projects are still dominated by Western-centred values and approaches, as most of their authors were educated in and are based in European or American universities. Thus, despite their geographic origin, most of these scholars have been trained in Western historiography. However, in the last two decades, a new canon is emerging in historiography – an expanded and enriched one, no doubt, but a canon nonetheless. Some of the scholars who have created a new globalized canon of history include N. Jayapalan (1999), Arif Dirlik, Vinay Bahl, and Peter

---

[38] Dipesh Chakrabarty, *Provincializing Europe: Postcolonial Thought and Historical Difference* (Princeton: Princeton University Press, 2007).

Gran (2000), Eckhardt Fuchs and Benedikt Stuchtey (2002), Tej Ram Sharma (2005), Edward Wang (2006), Georg Iggers, Edward Wang, and Supriya Mukherjee (2017), Daniel Woolf (2012) and Prasenjit Duara (2014).[39] The irony is that I doubt that any of these authors would argue that there is a global 'canon', even if with their works they are more or less deliberately proposing one.

Canonizing

After examining the phases of canon development, we can explore how the canon works and what the processes of canonization involve through some case studies. Though we might perceive the canon as a static reality, the circumstances surrounding its origins – the birth of a canonical book, its first reception, its durability, and its downshifts of validity through time – often change. Books such as Gibbon's *Decline and Fall of the Roman Empire* (1776–89) were perceived as canonical immediately upon their publication. Others, such as the five

---

[39] N. Jayapalan, *Historiography* (New Delhi: Atlantic Publishers and Distributors, 1999); Arif Dirlik, Vinay Bahl, and Peter Gran, *History after the Three Worlds: Post-Eurocentric Historiographies* (Lanham: Rowman & Littlefield, 2000); Eckhardt Fuchs and Benedikt Stuchtey, *Across Cultural Borders: Historiography in Global Perspective* (Lanham: Rowman & Littlefield, 2002); Tej Ram Sharma, *Historiography: A History of Historical Writing* (New Delhi: Concept Publishing, 2005); Edward Q. Wang and Georg G. Iggers, *Turning Points in Historiography: A Cross-Cultural Perspective* (Woodbridge: Boydell & Brewer, 2006); Prasenjit Duara, Viren Murthy, and Andrew Sartori, *A Companion to Global Historical Thought* (Chichester: Wiley Blackwell, 2014).

volumes of Macaulay's *History of England* (1848–1862), were enthusiastically received, became canonical very early on, were passionately read by a whole generation of nineteenth-century liberal intellectuals, but then fell into oblivion and were dropped from the canon by scholars, only to be reinstated later.[40] Finally, a third group, whose model would be White's *Metahistory* (1973), is initially rejected for their challenging and non-conventional proposals, but later become firmly established in the canon. These three case studies allow us to analyse the contexts wherein canonical books might be produced, spread and maintained.

We still consider Gibbon as 'the first of the historians of the Roman Empire', and a continued source of inspiration to understand not only Roman political and social structures but also the rules governing the dialectic between rise and decadence, permanence and change in history, as Roy Porter has argued.[41] His interest among the historians 'shows no sign of abating', following John Burrow.[42] Hugh Trevor-Roper considers *The Decline and Fall* the most majestic work of history ever written.[43] The ever-demanding G. M. Trevelyan thinks that 'Gibbon's work comes as near perfection as any human achievement'.[44] John Clive believes 'that *The Decline and Fall*

---

[40] Nathaniel Wolloch, *Macaulay and the Enlightenment* (Woodbridge: Boydell, 2022).

[41] Porter, *Edward Gibbon*, 164.

[42] Burrow, *A History of Histories*, 352.

[43] Hugh Trevor-Roper, 'Introduction', in *Gibbon: The Decline and Fall of the Roman Empire* (New York: Twayne, 1966), xxi.

[44] Quoted in David Womersley, *The Transformation of the Decline and Fall of the Roman Empire* (New York: Cambridge University Press, 1988), 43.

was a classic that was two hundred years young, one that had barely begun its majestic and assured journey into immortality' and advises us to 'turn to the modern as well as the older classics of historical writing', wondering 'what today's historians can learn about the rhetoric of history from the classical historians of *modern* times'.[45] Peter Brown adds that 'like all great books, *Decline and Fall of the Roman Empire* raises themes that stretch far deeper and far wider than a conventional interpretation of this title leads us to expect'.[46] Joseph M. Levine is persuaded that Gibbon's historiographical greatness lay in his ability to combine three current traditions of historical writing apparently antithetical: the narrative after the fashion of the ancients, particularly his admired Tacitus; the reflective history of the philosophers of his time, exemplified by the works of Hume and Voltaire; and the erudition of philologists and antiquarians 'who had been trying for three centuries to recover the lost worlds of antiquity by collecting and sifting evidence and assembling massive collections of facts and data'.[47] In 1976, a group of scholars gathered in a commemorative conference of *Decline and Fall*'s second centenary, and devoted a whole volume to an analysis of the work's relevance to modern scholarship, entitled *Edward Gibbon and the Decline and Fall of the Roman Empire.*'[48]

[45] Clive, *Not by Fact Alone*, 52, 306, and 298.

[46] Brown, *Society and the Holy*, 56.

[47] Joseph M. Levine, *The Autonomy of History: Truth and Method from Erasmus to Gibbon* (Chicago: The University of Chicago Press, 1999), 158.

[48] G. W. Bowersock, J. Clive, and S. R. Graubard (eds.), *Edward Gibbon and the Decline and Fall of the Roman Empire* (Cambridge: Harvard University Press, 1977).

Leo Braudy concludes that Gibbon's canonical status must be attributed to his literary quality rather than to his historical structuring:

> The shape of history in the *Decline and Fall* is preeminently a construction, a literary work with aesthetic rather than systematic order and coherence. In the course of the *Decline and Fall*, Gibbon's controlling presence becomes more and more palpable, ordering, assorting, varying, and qualifying. By its conclusion the *Decline and Fall* has become an enclosed object, to be contemplated as much for its formal and detailed beauty as for its accurate transcription of what was.[49]

In addition to the interest raised by Gibbon's *Decline and Fall* among his fellow historians, the work has been a continuing source of inspiration for literary critics, intellectual historians, and historians of ideas.[50] Perhaps the most impressive of them has been the five volumes

---

[49] Braudy, *Narrative Form*, 214.

[50] In chronological order of appearance: Guiseppe Girarrizzo, *Edward Gibbon e la cultura europea del settecento* (Naples: Istituto Italiano per gli Studi Istorici, 1954); Michel Baridon, *Edward Gibbon et le mythe de Rome: histoire et idéologie au siècle des lumières* (Paris: Honoré Champion, 1977); Harold Bond, *The Literary Art of Edward Gibbon* (Oxford: Clarendon, 1960), and the more recent books quoted on this section by Leo Braudy, Lionel Gossman, J. G. A. Pocock, Patricia B. Craddock, and David Womersley. See also H. R. Trevor-Roper, 'The Historical Philosophy of the Enlightenment', in *History and the Enlightenment* (New Haven: Yale University Press, 2010), 1–16; Charlotte Roberts, *Edward Gibbon and the Shape of History* (Oxford: Oxford University Press, 2014); and, on the work's reception, Christopher Kelly, 'Reading Gibbon's Decline and Fall', *Greece & Rome* 44, 1 (1997): 39–58.

that Pocock devoted to it in his *Barbarism and Religion* – a phrase coined by Gibbon himself. Pocock was driven by the conviction that at the end of the twentieth century, there were specialists and critics who could examine and even evaluate Gibbon, 'treating him as a contemporary and equal who may be paid the compliment of criticism'.[51] He used the canonical status of *Decline and Fall* to construct an imposing monograph on eighteenth-century European culture. This shows that Gibbon's work has a strictly contextual dimension – his specific analysis of the fall of the Empire – but also a universal and timeless dimension, since it allows critics to explore the tensions between the old and the new, the traditional and the modern, virtue and vice, barbarism and religion. At the same time, Pocock's analysis of *Decline and Fall* demonstrates that the significance of canonical works is not restricted to a historiographical dimension – that of the object of the past on which they focus – but also applies to historical (Gibbon's context), intellectual (the ideas of the English Enlightenment), and philosophical ones (the approach to the great questions of the past and the present).

This multiple meaning was made possible by Gibbon's ability to bring together the erudite or antiquarian scholarship derived from the Renaissance with the philosophical historiography resulting from the Enlightenment: erudition

[51] J. G. A. Pocock, *Barbarism and Religion. Volume One. The Enlightenments of Edward Gibbon, 1737–1764* (Cambridge: Cambridge University Press, 1999), 1. See also Rosamond McKitterick and Roland Quinault, *Gibbon and the Empire* (Cambridge: Cambridge University Press, 1997).

and philosophy interacted and changed one another's meanings.[52] But Pocock added a third seasoning, which is precisely that 'surplus of meaning' and the 'literariness' that I have argued for in the creation of a canonical work – narrative: 'Both philosophy and erudition required integration with a third component of the historiographical package: that is to say, with narrative, meaning in the first place that classical narrative of the exemplary actions of leading figures, derived from the Greco-Roman model as interpreted by Renaissance humanists.'[53]

The effectiveness of *Decline and Fall* is determined by its 'micronarrative of systemic change rather than the classical narrative of exemplary or arcana actions'.[54] Hence, in *Decline and Fall*, it seems that the literary author speaks more than the historical scientist: 'the true voice of control, the true organizer, the force that shapes and gives meaning to history is Gibbon's own narrative voice'.[55] Gibbon manages in his *Decline and Fall* to emphasize the authorial voice inherent in any durable text and that rises it to the stratum of the classic. The authorial voice, the tenor, and the style of the prose carries the presence of an individual narrator always present, colouring, and commenting on the history that establishes a special writer/reader relationship. One thinks of Thucydides, Tacitus, and of course, Gibbon who studied

[52] Arnaldo Momigliano, *Contributo alla Storia degli Studie Classici* (Rome: Edizioni di Storia e Letteratura, 1955), ch. viii.
[53] J. G. A. Pocock, *Barbarism and Religion. Volume Two. Narratives of Civil Government* (Cambridge: Cambridge University Press, 1999), 5.
[54] Pocock, *Barbarism and Religion: Narratives of Civil*, 397.
[55] Braudy, *Narrative Form*, 257.

Tacitus's prose style and made it his own. The authorial voice of the narrator who displays the history is crucial to works that invite rereading over time.

In Gibbon's *Decline*, the authorial 'I' incessantly prevails in the second part of the book, in which he presents himself more as an author than as an objective historian or, to use his own words, as a 'philosophical observer'.[56] However, his narrative qualities did not obfuscate the historical work. As Virginia Woolf has argued, '... Gibbon was an historian, so religiously devoted to the truth that he felt an aspersion upon his accuracy as an aspersion upon his character'.[57]

These judgements of modern critics support the reception the book has had since its publication, with the exception of a few clergymen unhappy with Gibbon's disparaging treatment of original Christianity.[58] The contemporary critic Horace Walpole (1717–1797) exclaimed 'Lo! A truly classic work has appeared' after reading its first volume in 1776.[59] The book was soon translated into French by the historian François Guizot. In the United States, it was revered from

---

[56] On the authorial 'I' of the historians, see Enzo Traverso, *Singular Pasts. The 'I' in Historiography* (New York: Columbia University Press, 2022); Jeremy D. Popkin, *History, Historians & Autobiography* (Chicago: The University of Chicago Press, 2005); Aurell, *Theoretical Perspectives*.

[57] Virginia Woolf, 'The Historian and "The Gibbon"', in Virginia Woolf (ed.), *The Death of the Moth and Other Essays* (London: The Hogarth Press, 1942), 55–63, here 57 (the text is from 1937).

[58] For an in-depth analysis of the popular and academic reception of Gibbon's *Decline and Fall*, see Craddock, *Edward Gibbon*, chapter five, 'Gibbon's Reputation', 343–365.

[59] Porter, *Edward Gibbon*, 2.

very early on by figures who went even beyond the strictly academic, such as William Prescott, Francis Parkman, and Henry Adams.

But the book also went through a dark period. There was a rejection of Gibbon and his *Decline and Fall* among the next generation of Romantic historians and philosophers of history, who postulated a reduced presence of the scientific aspect of history. As White explains,

> by the end of the Enlightenment, such thinkers as Gibbon, Hume, and Kant had effectively dissolved the distinction between history and fiction on which earlier thinkers such as Bayle, and Voltaire had based their historiographical enterprises. It was against this 'fictionalization' of history, this Ironic stance before the 'scientific' tasks which early eighteenth-century historians had set for themselves, that Herder, Burke, and the *Stürmer und Dränger* rebelled'.[60]

The book's fall into oblivion in Victorian England not only confirms the saying that 'no one is a prophet in his own land' but can be explained by the reality of canonical books: the shift in the reception depending on the historical period. Burrow explains that

> any general Victorian pronouncement on the historical sense of the historiography of the eighteenth century will be dismissive, ignorant and distorting. The mentality of that century which, more than any other, has established the category of the modern understanding of history of Europe is habitually characterized in nineteenth-century England as *unhistorical* ... In the nineteenth century,

---

[60] White, *Metahistory*, 48–49.

too, the categories of 'race' and 'nations' were reified and taken with extreme seriousness as bearers of precise and indelible qualities: eighteenth-century cosmopolitanism such as one finds in Hume and Gibbon could be regarded as more evidence of superficiality, whereas we would be inclined to see a sensible scepticism.[61]

These shifts in the reception over time are also explained by the fact that, though canonical books have something that makes them enduring, none of them can escape the historiographical circumstances of their time. *Decline and Fall* fit in well with the Enlightenment ideas prevailing in Europe in the second half of the eighteenth century, but not with the romanticism and Victorian modernism of the nineteenth. However, canonical books ultimately remain as such even in the countries where they were born: at the beginning of the twentieth century, Lytton Strachey and Winston Churchill made *Decline and Fall* the object of their admiration and imitation, and contributed to their re-establishment as canonical.

Gibbon inspired other historians in the canon as well since, as Macaulay acknowledges in his diary in 1838, he had 'read a good deal of Gibbon' and 'still the book, with all its great faults of substance and style, retains, and will retain, its place in our literature'.[62] Macaulay's *History of England*, published one century after *Decline and Fall*, became a bestseller in mid-Victorian England and continued to be in print for the rest of the century. Twenty-five years after its publication, the first of the five volumes alone had sold over

---

[61] Burrow, *A History of Histories*, 364–365.
[62] Clive, *Not by Facts Alone*, 74–75.

133,000 copies. It attracted many different kinds of readers, from lords and gentlemen to working-class people. Macaulay could write soon in his journal:

> At last I have attained true glory. As I walked through Fleet Street the day before yesterday, I saw a copy of (David) Hume at a bookseller's window with the following label: 'Only £2.20. Hume's *History of England* in eight volumes, highly valuable as an introduction to Macaulay'. I laughed so convulsively that the other people who were staring at the books took me for a poor demented gentleman. Alas for poor David'.[63]

Much of the immediate success of his publication and its longevity in the canon can be attributed to the fact that Macaulay

> wanted to make his *History* instructive, entertaining, and universally intelligible; and he rewrote and polished endlessly to achieve these goals … This imaginative capacity contributed in great measure to two important qualities that helped to lend *The History of England* its never-ending fascination: a strongly developed sense of the concrete in pictorial forma and the capacity to animate into forward motion in time motives, characters and situations – a capacity which at the same time that it benefited the style and general structure of *The History* also contributed to the strong sense of linkage between past and present that pervades it. This sense of linkage we have come to recognize, perhaps a little too readily, as characteristic of the 'Whig interpretation of history'.[64]

---

[63] Macaulay, quoted in Clive, *Not by Facts Alone*, 84.
[64] Clive, *Not by Facts Alone*, 67–69.

Macaulay was surprised by the success of his work in the United States, since it was a 'national history,' in contrast to Gibbon's and the Enlightened historians' more cosmopolitan history. Moreover, as he acknowledged: 'I do not at all understand how it should be acceptable to the body of peoples, who have no King, no lords, no knights, no established church, no Tories, nay, I might say, no Whigs in the English sense of the world.'[65] But these cultural circumstances could not overcome those that propelled him to universal appeal: his direct polished style – the *art* of every story. Macaulay's popular style certainly contrasted with Gibbon's elitism, which corresponded to their two different audiences, but both share that narrative style which makes for a compelling read.

Macaulay's case also presents a challenge in answering the question of the extent to which historical works of the canon are quoted rather than read and, more crucially, of its fragile and unstable existence. In an essay Gertrude Himmelfarb wonders,

> Who now reads Macaulay? Who, that is, except those who have a professional interest in him – and professional in a special sense: not historians who might be expected to take pride in one of their most illustrious ancestors, but only those who happen to be writing treatises about him. In fact, most professional historians have long since given up reading Macaulay, as they have given up writing the kind of history he wrote and thinking about history as he did.[66]

[65] Clive, *Not by Facts Alone*, 83.
[66] Himmelfarb, *The New History*, 143.

Perhaps this is the paradoxical fate of canonical books: their provisional and, in some cases, permanent oblivion and eventual expulsion from the canon. Even poets such as Virginia Woolf have wondered about the fragility of supposedly canonical historical works, referring to the cases of Gibbon, Macaulay, and Carlyle:

> Few people can read the whole of the [Gibbon's] *Decline and Fall* without admitting that some chapters have glided away without leaving a trace; that many pages are no more than a concussion of sonorous sounds; and that innumerable figures have passed across the stage without printing even their names upon our memories. We seem, for hours on end, mounted on a celestial rocking-horse which, as it gently sways up and down, remains rooted to a single spot. In the soporific idleness thus induced we recall with regret the vivid partisanship of Macaulay, the fitful and violent poetry of Carlyle. We suspect that the vast fame with which the great historian is surrounded is one of those vague diffusions of acquiescence which gather when people are too busy, too lazy or too timid to see things for themselves.[67]

Himmelfarb and Woolf's authoritative insights demystify the idea of a fixed canon: the canon is in fact flexible. No one doubts the scientific capacity or celebrity that Clarendon or Macaulay had in their time, to give two characteristic examples, but today that success has been lost. Yet this brings us back to the question of the singularity or plurality of the canon: is there one criterion for

---

[67] Woolf, 'The Historian', 56.

considering certain historical works – such as Macaulay's and Clarendon's – or are there several? These two historians were massively recognised and read at his time, but the same cannot be said of other historians who were equally respected but more restricted to a specialist public, such as many of those cited in these pages – for example Bloch, Braudel, Thompson, Ginzburg, or Davis. Therefore, there can be two canons of historical works if we go by the criterion of their audience.

But a canon can also be articulated according to its subject matter: the canon of relevant works for an economic and cultural historian would be different from that of a political or military historian. Moreover, many of the works of historians of antiquity and the Middle Ages – Eusebius and Bede among them – may have entered the canon of the most widely read historical works as our only source on particular events, such as Herodotus for the Persian invasion, Thucydides for the Peloponnesian wars, Sallust for Catilinarian conspiracy, all of Tacitus, and Bede for Anglo-Saxon England, among others. The reading and rereading of these works will continue for sheer information although the importance of their intellectual and literary qualities is also crucial and raises them above the status of evidentiary documents. The classic status or canonicity of these histories is different from that of, for instance, Gibbon on Rome, Michelet on the French Revolution, Burckhardt on the Renaissance, Huizinga on the Middle Ages, or Thompson on the English working class.

Similarly, as we shall see in the chapter on historical genres, other historical works such as Gibbon's *Decline and Fall*, Burckhardt's *Renaissance*, or Kantorowicz's *Two Bodies* have entered the canon by being the first to explore a particular *mode* of historical approach. In many cases, they are not even original in their treatment of a subject, but their approach makes them unique. As Pocock has argued, 'Gibbon declared that Constantine, in addition to perpetuating the changes wrought by Diocletian, had taken two revolutionary steps: the foundation of the new capital city that bore his name on the Bosphorus, and the establishment of Christianity as the state religion on the empire. Neither statement was in any way new in European historiography.'[68]

Macaulay's case is particularly relevant to the question of the plurality and polyvalence of the canon. It refers to another dimension of this variety: canons have both a synchronic and a diachronic existence – they reflect the difference between a freeze frame of a canon at a particular moment in time (single-moment) and a film tracing its evolution and membership over time. My book on the canon 'in' history focuses on the latter, but any presentation of a particular canon – for example, any history of historiography – refers to the former (the canon 'of' history). This is why the question developed by Himmelfarb in one of her essays is so pertinent: 'Who Now Reads Macaulay?'[69] Macaulay was an author who enjoyed a wide popular readership for a time, only to be confined to readers with a specifically historical, if not exclusively historiographical, interest, as is the case with

---

[68] Pocock, *Barbarism and Religion: Triumph in the West*, 1.
[69] Gertrude Himmelfarb, 'Who Now Reads Macaulay?', in *The New History and the Old*, 143–154.

the present author. This brings up an important point, developed earlier in this book: a *durable* text like Macaulay's is not necessarily a canonical one.

Finally, the fragility and evanescence of the canon may be the result of the historian's over-attachment to context. For example, some French historians such as Auguste Thierry, François-Auguste Mignet, François Guizot, Louis Adolphe Thiers, Amable Guillaume Prosper Brugière (Baron de Barante), and Amédée Thierry – all of them belonging to the generation that followed the Romantics, such as Michelet – were popular in their time largely because of their political activism. But once the particular conditions under which their nineteenth-century liberal creed lost vigour in France, they ceased to appear on the lists of the most renowned historians.[70] All these examples show that the canonicity of a historical work, as opposed to its durability, depends on its audience, content and genre, and on the anachronistic and diachronic dynamics at play.

Hayden White serves as a third model of the place of the canon in history. Half a century after its publication, few doubt that his *Metahistory* has changed the course of historiography, or at least contributed decisively to the consolidation of postmodernism and narrative history and the subfield of historiography itself. White, originally trained

---

[70] Stanley Mellon, *The Political Uses of History: A Study of Historians in the French Restoration* (Stanford: Stanford University Press, 1958); Rulon N. Smithson, *Augustin Thierry: Social and Political Consciousness in the Evolution of a Historical Method* (Genève: Droz, 1973); Lionel Gossman, 'Augustin Thierry and Liberal Historiography', *History and Theory* 15, 4 (1976): 3–83.

as a medievalist, wanted to write a book on intellectual history through the analysis of the 'classics of the nineteenth-
century European historical thought' of the last two centuries:
G. W. F. Hegel, Jules Michelet, Leopold von Ranke, Alexis
de Tocqueville, Jacob Burckhardt, Karl Marx, Friedrich
Nietzsche, Benedetto Croce.[71] Despite the ambition of his
project – or perhaps because of it – the book was not well
received and had to make its way with much effort. The manuscript was rejected several times before it was published by
the Johns Hopkins University Press. Historians reviewed the
book harshly: Phyllis Grosskurth called it 'irritating and pre-
tentious' and Eric Monkkonen suggested that 'only the tiniest
handful of historians would concur with White'.[72] Andrew
Ezergailis even went so far as to classify it as 'the most damaging undertaking ever performed by a historian on his
profession'.[73]

The book did, however, receive more generous praise
from literary critics and from the part of a minority of historical theorists. The historian Hans Kellner was able to detect, as
early as 1980, an 'enthusiastic reception' among historians.[74]
Fifteen years after its publication, Richard Vann considered
it a 'decisive turn in philosophical thinking about history'.[75]

---

[71] White, *Metahistory*, ix.
[72] Phyllis Grosskurth, review of *Metahistory* in *Canadian Historical Review* 56 (1975): 193 and Eric H. Monkkonen, 'The Challenge of Quantitative History', *Historical Methods* 17 (1984): 86–94, here 86.
[73] Andrew Ezergailis, review of *Metahistory* in *Clio* 5 (Winter 1976): 240.
[74] Hans Kellner, 'A Bedrock of Order: Hayden White's Linguistic Humanism', *History and Theory* 19 (1980): 1–29, here 13.
[75] Richard T. Vann, 'The Reception of Hayden White', *History and Theory* 37 (1998): 143–161, here 143.

Its place in the canon was consolidated when, a quarter of a century after its appearance, one of the leading journals in historiography, *History and Theory*, published a monograph commemorating its twenty-fifth anniversary: 'Hayden White: Twenty-Five Years on.'[76] The authors participating in this volume (Richard T. Vann, Nancy Partner, Ewa Domanska, Frank Ankersmit) emphasized the rupture that *Metahistory* meant for historiography, but, at the same time, they perceived that White's theses responded to the concerns that, in those years, were sweeping the entire field of historiography. Moreover, either because of this good reception or simply because of the intense controversy it generated, the book was soon translated into Italian, Spanish, Dutch, Russian, Portuguese, and French. Its influence in Latin America has also been profound. Today no one doubts that *Metahistory* has marked a decisive turning point in the theory of history, among other things because the book was able to bring together, in a single volume, an approach that blended the methodologies of the philosophy of history, intellectual history, and the history of historiography, thus inaugurating postmodern historiography – despite the disagreement that this label raises among theorists.

From the celebrity and durability gained and sustained over time by Gibbon's *Decline and Fall*, Macaulay's *History of England*, and White's *Metahistory*, three of the most reliable characteristics of the canon of/in history emerge.

---

[76] *History and Theory*, 37, 2 (1998). Interest in Hayden White's work seems to have continued to this day: see the review of a new collection of White writings by Michael S. Roth, 'The Ironic Radical: On Hayden White's "The Ethics of Narrative"', *Los Angeles Review of Books*, 2 June 2023.

First, it shows that canonical books, though firmly located in their intellectual time, offer perspectives that transcend particular historical periods, since, as White argues, 'Every great historical narrative is an allegory of temporality.'[77] Second, it confirms the dual nature of history – at once science and art – which emerges from the paradox that history is at the same time 'a progressive discipline and a treasure house of classics,' in Peter Gay's phrase.[78] Today, historians do not base their studies of ancient Rome on Gibbon, the history of England on Macaulay, or the history of historiography on White. But their texts are 'imperishable masterpieces which no amount of fresh facts or revisionist interpretations will eject from the pantheon'.[79] Third, it highlights the unconventionality of canonical historical books, their commitment to disciplinary innovation, and their status as the hinge or turning point of historiography. As John Burrow explains, regarding *Decline and Fall*,

> It is difficult now to recognize how innovative was Gibbon's choice of his life's work. It was not the practice to write histories of the ancient world (though Adam Ferguson had published a history of the Roman republic), because the ancient historians were thought unsurpassable, but through merit and through superior access. … In its time Gibbon's work was unique, and not only in this scale. To attempt it was undoubtedly a bold step, which Gibbon came to take only gradually.[80]

[77] White, *The Content of the Form*, 181.
[78] Gay, *Style in History*, 215.
[79] Gay, *Style in History*, 215–216.
[80] Burrow, *A History of Histories*, 354.

Arnaldo Momigliano confirms this assertion, looking at another aspect of the innovation, since

> Gibbon broke new ground not by his ideas on the decline of Rome, but by offering the treasures of erudition to the contemplation of the philosophic historian. By doing so, he unexpectedly reconciled two methods of writing history which so far had seemed to be inevitably opposed ... a new type of philosophic history emerged. It combined the learning of one school of thought with the philosophic imagination of the other.[81]

Regarding Macaulay's *History of England*, Peter Gay adds that the author anticipated twentieth-century social history, since one of the chapters contains an analysis of social classes, standards of living, the condition of the poor, the state of agriculture and industry, the growth of population, life in the towns, child labour, poverty, and people's cultural interests.[82]

Burrow, Momigliano, and Gay argue in favour of a certain 'unorthodoxy' and 'unconventionality' among the historians able to create a canonical work of history. Peter Brown concludes that,

> It may well be that it is those aspects which make Gibbon appear to be most alien to the sympathies of modern scholars that he has remained most relevant: for behind his dismissal of much of the evidence and many of the phenomena that have come to interest us, there lies a

[81] Arnaldo Momigliano, *Studies in Historiography* (London: Weidenfeld and Nicolson, 1966), 51.
[82] Gay, *Style in History*, 117.

theory of the relation between the ideas and society of a large empire which still merits our careful attention.[83]

To confirm this point, in the last two centuries, some of the books most often cited in the canon have been usually written by mavericks of the historical discipline, such as Jacob Burckhardt and Arnold J. Toynbee since they were not counted among the practitioners of *professional* history. In other cases, they have been at least books that contravened the hitherto established conventions, such as Marc Bloch's *Les Rois Thaumaturges*, Hayden White's *Metahistory*, Georges Duby's *Le Dimanche de Bouvines*, or Natalie Zemon Davis's *The Return of Martin Guerre*. This allows us to better understand what I consider the great paradox of the canon in history: those who have become established in the canon of history, from Herodotus and Thucydides to White and Davis, have done so not because they have preserved the convention of the discipline, but precisely because they have not. They have achieved relevance open to the present because they placed themselves in a genealogical chain of historiography conveying both continuity and disruption at the same time.

Indeed, it might seem counterproductive to introduce Bloch, Braudel, Thompson, White, and Davis into a canon that they contributed so much to demolish. But it was precisely their annalistic, structuralist, metahistorical, narrative, and postcolonial critiques of the Western canon, and their breaks with convention, that gave them historiographic legitimacy and entry into the canon of history. And surely the same is true of literature, where late modernists like Virginia Woolf demonstrated

---

[83] Brown, *Society and the Holy*, 25.

the capacity of the novel to be more than a linear narrative of events, or someone like Marquez inspired magical realism. Their rupture with convention did not signify, in the end, the destruction of the canon, but simply its theoretical revision, its global updating, and its geographical expansion. Here we see how the canon operates as a critical tool of historiographical exploration as it allows the location of an author or a text at the beginning of a certain turn, as well as the attempt to impose a definitive meaning and shape on that tradition.[84]

At this point there are some analogies to be drawn between historiography and other fields of artistic creation, such as music and painting. Some authors are canonical because they so clearly sum up their own time, as they are on the threshold between the end of a tradition and the emergence of a new one. Bach and Mozart epitomize Baroque and classical composition, as Beethoven and Schoenberg are revolutionaries. In historiography, Gibbon is probably more like Bach, and Ranke like Beethoven.[85] In more contemporary terms, and applied to painting, the ardent romantic Jules Michelet would be to Francisco de Goya what the modernist and impressionist Johan Huizinga was to Claude Monet, the creative multifaceted Georges Duby to Pablo Picasso and the theorist Hayden White to Wassily Kandinsky. All of them – historians, musicians, and painters – contributed to new modes of expression in their respective fields, driven

---

[84] Joseph Blenkinsopp, *Prophecy and Canon: A Contribution to the Study of Jewish Origins* (Notre Dame: University of Notre Dame Press, 1977), 9.

[85] I am grateful to one of the reviewers of the manuscript for this interesting comment.

by their untamed creativity, while at the same time remaining well rooted in the epistemic, or artistic, tradition of their discipline.

This liminal character of canonical works is reflected, for instance, in the work of Gibbon. As Pocock argues, the *Decline and Fall*,

> was written and published at the last moment when a history of this kind could have been conceived and constructed: as a product of Franco Venturi's *prima crisi dell'Antico Regime* [1979], the years after 1763 when Hume, [Guillaume-Thomas] Raynal, and [Adam] Ferguson thought that the struggle between the British and French empires had subverted the order of the European states and would lead to revolutionary consequences for one of the other.[86]

Gibbon's work, while epitomizing the end of one historical and historiographical era, also announced, almost prophetically, the beginning of a new one:

> He published his [*Decline and Fall*'s] last volumes under the date 1 May 1788 with the remark 'next summer and the following winter will rapidly pass away'. They did; and by the end of his life six years later, Europe would be faced with a new history culminating not in Enlightenment, but in revolution, to be followed by counter-revolution and the profound changes which would lead historiography from its early modern to its modern condition – from humanism to historicism, and from the status of a leisurely pursuit for men of letters, to

---

[86] Pocock, *Barbarism and Religion: Triumph in the West*, 509.

that of a public discourse by university professors deeply concerned with the state.[87]

Put in historiographical terms, the key to the potential canonicity of a historical work lies in its capacity to simultaneously combine conventionality – one that inserts it into a community of historians linked by essential heuristic values – and disruption, one that endows it with singularity within that community, as Foucault argued in his concept of genealogy. A text becomes canonical when it creates a strategic conceptual tension with texts of the past and opens up a new way of thinking about the world in the future. Much here connects to the concept of 'essential tension' argued by Thomas Kuhn, and of 'historical genres' and 'genealogy', which I will analyse in more detail in the next chapters in relation to these paradoxes resulting from the canon.

Resistances

Yet, beyond the permanence of historians such as Gibbon, Macaulay, and White, resistance and scepticism to the canon – at least, in its Western version, as conceived and sanctioned by Croce and Collingwood – began to spread in historiography during the 1970s. As William Franke explains, 'it is not as if the literary canon went unchallenged for thousands of years until critics suddenly woke up in 1968 and declared the need for a change.'[88]

---

[87] Pocock, *Barbarism and Religion: Triumph in the West*, 509.

[88] William Franke, 'The Canon Question and the Value of Theory: Towards a New (Non-) Concept of Universality', in Liviu Papadima, David Damrosch, and Theo D'Haen (eds.), *The Canonical Debate Today* (Amsterdam: Rodopi, 2011), 55–71, here 55.

The canon has been constructed and deconstructed throughout history, changing its bases, and generating an intense debate about its very existence. But its legitimacy has never been as challenged as it has in the last decades. How can we then explain this current distrust of historiography towards the canon? Beyond the general tendency of postcolonial studies, mentioned in the first section of this chapter, three other motivations, specific to historiography, explain this apparent rejection.

First, unlike literature and art, historians have not yet accepted the existence of a critical sub-discipline within their field (historical criticism) or of a group of historians acting exclusively as history critics. This fact was denounced by White, as he asked, 'what is the use of criticism and especially meta-criticism in a field of study like history?'[89] This question led him to the conclusion that this absence of meta-criticism has prevented history from possessing that minimal community of theorists that would enriche history and the other humanistic disciplines and would allow them a greater connection with the surrounding community:

> it is imperative to have cadres of scholars and intellectuals who specialize in what might be called the social import of fields of creative production like literature and the rest of the arts. Not in order to regulate them, but to provide opinions on the nature and consequences of their products. Thus, [Frank] Kermode concluded, literary critics and theorists do the serious reading for community.[90]

[89] White, 'Foreword', xi.
[90] White, 'Foreword', xi.

Without reference to theory, history becomes, as I have argued elsewhere, 'archaeological', and therefore without any reference to the problems of the present.[91] Unsurprisingly, most historians would probably not be interested in the 'classic' and 'canon' of history that I propose in this book, because they consider these concepts something related to literature or art, and therefore alien to the *scientific* discipline of history. But without the distinction between 'practice' and 'critical' production – clearly defined in other disciplines – historical writings merge with critical approaches so that they cannot enter into a permanent canon because they always tend towards provisionality. This was emphasized by Said, referring to Auerbach's *Mimesis*, as one of the few critical works that have gained a place in the canon:

> The influence and enduring reputation of books of criticism are, for the critics who write them and hope to be read for more than one season, dispiritingly short. Since World War Two the sheer volume of books appearing in English has risen to huge numbers, thus further ensuring if not ephemerality, then a relatively short life and hardly any influence at all. Books of criticism have usually come in waves associated with academic trends, most of which are quickly replaced by successive shifts in taste, fashion, or genuine intellectual discovery. Thus only a small number of books seem perennially present and, by comparison with the vast majority of their counterparts, to have an amazing staying power.[92]

---

[91] Jaume Aurell, 'Practicing Theory and Theorizing Practice', *Rethinking History* 24 (2020): 229–251.

[92] Edward Said, 'Introduction to the Fiftieth-Anniversary Edition', in Auerbach, *Mimesis*, ix.

Books of criticism connect with academic trends. They are soon replaced by successive shifts in taste, fashion, methodologies, or new intellectual discoveries. Indeed, it is a paradox of postmodern times that, for the first time, a theorist of history such as White – mentioned as one of the case studies for this chapter – may have entered the canon of history. Only time will test its validity, but White's dual role as a theorist of history and intellectual historian has contributed decisively to his permanence in the canon. The discipline of history appears to assume the convenience of theory and criticism, which would imply a greater acceptance of the canon in the future.

The second reason for historians' reluctance in accepting a canon is that history, unlike poetry and music, is a cumulative discipline, and therefore suspicious of any canonical stability. The canon in history has a different nature, more prone to elision,[93] since it lacks that permanent spirit of art, that something permanent, described by Eliot: 'What happens when a new work of art is created is something that happens simultaneously to all the worlds of art which preceded it. The existing monument forms an ideal order among themselves, which is modified by the introduction of the new (the really new) work of art among them.'[94]

This non-artistic condition of history and its dual nature (practical and critical at the same time) is what Croce

---

[93] Eva Illouz, 'Redeeming Consumption: On Lowenthal's "The Triumph of the Mass Idols"', in *Canonic Texts,* 91–92.

[94] T. S. Eliot, 'The Function of Criticism', in *Selected Essays* (New York: Harcourt, 1950), 12–22, here 12.

defined as 'work of thought', different from the 'work of imagination' of literature and art:

> Art, which is the work of the imagination, can be well distinguished from the theory of art, which is the work of reflection; artistic genius produces the former, the speculative intellect the latter, and it often happens with artists that the speculative intellect is inferior to their genius. … But history and theory of history are both of them works of thought, bound to one another in the same way as thought is bound to itself, since it is one.[95]

As historical practice merges with criticism, any interpretation of the past becomes a critical artefact. In literature, for example, Erich Auerbach and Frank Kermode are considered literary critics, like Dante and Shakespeare literary authors – although, as an exception, some of them may act as 'double agents' (producing literature and criticism at the same time or as separate activities). The same is true in art: Giorgio Vasari and Ernst Gombrich are art critics, while Giotto and Picasso are artists. However, any historian continuously exercises the function of 'critic of the past', and there is no discipline properly called historical criticism. Croce based his influential history of historiography on the assumption that, 'Beginning with methodical delimitations, I shall note in the first place that in a history of historiography as such, historical writings cannot be looked upon from the point of view proper to a history of literature—that is to say, as expressions of individual sentiments, as forms of art.'[96]

[95] Croce, *Theory and History of Historiography*, 172.
[96] Croce, *Theory and History of Historiography*, 166.

The third reason for history's reluctance to recognize the canon lies in the discipline's ambiguous epistemological status, which straddles the line between the humanities and the social sciences, between the arts and the sciences, as Ernst Gombrich and Carlo Ginzburg have pointed out.[97] On the one hand, the closer it appears to literature and the arts, the more the discipline values the quality, originality, uniqueness, and creativity of historical works because it appreciates them as models of writing and creative methodologies – Eliot's 'ideal order.' All of these qualities affect the form and transcend simple historical evidence, thus offering enduring validity, despite the possibility of research providing new data. Although the historical data and most of the interpretations of Herodotus, Thucydides, Eusebius, Gibbon, Michelet, Ranke, Burckhardt, and Huizinga, are now outdated, we still consider them a continuing source of inspiration for anyone trying to understand not only their specific historical subjects but also the rules governing the dialectic between rise and decline, personal and collective action, permanence and change. On the other hand, as the discipline increasingly adopts scientific methodologies, form loses relevance with respect to content, and the criterion of novelty predominates, increasing its intolerance of the permanence of certain works of reference sustained over time: the canon becomes irrelevant. Hayden White famously defined this tension as the *burden of history*:

> When criticized by social scientists for the softness of his method, the crudity of his organizing metaphors,

---

[97] Ernst H. Gombrich, 'Research in the Humanities: Ideals and Idols', *Daedalus* 102 (1973): 1–10, and Ginzburg, 'Roots of Scientific Paradigm', 273–288.

or the ambiguity of his sociological and psychological presuppositions, the historian responds that history has never claimed the status of a pure science, that it depends as much upon intuitive as upon analytical methods, and that historical judgments should not therefore be evaluated by critical standards properly applied only in the mathematical and experimental disciplines. All of which suggests that history is a kind of art. But when reproached by literary artists for his failure to probe the more arcane strata of human consciousness and his unwillingness to utilize contemporary modes of literary representation, the historian falls back upon the view that history is after all a semi-science, that historical data do not lend themselves to 'free' artistic manipulation, and that the form of his narratives is not a matter of choice, but is required by the nature of historical materials themselves.[98]

This balance between science and art, between the cumulative and the artistic, between tradition and modernity, does not pose a particular problem in activities such as art and literature, in which the past exerts a continuous fascination and does not constitute, in itself, a reduction of authority. But in history, which is supposedly scientific and therefore shares the inexorable law of the sciences that the present must surpass the past – form subordinated to content, and method privileged over creativity – the paradox of the canon grows exponentially.

[98] Hayden White, 'The Burden of History', *History and Theory* 5 (1966): 111–134, here 111.

Paradoxes

We note this paradox in some of the examples of canonical works in history analysed in this chapter. Successive criticism of the canon – modernist, postmodernist, postcolonial – have followed one another, but one or the other canon prevails, as these criticisms shape new canonical configurations and their unconventionality turns into conventionality.

This confirms some of the parallelisms and differences between historiographical and biblical canon. The theorists of the biblical canon, who have approached this subject in greater depth, emphasize two basic rules for the consolidation of a work in a canon: conventionality and continuity. Conventionality is 'a basic prerequisite for canonicity in conformity to what was called the *rule of faith* (*kerygma*), that is, the congruity of a given document with the basic Christian tradition recognized as normative by the Church'.[99]

However, if we exchange this 'Christian tradition' for the 'historiographical tradition,' that is, the convention established by the discipline from its nineteenth-century scientific foundations, we see that just the opposite is true. Historiography is wary of the biblical rule – conventionality – since, unlike what happened in ancient Christianity, which had the Magisterium of the Church as its normative source, history has no centralized academic authority to impose a common norm.

In its resistance to conventionality, the historical canon tends towards discontinuity, rupture, and innovation, as opposed to continuity and respect for tradition: 'a canon

[99] Bruce Metzger, *The Canon of the New Testament: Its Origin, Development, and Significance* (Oxford: Clarendon Press, 1987), 251.

changes, and the changes renew the supply of both pleasure and its potent derivative, dismay'.[100] By defending the canon as rupture – the hermeneutics of discontinuity – we turn to the concept of post-structural genealogy as articulated by Michel Foucault.[101] But by defending the canon as continuity and conventionality, we turn to the concept of medieval gene-alogy as examined by Gabrielle M. Spiegel.[102] As I will explain in more detail in the last chapter, the former refers to the 'logos', while the latter to the 'genesis'. The intrinsic connec-tion between these two notions of genealogy may shape our understanding of canonical dynamics in history. Their asso-ciation demonstrates that criticisms of the canon as essen-tialist, hegemonic, and normative are argumentatively weak because experience has shown that, in reality, this aspiration to demolish the canon has culminated in its revision in order to impose a new canon, rather than its mere disappearance.

Tending to the post-structural genealogy, the histo-riographical canon connects here with a solvent of historical continuity and linearity, potentially disruptive and delegiti-mizing, which 'demands a battle of knowledge against the "power effects" of scientific discourse and takes its place in this battle as a tactic, deployed to put into play the forms of knowledge (*savoirs*) thus engaged, as a result of which they are "desubjugated" and rendered free'.[103]

---

[100] Frank Kermode, *Pleasure and Change: The Aesthetics of Canon* (Oxford: Oxford University Press, 2004), 50.

[101] Foucault, 'Nietzsche', 139–164.

[102] Gabrielle M. Spiegel, 'Foucault and the Problem of Genealogy', *The Medieval History Journal* 4 (2001): 1–14.

[103] Spiegel, 'Foucault', 10.

Consequently, the paradox of the canon in history is that historians and their most celebrated works are remembered precisely for having broken with tradition, representing a disruption rather than a continuity of the reigning conventionality. In the canonical historiographical narrative that – whether we agree or not – most of us have received in our classes, Herodotus was the 'founding father of history' who foregrounded the emergence of historiography as a branch of knowledge, Thucydides created the concept of 'history' which was not available before, Polybius proposed the concept 'the writing of history', Gibbon practised a new philosophical history, Michelet wrote Romanticist history analogous to that of his colleagues in literature, Ranke proposed a renewed philological–critical method, Burckhardt inspired a new approach to cultural history, Braudel negotiated with a long-durée approach, Ginzburg opted for microhistory in a hegemonic context of macrohistory, Natalie Z. Davis reintroduced narrative history, and White championed the philosophy of history recovered by historians.

Each new generation of historians questions the previous paradigms, and the labels assigned to the old historians are considered outdated. The aforementioned list is seen today, for example, as one more sign of the patriarchal and hegemonic domination of the West. But nothing prevents them from remaining fixed in a canon that only rarely is lost – Macaulay is the paradigmatic example of a 'lost canon', but is really unusual.[104]

As a result of this 'discontinuity within continuity,' which fits well with the cycle argued by Thomas Kuhn in his

---

[104] Himmelfarb, *The New History*, 143–154.

The Structure of Scientific Revolutions (1962), the historiographical canon subsumes the two senses of genealogy: the medieval and the Foucauldian. On the one hand, medieval genealogies sought continuity and legitimization, combining historical and symbolic meaning.[105] The rhythmical repetition of the verb *genuit* ('he engendered') in medieval genealogies serves as the grammatical and semantic key of a given history, giving it internal coherence and structure since each link of the chain establishes continuity.[106] The historical practice needs to explain itself through those genealogies that have been transmitted from generation to generation, first through oral tradition and later in a more formalized way through academic essays on the history of historiography and university syllabi. The modern footnotes are an almost literal reverberation of the function that the *genuit* had in medieval genealogies.[107] But, on the other hand, a rupture necessarily occurs at the moment of the inclusion of a new component in that genealogy – in the Foucauldian sense – which has made it possible to consider authors who in the 1970s–1980s were as subversive to the discipline as Natalie Zemon Davis, Hayden White, and Edward Said, as an essential part of the canon of history. And this is where the sense that Foucault gave to genealogy appears: that of rupture, disruption, discontinuity, and delegitimization.

[105] Spiegel, 'Foucault', 2–3.
[106] Gabrielle M. Spiegel, 'Genealogy: Form and Function in Medieval Historical Narrative', *History and Theory* 22 (1983): 43–53; Aurell, *Authoring the Past*, 111–132; Romila Thapar, 'Genealogy as a Source of Social History', in *Ancient Indian Social History: Some Interpretations* (New Delhi: Orient Longman, 1978), 286–316.
[107] Anthony Grafton, *The Footnote: A Curious History* (Cambridge: Harvard University Press, 1997).

The binary capacity of the canon of history – continuity and discontinuity – gives it a peculiar shape. It is not hegemonic or supremacist, because none of the authors who have finally imposed themselves in the canon were hegemonic when they started working – rather, they had to overcome the difficulties of being anti-hegemonic. We should value these canonical historical texts because, in their simultaneously conventional and subversive dimension, they contribute to mobilizing and organizing the community of knowledge of historians. In this respect, history behaves as a critical rather than creative discipline. For example, Foucault, Bourdieu, Geertz, White, and Said have, in this last century, each provided their own set of metaphors to deconstruct the assumptions that animate the traditional canon in their respective social disciplines, and to discuss the ways in which social and cultural value is reconstructed. They have become canonical, and will most likely remain so for a long time.[108]

With this doubly genealogical dimension, the idea of canon implies a dialectic. Canonical texts were originally a revelation, often a revolution – like these 'revolutions in sensibility' which affect from time to time some disciplines, as Ernst Gombrich argued for the history of art, Thomas Kuhn for the history of science, and Lucien Goldman for the history of literature: 'Those works which are canonic in the most important sense are those whose individuality is achieved through refinement or innovation in relation to factors which are fundamental to their medium's syntactic and semantic structures.'[109]

---

[108] Illouz, 'Redeeming Consumption', 91–92.
[109] Crowther, *Defining Art*, 87. See White, *The Fiction of Narrative*, 91.

The canonical work carries within it a mechanism of adaptation and a generator of rupture that, if it works properly, may provide for a legitimate adaptation to changing circumstances and sensibilities. To give a few recent examples, no one can imagine historians such as Natalie Zemon Davis, Georges Duby, or Hayden White as 'guardians of tradition', equipped to prevent the successive innovations that came after their works. Duby's case is particularly illustrative, since, as he himself acknowledged in his intellectual autobiography, he always sought to break new ground in each of his projects, from his early work on socioeconomics to his examination of *mentalités*, his narrative texts, and the history of women.[110] The canonical figures are usually themselves respectful not only of the tradition, but also of the novelty that succeeds them, and this has always been the case in history, except when the discipline was somewhat imprisoned by ideology – something well visible in the most intense moments of historical materialism of the 1950s and 1960s.

We can only understand the canon from the juxtaposition of its permanence and transience. The interplay between the absolute and the relative, between the permanent and the contextual, and between the structural and the conjectural, results in an 'eternal inconclusiveness' of the legacy of canonical works, endowing it with a permanent potential for renewal. This paradox gives relevance to the canon. As Menahem Blondheim explains, in the context of communication sciences, canonical works are all about: 'relevance, in the sense of the flexibility of his work, its inconclusiveness, and

---

[110] Aurell, *Theoretical Perspectives on Historians' Autobiographies*, 119–122.

its potential for renewal', and this is what qualifies and legitimizes them as sources and origins of scholarship.[111] Perhaps Thucydides was aware of this 'paradox of inconclusiveness' when he wrote that his work was not composed 'for the applause of today's hearing, but as a possession for all time'.[112]

Within the duality between the two genealogical dimensions of the canon, the most *visible* is the tendency of the canon of history to perpetuate the conventional part of historical works – its *medieval* genealogical dimension. This tendency is understood by the experience that 'history is perhaps the conservative discipline *par excellence*'.[113] As Bruce Metzger explains from a theological perspective, 'another obvious test of authority for a book was its continuous acceptance and usage by the Church at large. This was, of course, based on the principle that a book that had enjoyed acceptance by many churches over a long period of time was in a stronger position than one accepted by only a few churches, and then only recently.'[114]

Metzger explains that Jerome emphasized the verdict of eminent and ancient authors and, when asked about the author of the epistle to Hebrews he declared, 'it does not matter, for in any case it is the work of a church-writer (*ecclesiastici viri*) and is constantly read in the Churches'.[115] The appeal to authorities of the past has been recognized in historiography

---

[111] Menahem Blondheim, 'Harold Adams Innis and His Bias in Communication', in *Canonic Texts*, 156–158.
[112] Edmunds, *Chance and Intelligence*, 150.
[113] White, 'The Burden of History', 112.
[114] Metzger, *The Canon*, 253.
[115] *Epist.* Cxxix, quoted by Metzger, *The Canon*, 253.

since ancient times. Dionysius of Halicarnassus advised reading the works of the ancients not only to obtain the subject matter but also for the emulation of their peculiar forms of expression. Jerome and Isidore construct their key works – the *Vulgate* and the *Etymologies* – as a tribute, remembrance, and preservation of the authority of the past. In the Middle Ages, this aspiration was taken up by genealogical chronicles. In the genealogies of the counts of Barcelona (twelfth century), for example, the chronicler declares that he has based himself on the 'account of the Ancients' (*Antiquorum nobis relatione*).[116] Since modernity, this dependence on authorities, far from abating, has been consolidated, and formalized in the footnotes as an instrument in the service of canonicity, as Anthony Grafton explains: '[F]ootnotes form an indispensable if messy part of that indispensable, messy mixture of art and science: modern history.'[117]

This tendency of historiography to seek an external authority to legitimize its texts responds, on the one hand, to a deep-rooted norm in science. But it also reflects the fact that the canon is a living category, because it does not refer to the past from which the authority referred to was created, but to the present within which the historian writes. In this aspect, the canon is presented as a myth, since, once a historical work is established, it is uncritically cited as a reference, when perhaps it has not even been read: think, for example, of Gibbon's *Rise and Decline*, Michelet's *History of the French*

---

[116] *Gesta Comitum Barchinonensium*: Critical edition: *Cròniques Catalanes. II. Gesta Comitum Barchinonensium*, L. Barrau-Dihigo and J. M. Torrents (eds.) (Barcelona: Institut d'Estudis Catalans, 1925), 3.
[117] Grafton, *The Footnote*, 235.

Revolution, and Hayden White's *Metahistory*. These works preserve something of the 'eternal present', to adapt the expression popularized by Max Weber, and also refer to that quality mentioned by Geertz in his autobiography: 'Myth, it has been said, I think by Northrop Frye, describes not what happened but what happens'.[118] Its relevance goes beyond a specific historical circumstance: 'Contemporary relevance is clearly related to non-ephemerality: a non-ephemeral work is one relevant to every generation, to all people at all times.'[119]

Thus, the study of the canon raises questions related to the present, such as the assignment of authority or the essential mechanisms governing the historiographical transmission, the relations between the centre and the periphery of the profession, and the tensions between tradition and innovation. As Gadamer posits, the canon is 'a consciousness of something enduring, of significance that cannot be lost and that is independent of all the circumstances of time – a kind of timeless present that is contemporaneous with every other present'.[120] The recognition of the presentism of the canon unmasks the hypocrisy of overemphasizing criticism of the dominance of historiographical centres that exercised hegemony in the past since there is always someone who occupies that place – and it appears at that moment a new aspirant fighting to fill that place. The resistance of the old canon is as defensible as the struggle of the new one to become hegemonic, so it seems advisable to maintain a

---

[118]   Clifford Geertz, *After the Fact: Two Countries, Four Decades, One Anthropologist* (Cambridge: Harvard University Press., 1995), 3.
[119]   John Barton, *Holy Writings, Sacred Text: The Canon in Early Christianity* (Louisville: Westminster John Knox Press, 1997), 137.
[120]   Gadamer, *Truth and Method*, 299.

balance between respect for the historiographical tradition and the search for new paths. The canon can contribute precisely to the awareness of the need for this flexibility and weighting.

Inescapability

The canon in history is sanctioned by tradition, repetition, and preservation, but originates in a genealogical rupture, as shown in the cases studied in this chapter such as Gibbon, Macaulay, and White, but also obvious in the innovations brought by historians such as Thucydides, Eusebius, Froissart, Michelet, Ranke, Marc Bloch, Braudel, Thomson, and Natalie Zemon Davis. Their most important works broke new ground for historiography, thus implying a break with tradition. But these were also inserted in a line of canonical continuity that made them identifiable with historical convention by their readers. As their itineraries show, the canon thus conveys continuity and discontinuity simultaneously: it pushes forward while nonetheless it is cloaked and takes refuge in convention. It establishes authoritative tradition over time, even as it seeks relevance in the present. This paradox rejects acritical preconceived and aprioristic or ideological approaches. It develops, not from a centrally organized conspiracy and formalized classification, but from a complex and random process in which a selection of the works remains in the collective mind of a culture as the result of multifaceted interactions of numerous individuals, and intentional efforts at the micro-level.[121] It provides systems

---

[121] Franke, 'The Canon Question', 61 and S. Simone Winko, 'Literatur-Kanon als invisible hand-Phänomen', in Heinz L. Arnold (ed.), *Literarische Kanonbildung* (München: R. Boorberg Verlag, 2002), 9–24.

or frameworks of meaning which serve both to read the word and guide future interpretations. Nevertheless, the canon is not a rigid and close category but a flexible and open one. As Gregor Langfeld argues, 'the canon and processes of canon formation are not, as used to be assumed, static but are rather characterized by an incredible dynamism'.[122] This dynamism leads to the flexibility of the canon: 'canon is a dynamic transhistorical textual community and not a timeless inscription of fixed meanings'.[123]

For these reasons, I argue that the canon plays – or should play – a key role in history and in historical criticism. It was clearly more necessary in the premodern world, in which 'each profession constructed a canon, mastery of which was both the price of admission to practice' while nowadays canon only matters 'in a relatively limited number of areas'.[124] Yet, modern communities of knowledge, including the discipline of history, demand a set of rules and agreed-upon references. Otherwise, they run the risk of becoming formless, or of being forced to rely exclusively on scientific modes of data collection and discussion, or what Nietzsche would call an 'archaeological history', which stifles history's necessary interpretative dimension.

The canon becomes a privileged observatory of the diversity of perspectives deployed by historians through the

---

[122] Gregor Langfeld, 'The Canon in Art History: Concepts and Approaches', *Journal of Art Historiography* 19 (2018): 1–18, here 18.
[123] Alter, *Canon and Creativity*, 18.
[124] A. Anthony Grafton and Glenn W. Most, 'How to Do Things with Texts: An Introduction', in A. Grafton and W. M. Glenn (eds.), *Canonical Texts and Scholarly Practices* (Cambridge: Cambridge University Press, 2016), 1–13, here 7.

centuries and, as such, allows us to grasp the same object through a variety of points of view and positions. When we talk to our students about 'war and power' from Herodotus, Thucydides, Froissart, Gibbon, and Michelet, or about 'culture and power' from Machiavelli, Burckhardt, Bloch, Thompson, Duby, and Foucault, we are in fact teaching a set of perspectives that dialogue with each other – valuing the commonalities and differences in each of their interpretations.

The canon is indispensable for an interpretative and cumulative discipline such as history, in which such milestones exist. The main argument for the existence of the canon is that these enduring works *are there*, and historians and their readers still have them as a point of reference. Knowledge communities develop best when they have at their disposal an array of conceptual perspectives developed over time, which also allows them to recognize the tensions between them. Although some of the data, interpretations, and conclusions of the canonical books of the past have been refuted by later research, their approaches remain canonical for our fields because the texts remain embedded in fundamental conceptual tensions: they are alive in the central debates of the discipline that move in a broader framework than circumstance and context. As Eva Illouz concludes, 'what makes a text *canonic* is … its ability to invoke dilemmas that are still central to our field'.[125] Thus, Eusebius is identified with the great dilemma of providence in history, Gibbon with the rules of the rise and fall of civilizations, Michelet with the condition of nations, Ranke with the method of history itself, Burckhardt

---

[125] Illouz, 'Redeeming Consumption', 91–92.

with the centrality of culture, Braudel with the relationship between space and time, and Davis with the essential role of narrative in history and society. They were able to approach the great historical questions, beyond the specific topics that their works dealt with.

The criticism of the canon as an imposition or norm fails since the canon is not constructed but emerges from the analysis of the most cited and referenced books. Borges concludes that 'writers invent their predecessors', making the process of canon formation organic.[126] The canon then works as a narrative rather than as a closed and schematic list of names, as Hugh Kenner suggests: 'For a canon is not a list but a narrative of some intricacy, depending on places and times and opportunities.'[127] Moreover, as Charles Altieri argues: 'Canons are shared metanarratives or models of rationality.'[128]

This metanarrative character implies that the canon in history possesses a storyline that goes beyond an enumeration of historical works based on a specific era or theme, and constitutes a historiographical narrative in itself. If the canon did not exist, there would be no way to transmit in the same storyline such diverse works as Herodotus' *History*, Thucydides' *Peloponnesian War*, Eusebius' *Ecclesiastical History*, Froissart's account of the *Hundred Years' War*,

---

[126] Hugh Kenner, 'The Making of the Modernist Canon', in R. von Hallberg (ed.), *Canons* (Chicago: The University of Chicago Press, 1984), 363–375, here 363.

[127] Kenner, 'The Making of the Modernist Canon', 373.

[128] Charles Altieri, *Canon and Consequences: Reflections on the Ethical Force of Imaginative Ideals* (Illinois: North-Wester University Press, 1990), 223.

Guicciardini's *History of Florence*, Gibbon's *Decline and Fall*, Michelet's *History of France*, Burckhardt's *Civilization of the Renaissance in Italy*, Bloch's *Feudal Society*, Braudel's *Mediterranean World*, and Thompson's *Making of the English Working Class*. Nor would it have been possible to construct a coherent history of historiography. Beyond their heterogeneity in time and subject, we historians identify in this enumeration a narrative coherence, governed by the fact of belonging to an implicit but patent canon – the central nerve of this narrative constituted by their ability to take their approaches universally, beyond the specific topics they address.

The metanarrative of the canon frames it in teaching, another of its evident – and, again, inescapable – functions. Without a canon, teaching history, both at the secondary and university level, would be extremely difficult: 'For pedagogical purposes, some principle of selection and organization among the vast amounts of print is indispensable. No such principle will ever be sociologically neutral, but no scholarly or artistic institution will be able to operate practically without one either.'[129] Indeed, Roland Barthes defined the canon in neutral terms, strictly related to teaching: a canonical text is what we read in class. Pierre Bourdieu had already detected this function even in the most predominantly post-structuralist years – the apparently most anti-canonical period:

> Sustained by all the authority of the academy, and by the facilities that the academy procures for the fulfillment of its tasks (the famous 'explication de textes' of professors in the French educational system), this tradition does not

[129] Katz, 'Introduction', 4.

need to set itself up as a doctrine. With a few exceptions (like New Criticism), it can remain a doxa, able to perpetuate itself surreptitiously, through and beyond the apparent refurbishing of the academic liturgy like 'structuralist' or 'de-constructionist' readings of isolated texts. Or again this tradition finds sustenance in the commentary on canons of 'pure' reading as in *The Sacred Wood* of T. S. Eliot or by writers of the *Nouvelle Revue Françoise*, notably Paul Valery.[130]

The narrative form and function of the canon, and its pedagogical potential also allow us to connect with those who have preceded us in the discipline, links in a chain of continuity. Communication theorists have compared the canon to a correspondence company that facilitates contact with those who came before us, with whom we connect intellectually: 'Work in the humanities and social sciences is inevitable in dialogue with previous work (and though the hermeneutic element in natural science is often suppressed or irrelevant, it is still often surprisingly important) … Scholarship, like most forms of creative work, involves long-distance correspondence with imaginary pen pals. Canon helps us select our correspondents.'[131]

Inquiring into the double genealogical dimension – continuity and discontinuity, permanence and change – that every canon implies, allows us to discern between the part that remains constant throughout history, as Herbert Marcuse acknowledges: '[T]hroughout the long history of art, and in

---

[130] Bourdieu, 'Flaubert's Point of View', *Critical Inquiry* 14 (1988): 539–562, here 542.
[131] Katz, 'Introduction', 5.

spite of changes in taste, there is a standard which remains constant.'[132] At the same time, we can locate the break and turning points that mark this line of continuity and address one of the essential inquiries: the question of what we should read and why.

In the end, the recognition of the inescapability of the canon, its intellectual properties, its metanarrative condition, its pedagogical dimension, and its linking function are compatible with the antagonism that the idea of the canon generates today – especially for those who would like to subvert or enter it. We will never know to what extent medievalists like myself read and reread Huizinga, Bloch, Kantorowicz, Duby, and Le Goff because they provide the most compelling analyses, interpretations, and narratives of their subjects, or because they are on the canonical list transmitted via university teaching, footnotes, and conversations. As the popular saying goes, 'the busiest roads in Europe are the best; that is why they are so busy.' Here is a key, but perhaps unresolvable, question: does the authority of Kantorowicz's *The King's Two Bodies* derive from its inherent historiographical authority (the canon *in* history) or from the authority that comes from being included in a canonical list of history books to read (the canon *of* history)? Paul Lauter calls this conundrum the *dialectics of validation*: 'certain historical constructs gave importance to a body of texts, while the weight attributed to the texts sustained the very credibility of received version of history'.[133]

---

[132] Herbert Marcuse, *The Aesthetic Dimension: Towards a Critique of Marxist Aesthetics* (Boston: Beacon Press, 1979), x.

[133] Paul Lauter, 'History and the Canon', *Social Text* 12 (1985): 94–101, here 94.

The content (the canon itself) and form (the fixed list) of the canon interact in a continuous dynamic relationship:

> The notion of canon as authority and list (function and shape) were never at odds and notions of functions or shape (fixed lists) were never mutually exclusive. While function always preceded shape and lists were never possible before widespread recognition of the authority of a collection of sacred texts, shape also has become subsequently an important feature that identifies the sacred texts.[134]

The canon does not imply its own self-justification but redirects our attention to the tradition it mediates. Clearly, a certain common experience of tradition is required for any social, professional, cognitive, or scholarly community, as this provides a sense of disciplinary cohesion. But this dependence of the canon on tradition increases its weakness and vulnerability in the current intellectual and social context. This singular and dominant condition of our time has been defined by some authoritative critics as *presentism*.[135] Postcolonial tendencies criticize the canon's links to the Western tradition and its inextricable implication in European colonial power. This embodies the most important arguments in the contemporary contestation of the canon but also illustrates the great paradox of the canon: the difficulty of conducting cultural and intellectual exchanges without it. By containing

---

[134] Lee M. McDonald, *The Formation of the Biblical Canon. Volume I: The Old Testament: Its Authority and Canonicity* (London: Bloomsbury, 2017), 79.

[135] Hartog, *Chronos: The West*, ix.

within themselves cells of the past and of the present – of the genealogy of continuity and of the genealogy of disruption – the canon helps generate the conceptual tensions from which paradigms of knowledge evolve. This double dependence of the canon on the past and the present, on tradition and innovation, calls for a deeper analysis of the concept of genres and genealogies, which summarizes both, as I will try to show in the following chapters.

4

The Canonical Function of Historical Genres

To some extent the historian and the chronicler
have the same goals and use the same material,
but their method of handling it is different,
as is their form.

Gervase of Canterbury, *Chronicle*

The historical genres are the most visible part of the continuity and permanence that the classic and the canon provide to historiography.[1] Yet, the irruption of a new historical genre, of a new way of representing history, immediately implies a discontinuity with the past. Paradoxically, this discontinuity, as I will argue in this chapter, provides durability to the authors and books that have renewed historiography with these new ways of representing the past. Therefore, historical genres carry within them a seed of continuity and discontinuity and, in this respect, their behaviour is analogous to that of the classic: 'From day to day we must cope with the paradox that the classic changes, yet retains its identity. It would be not read, and so would not be a classic, if we could not in some way believe it to be capable of saying more than its authors meant.'[2] For this reason, the analysis of historical genres is relevant in an investigation of classics and the canon such as I am proposing in this book.

---

[1] Earlier versions of portions of this chapter appeared as 'The Historicity of Historical Genres', *Storia della Storiografia* 80, 2 (2021): 65–86.

[2] Kermode, *Classic*, 80.

Gadamer has confirmed the essential role that genres play in the discernment of the classical. The permanence of the classical is perfectly compatible with the variability of genres. The close relationship between the two, in fact, makes the durability of the classics visible:

> The authors regarded as classical are always the representatives of particular literary genres. They were considered the culmination of the norm of that literary genre, and ideal that literary criticism makes plain in retrospect. If we now examine these generic norms historically – i.e., if we consider their history – then the classical is seen as a stylistic phase, a climax that articulates the history of the genre in terms of before and after. Insofar as the climatic points in the history of genres belong largely within the same brief period of time, within the totality of the historical development of classical antiquity, the classical refers to such a period and thus also becomes a concept denoting a period and fuses with a concept of style.[3]

In addition, the genres chosen by historians become a privileged site for the analysis of the relationship between content and form in the historical operation. At first, it might appear that historians choose a specific genre because they think that story is best told that way. Even today, most historians remain convinced that the monograph is the most effective way to represent the past. The monograph has always been particularly useful to historians because it allowed them to include primary sources, go in-depth and

---

[3] Gadamer, *Truth and Method*, 288–289.

give substantial details about events, and offer multiple interpretations. As some theorists on scholarship argue, 'the monograph has become a catch-all term for a book that is not of a reference type, that is of primary material.'[4] Other historians are persuaded that biography is the second most conventional genre for a representation of the past, and the one which best connects with readers. Jill Ker Conway points out that the 'magical opportunity of entering another life is what really sets us thinking about our own'.[5] Historians have also used different forms of autobiography as historical representation since they aim to recreate the past, as Albert E. Stone argues, not by literal reproduction of remembered and recorded facts but by patterning the past into a present symbolic truth.[6] They feel that autobiography is 'historically useful', as Walter Laqueur puts it.[7] They are also attracted by the 'performative mode of autobiography' which allows historians to transcend 'the conventional limited strategies of writing autobiography' to promote a social or cultural agenda, as Rocio G. Davis suggests.[8]

---

[4] David Green and Rod Cookson, 'Publishing and Communication Strategies', in R. Campbell, E. Pentz, and I. Borthwick (eds.), *Academic and Professional Publishing* (Oxford: Chandos 2012), 115.

[5] Jill K. Conway, *When Memory Speaks: Exploring the Art of Autobiography* (New York: Vintage, 1999), 18.

[6] Albert E. Stone, *The American Autobiography* (Englewood Cliffs: Prentice-Hall, 1981), 6.

[7] Walter Laqueur, *Thursday's Child Has Far to Go: A Memoir of the Journeying Years* (New York: Charles Scribner's Sons, 1995), 4.

[8] Rocio G. Davis, 'Academic Autobiography as Women's History: Jill Ker Conway's True North and Leila Ahmed's A Border Passage', *Rethinking History* 13, 1 (2009): 109–123, here 114.

Yet these three historical genres – monography, biography, and autobiography – do not encompass all the genres selected by historians. Carolyn Steedman used her own and her mother's stories to challenge some of the main scenarios in which modern British history had been conceived and 'to argue against some of the primary ways in which histories tend to be written' and to present an alternative to the 'very process through which historical accounts are conventionally put together'.[9] Persuaded that 'ultimately it is not the facts that make us what we are, but the stories we have been told and the stories we believe',[10] and in order to show that these stories cannot be told through a rigid generic platform, Robert A. Rosenstone has practised different non-conventional historical genres to reproduce the past in a way he felt he cannot say within the framework of the other traditional historical genres.[11] I have discussed elsewhere this attitude of the most recent experimental historians:

> In the end, it is possible that historians have turned to self-writing simply to say things that they feel they cannot say within the framework of the scholarly text. In fact, academia may become for some historians a kind of straitjacket that precludes their saying what

[9] Geoff Eley, *A Crooked Line: From Cultural History to the History of Society* (Ann Arbor: University of Michigan Press, 2005), 174 on Carlyn Steedman, *Landscape for a Good Woman: A Story of Two Lives* (New Brunswick: Rutgers University Press, 1986).

[10] Robert A. Rosenstone, *The Man Who Swam into History* (Austin: University of Texas Press, 2005), xv.

[11] See, for instance, his experimental autobiography, Robert A. Rosenstone, *Adventures of a Postmodern Historian* (London: Bloomsbury Academic, 2016).

they want about the world, past and present. Thus, historians turned autobiographers seem to deliberately break the rules of the game with conventional (and in some sense arbitrary) boundaries that keep them and other scholars from sharing things they know (or think they know). Some of these writings, particularly postmodern and interventional styles, are just an attempt to get out of that game, spread the wings and fly a little.[12]

Historians such as Sheila Fitzpatrick advocate for the necessary flexibility in historical genres, depending on the topic: '[I]f someone else were to write the history of my life on the basis of all the sources except my memory, they would (in my mother's habitual phrase) get it all wrong.'[13] Other historians, such as Hans A. Schmitt, sought liberation from the formal constrictions of academic structures, and decided to choose a narrative rather than a scientific language: '[F]or a scholar it is a marvellous release to be able to write sentence after sentence, and page after page, without stopping for footnotes.'[14] Carlos Eire chose autobiography to delve into the injustices of dictatorships, which allowed him to free himself from some academic conventions that could have hindered the reception of his message.[15] Natalie Zemon Davis led the

---

[12] Aurell, *Theoretical Perspectives on Historians' Autobiographies*, 265.

[13] Sheila Fitzpatrick, 'Can You Write a History of Yourself? Thoughts of a Historian Turned Memoirist', *Griffith Review (Brisbane)* 33 (2011): 1–7, here 4.

[14] Hans A. Schimtt, *Lucky Victim: An Ordinary Life in Extraordinary Times, 1933–1946* (Baton Rouge: Louisiana State University Press, 1989), 242.

[15] Carlos Eire, *Waiting for Snow in Havana: Confessions of a Cuban Boy* (New York: Free Press, 2003), 388.

late twentieth-century generation of narrative historians, who argued for a certain return of narrative in history which facilitated to 'play with the idea of "margins", an idea important to me not because of recent de-constructionist use à la Derrida, but because of my own lifelong ambivalence about centres.'[16]

Today, in the context of the freedoms inspired by postmodernism and enabled by the development of innovative textual and graphic platforms, creative historical writing challenges conventional genre categorization as new mediums of representing the past are being used, including comics, cinema, media, or virtual constructions.

All these historians' choices show that genres had no pre-established substances or essences, but had to be seen as systems of practical classifications – open systems – subject to blending, change, and displacement according to the exigencies of different social and cultural situations. Yet, although genres had no substances, they had histories. This meant that the best way to study the forms and contents of any mode of cultural expression, and the ways in which forms and contents were fused in any given moment of a society's evolution, is historical: '[T]he history of genres provides the basis for a history of literature in a way that the other aspects of the literary work of art do not.'[17] White concludes that genre theory could be very useful for the analysis of historical texts, as he had done in his *Metahistory* (1973): 'If the history of genres provides us with a way of conceiving the history of literature

---

[16] Natalie Zemon Davis, *A Life of Learning* (New York: American Council of Learned Societies Occasional Paper, no. 39, 1997), 22.

[17] White, 'Reflections', 868.

in open and cosmopolitan ways, what happens if we extend this principle to the writing of history itself?'[18]

To complete this brief introductory genealogy, Northrop Frye's transhistorical conception of genres has recently been replaced – or, perhaps, enriched and revitalized – by Ralph Cohen's historicist conception of genres and, crucially for historiography, by White's narrativization of history. Mark S. Phillips argues that, for an intellectual historian engaged in tracing the history of historical narrative, genre becomes an attractive category since, 'by reconceiving genre as a structure that is historically conditioned, we make it into an instrument of historical investigation, replacing structuralist abstractions with an opportunity to explore concrete practices in their own specific literary and social settings'.[19]

Based on these perspectives, this chapter discusses the question of the plurality of historical genres practised by historians, and their function as a galvanizer of the classics. This diversity shows that history is perhaps a more complex rhetorical activity than the nineteenth-century founders of this academic discipline imagined. As Alun Munslow notes, 'history is a highly complex process of authorial insight, invention, and experimentation that is not in thrall to the exclusivity of the understanding that history is wholly an empirical, analytical, and representationalist undertaking'.[20] The shifting nature of historians' genre choices may be defined

---

[18] White, 'Reflections', 868.

[19] Mark S. Phillips, 'Histories, Micro- and Literary: Problems of Genre and Distance', *New Literary History* 34 (2003): 211–229, here 213.

[20] Alun Munslow, 'Introduction', in Alun Munslow (ed.), *Authoring the Past: Writing and Rethinking History* (New York, 2013), 1–6, here 3.

as historicist, challenging the supposed formal stability of the historical narratives – automatically related to their realistic content, which distinguishes them from literary texts.

This peculiar connection between the content and form of historical narratives is precisely what gives rise to the difficult paradox of historical genres. As Gian Biagio Conte has argued, 'a category of genre based exclusively upon formal feature is clearly unacceptable; a classification by contents runs the danger of never indicating the boundary between the general and particular.'[21]

The examination of the variety of genres through which history is represented immediately leads to the questions I address in this chapter: why are some historical genres privileged in a given period, and then discarded as unreliable, unscientific, extra-academic, unconventional, or ahistorical by the next generation of historians? Based on what we have seen in the previous chapters, are historical genres connected with the notions of the classic and the canon? Is the change of a genre due to the authorial intention or to the changes in the audience or the context? What might explain one genre's temporal or definitive hegemony and the genre preference of historians – that is, patrons' requests, readers' preferences, scholarly conventions, or aesthetic fashions? Are shifting perspectives on the utility or validity of particular genre signs of a 'paradigm change'? Does genre *inform* and *conform* to or even *transform* the content of the story itself? Does this

---

[21] Gian Biagio Conte, *Genres and Readers: Lucretius, Love Elegy, Pliny's Encyclopedia* (Baltimore: Johns Hopkins University Press, 1994), 106–107.

transformative operation fit with Marshall McLuhan's notion that 'the medium is the message'? What makes one genre ostensibly more reliable than others? Can we use the category of 'historical genres' for a critical analysis of historical practice? In the end, is genre a useful category for historical and historiographical analysis?[22]

I will proceed first ('Taxonomies') by analysing the theories, definitions, and classifications of historical genres developed by scholars of ancient and medieval periods such as Cicero, Dionysius of Halicarnassus, Lucian of Samosata, Isidore of Seville, and Gervase of Canterbury, connecting with the taxonomical project of *modern* scholarship from Felix Jacoby. This project became obsolete after the change of direction of genre study carried out by Bakhtin and Todorov arguing for a shift from classification to its functions in human speech and behaviour.[23] In the second section ('Developments'), I provide a brief history of the development of historical genres over time from old logographers to modern digital platforms, focusing especially on the moment of their emergence. In the last section ('Reappraisals'), I combine the premodern and modern approaches described in the two first sections, assuming postmodern theories to apply them to the discernment of the classic and the canon in history/historiography.

---

[22] I am using here an analogy with Joan Scott's phrase used in her foundational article, 'Gender: A Useful Category of Historical Analysis', *American Historical Review* 91 (1986): 1053–1075.

[23] Mikhail M. Bakhtin, 'The Problem of Speech Genres', in Caryl Emerson and Michael Holquist (eds.), *Speech Genres and Other Late Essays* (Austin: University of Texas Press, 1986), 60, and Tzvetan Todorov, 'The Origin of Genres', in *Genres in Discourse* (Cambridge: Cambridge University Press, 1990), 18.

Taxonomies

The interest in the study of historical genres is not only patrimony of modern scholarship. Cicero deploys a remarkably
explicit use of the term in his defence of the use of memoirs as
a method of historical knowledge:

> I will write about myself, on the model of many noble
> men. But as you know, there are problems associated with
> this genre [*in hoc genere vitia*]: [1] one has to write with
> greater sensitivity about oneself when something is to be
> praised and not write at all if there is cause for criticism.
> [2] Authority and trustworthiness are reduced. [3] Many
> even complain, saying that even the heralds at games are
> more sensitive, since they bring in another herald when
> they themselves are crowned at the end of the games, so
> that they do not announce themselves as victors with their
> own voices.[24]

Here Cicero uses the word *genus*, in the inflected form
genere. The basic meaning of the word is something like type
or kind or category, but Cicero uses it to mean something very
much like the modern *genre*. However, despite the clear importance of what we would call genres in ancient literary thought,
the word itself never became part of critical discourse, nor did
others appear to discuss it in any depth.[25] Yet, ancient authors
emphasized some common features among some historical

---

[24] Cicero, *Epistulae ad Familiares*, 5.12.8, quoted by Andrew M. Riggsby,
'Memoir and Autobiography in Republican Rome', in *A Companion to
Greek*, 266–274, here 267.
[25] I am grateful to Andrew M. Riggsby for his interpretation of the Cicero
quotation.

texts, starting with the distinction between history and myth, as emphasized by Dionysius. He remarks in his essay on Thucydides, written at the end of the first century BC, that the early writers before Herodotus had compiled old traditions from records 'in which there were some myths believed from time long ago, and some dramatic reversals, which seems foolish to people today'. Thucydides, conversely, proceeded 'by adding no mythic material to it, nor using this history for deceiving and bewitching the many, as all those before him had done, [including] stories which seem incredible and very ridiculous to us today'.[26]

Dionysius of Halicarnassus' *On Thucydides* is one of the first attempts to trace the history of historiography and historical genres, based on material preserved in temples and archives. He proceeds from the earlier Greek logographers and the *historians* Herodotus and Thucydides to his own age, focusing on literary skill, selective method, and genres comprehensively. All later historians – whether they are aware of it or not – were conditioned by Dionysius' historiographical readings and interpretations, and take Herodotus and Thucydides as a model of historical writing, such that their writing might be seen as variations of their original method. More specifically for historical genres in thematic terms, Herodotus represents the path to cultural history, while Thucydides epitomizes the via of political history.[27]

---

[26] Dionysius of Halicarnassus, *On Thucydides*, 5–6, quoted by John Marincola, *Authority and Tradition in Ancient Historiography* (Cambridge: Cambridge University Press, 1997), 122.

[27] Sandra Gozzoli, 'Una teoria antica sull'origine della storiografia greca', *Studi Classici e Orientali* 19/20 (1970–71): 158–211 and Toye, 'Dionysius of Halicarnassus', 279–302.

A few decades later, Lucian's *How to Write History* inaugurated the reflection of the writing of history itself. The first chapter details faults to be avoided when writing history. He also discusses the ruinous effect in the history of flattery. He criticizes those who pass over the events and instead spend their time flattering their own generals and denigrating those of the enemies. Lucian's work exemplifies the appropriation of multiple genres, since his intertextual work says many things simultaneously.[28] For example, he examines the distinction between poetry and history, commenting on a series of passages from the *Iliad* and enumerating what is appropriate for poetry, specifically, the wonderful stories of the gods. But, he insists, such flattery is inappropriate in history, when transforming these stories into poetry without metre, and blending the two genres – history and myth – by failing to observe the conventional boundaries. He considers a grievous error the incorporation into historical writing of 'the embellishments of poetry: myth and encomium, and the excesses in both', which he likens to dressing an athlete in finery and painting his face.[29]

Among these authors of antiquity, Polybius functions as a metageneric commentator. He conceived his own work as a universal history, in geographical terms. If earlier historians had dealt with the history of one nation or race, such as Greece or Persia, he had 'undertaken to describe the events

---

[28] Adam Bartley, 'The Implications of the Reception of Thucydides within Lucian's Vera Historia', *Hermes* 131 (2003): 222–234.

[29] Lucian, *Quomodo Historia Conscribenda Sit*, c. 8, quoted in Marincola, *Authority*, 126.

occurring in all known parts of the world'.[30] He seems to assume the impossibility of writing a universal history before the rise of the Roman Empire:

> Thus I regard the war with Antiochus as deriving its origin from that with Philip, the latter as resulting from that with Hannibal, and the Hannibalic war as a consequence of that about Sicily, the intermediate events, however many and various their character, all tending to the same purpose. ... My history differs to its advantage as much from the works on particular episodes as learning does from listening.[31]

Universal history was highly qualified in antiquity as a genre, as argued by Diodorus Siculus in his *Library*, some decades after Polybius: 'It is fitting that all men should accord great gratitude to those writers who have composed universal histories, since by their individual labours they have aspired to help human society as a whole.'[32] In the third century, Marcus Junianus Justinus praised the herculean effort of Pompeius Trogus' universal history: 'Since most authors engaged in the history of single rulers or peoples find that Pompeius demonstrated an enterprise worthy of Hercules in undertaking a universal history, his books encompassing the annals of every period, king, nation, and people.'[33] Justinus is clearly

---

[30] Polybius, *The Histories*, 2.37.4, in trans. W. R. Paton (Cambridge: Harvard University Press, 2014), I: 365.

[31] Polybius, *The Histories*, 3.32.7–10, in trans. Paton, II: 83.

[32] Diodorus Siculus, *The Library of History*, 1,1, in trans. Charles H. Oldfather (Cambridge: Harvard University Press, 2014), 1: 5.

[33] Quoted in Katherine Clarke, 'Universal Perspectives', in C. Shuttleworth Kraus (ed.), *The Limits of Historiography: Genre and Narrative in Ancient Historical Texts* (Leiden: Brill, 1999), 254.

juxtaposing annals with universal history. If we believe that one best understands generic boundaries when faced with the limits of another, here we note how these two genres were envisioned by ancient critics.

In late antiquity, Isidore of Seville, in his *Etymologies*, distinguished among *historia, chronica, annales*, and *kalendaria*. This taxonomy, as well as many other of his ideas, was maintained for over four centuries. But the problem of genre resurfaced, prompted most often by the differences between *historia* and *chronica*. The criterion of distinction was the manner of narration: bare in the chronicle; elaborate, descriptive, and even interpretative in history.

After Isidore, some medieval authors discussed which historical genres were more suitable for their time. Writing in the second half of the twelfth century, Huguccio of Pisa, in his influential *Derivationes*, provided separate entries for annals (*annales*), the book that collected the deeds done in a particular year; chronicles (*cronica*) and chronography (*cronographia*), a record of deeds done in various times, written in chronological order; and history (*hystoria*) and historiography (*hystoriographia*), the description or depiction (*describere vel depingere*) of deeds (*res gesta*). Huguccio was probably based on the work of the Roman grammarians: Aulus Gellius, writing in the second century, added the detail that history focuses strictly on those deeds realized in the lifetime of the narrator, whereas the annals include the deeds of several years, set down in yearly sequence (testimonial vs observatory source, and recent vs remote past). Scholars such as Ralph de Diceto, Hugh of Fleury, Geoffrey of Viterbo, Gervase of Canterbury, Thomas of Pavia, and Paulinus of Venice, most of them working in the second half of the twelfth century, used analogous taxonomies.[34]

The most explicit of them is Gervase of Canterbury, who distinguishes in his *Chronicon* between *historicus*, which uses a specific narrative prose that illustrates the rhetorical view of history as a form of narration, and *chronicus*, which concentrates primarily on the flow of years. But he is also sceptical regarding the utility of a rigid distinction in practice:

> The glorious and commendable examples of the holy and orthodox fathers are found in histories and annals, which by another name are called chronicles. ... To some extent the historian and the chronicler have the same goals and use the same material, but their method of handling it is different, as is their form. They share a common purpose, because both strive for truth. The form of their work is different because the historian proceeds in a roundabout and elegant manner, while the chronicler adopts a direct and straightforward course. The historian 'employs rhetorical flourishes and long-winded words' [Horace, *Ars Poetica*, 97], while the chronicler 'practices the rustic muse upon a slender reed' [Virgil, *Eclogues*, 1.2]. The historian sits 'among the lofty speaker who sows grandiose words', while the chronicler rests beneath the hut of poor Amyclas [reference to Lucan, *Bellum Civile*, 5.515–559] so that there will be no a battle before his meager dwelling.[35]

---

[34] Some examples in Matthew Kempshall, *Rhetoric and the Writing of History, 400–1500* (Manchester: Manchester University Press, 2011), 441–444 and Bernard Guenée, 'Histoires, Annales, Chroniques. Essai sur les genres historiques au Moyen Age', *Annales* 28 (1973): 997–1016.

[35] Gervase of Canterbury, *Chronicle*, Lake, *Prologues*, 266.

In addition to these metahistorical reflections, medieval authors occasionally specify, usually in their prefaces, the kind of history they aim to write. These distinctions served as a formative conceptual tool, which enabled late medieval historians to make fundamental choices about forms of presentation and about the actual format of their historical writings. In a famous passage of his *Gesta Imperatorum*, Thomas of Pavia, for instance, announced the purpose of writing gestae ('Scripturi gesta imperatorum sublimium') trying to avoid both the chronic propensity to brevity and the historical tendency to verbosity.[36] These medieval chroniclers differed little in their generic classification and their reflection of history was influenced by the emergence of biblical exegesis which placed renewed emphasis on the literal sense of Scripture, as a truth to be uncovered, as well as its subsequent taxonomical interest.

Early modernity witnessed the rise of debates around the rhetorical nature of the *ars historical*. But these discussions did not focus on the historical genres, due to the pragmatic nature of history of that time and, more importantly, because of its antiquarian and archaeologist dimension, which blocked theoretical discussions.[37] In the nineteenth century the theory returned, but, according to the new rules of German historicism, formal–rhetorical debates were replaced by those related to the epistemic nature of history and its

---

[36] Quoted in Bert Roest, 'Medieval Historiography – About Generic Constraints and Scholarly Constructions', in B. Roest and H. Vanstiphout (eds.), *Aspects of Genre and Type in Pre-Modern Literary Cultures* (Leiden: Brill, 1999), 47–61, here 54.

[37] Burke, *The Renaissance*; Grafton, *What Was History?*

referentiality, so discussions on historical genres no longer inspired interest.[38] The disciplinary concurrence in Scripture and historiography promoted the renovation of history, and more specifically the development of genre theory.[39]

From the beginning of the twentieth century, modernist historical and literary scholarship showed great interest in historical genres, thanks to the foundational article on Greek historiography published by the classicist Felix Jacoby in 1909.[40] He distinguishes five types of historical writing, each with its own rules, conventions, and focuses: genealogy, ethnography, horography, chronography, and history. Some more recent critics, such as John Marincola, have distrusted the linear progressiveness of Jacoby's generic model, in which each new genre adds something, as though on a path to 'perfected' historiography, and they call for a more 'fluid and problematic' approach to classical genres.[41] Thomas F. Scanlon argues that 'the journey from Homer to Hellanicus

---

[38] Iggers, *The German Conception of History*.

[39] Marie-Dominique Chenu, 'Theology and the New Awareness of History', in *Nature, Man and Society in the Twelfth Century* (Chicago: The University of Chicago Press, 1968), 162–201.

[40] Felix Jacoby, 'Über die Entwicklung der griechischen Historiographie', in *Abhandlungen zur griechischen Geschichtsschreibung* (Leiden, 1956), 16–64 (original from 1909 in *Klio* 9 (1909): 80–123). Jacoby's taxonomy laid the foundation for a fruitful tradition of the study of historical genres in classical studies, including Charles W. Fornara, *The Nature of History in Ancient Greece and Rome* (Berkeley: University of California Press, 1983), 1–10, and John Marincola, 'Genre, Convention and Innovation in Greco-Roman Historiography', in *The Limits of Historiography*, 281–324.

[41] John Marincola, *Greek Historians* (Oxford: Oxford University Press, 2001), 2.

is not a straight line but an evolution of genres competing and complementing one another, all at the service of audience and authorial interest'.[42] Marincola and Scanlon are right, and their model applies not only to ancient historiography but also to medieval and modern historiography. But synchronic and anachronistic approaches should combine in any genre analysis since it is also evident that historical genres depend on their historical contexts. The less we know about the context, the more prudent we must be in assigning the text to a genre, type, or category. Genres are dynamic structures of narration rather than rigid rhetorical compartments so we cannot canonize or fix them in an essential moment beyond a particular context.

Already in the late twentieth century, Hayden White began his *Metahistory* by emphasizing the distinction between an analytical–descriptive chronicle and a narrative–interpretative story.[43] White assumes three main types of historical representation: annals, chronicles, and history proper. Yet he emphasizes the convention involved in distinguishing between these genres because '[it] is the modern historiographical community which has distinguished between annals, chronicle, and history forms of discourse on the basis of their attainment of narrative fullness or failure to attain it'.[44] These diverse forms of historical representation respond to specific contexts and cannot be reduced to a

[42] Thomas F. Scanlon, *Greek Historiography* (Chichester: Wiley Blackwell, 2015), 21.

[43] White, *Metahistory*, 5.

[44] Hayden White, 'The Value of Narrativity in the Representation of Reality', *Critical Inquiry* 7, 1 (1980): 5–27, here 27.

simple function of 'incomplete' or 'complete' histories from a modern perspective. Rather, they are 'particular products of possible conceptions of historical reality, conceptions that are alternatives to, rather than failed anticipations of, the fully realized historical discourse that the modern history form is supposed to embody'.[45]

Jacoby and White have made a decisive contribution to the contextualization of historical genres and thus to their correct interpretation. But these scholars had to confront that dilemma so acutely expressed by Spiegel:

> Efforts to rehabilitate genre as a concept governing the production of history throughout the medieval period, have been, in my view, equally unsuccessful in sustaining generic differences beyond the labels used to designate specific works. That is, while medieval texts themselves would appear to deploy genre as a useful category for discriminating between different forms of historiography, the actual texts, as in the case of the works studied here, fail to maintain these distinctions in practice.[46]

The paradox that Spiegel brings to light arises, in one way or another, for all the authors quoted in this section who have tried a systematic approach to the historical genres, from Cicero and Isidore to Jacoby and White. The challenge for the critical scholarship on historical genres lies in the task

---

[45] White, 'The Value', 10.
[46] Spiegel, Gabrielle M., 'Introduction', in R. Maxwell (ed.), *Representations of History: Art, History, Music* (Philadelphia: Pennsylvania University Press, 2010), 209. 'As in the case of the works studied here' Spiegel is referring to the texts compiled in the collective volume *Historiography in the Middle Ages*, Deborah M. Deliyannis (ed.) (Leiden: Brill, 2002).

of finding an authoritative voice between the genres as they were conceived and perceived by the contemporaries authors and readers of these texts *and* what modern scholarship considers, assuming an *a posteriori* critical vision, to be texts that can be grouped into categories that literary critics call *genres*. Therefore, in the following section, I present a synthesis of the historical evolution of historical genres, trying to attend as closely as possible to the concept of genre as it was perceived at the time. In this way, we highlight some of the historical works which have achieved durability because, by creating new ways of representing the past through new historical genres, they become signs of inescapable historiographical notoriety.

Developments

In the alleged origins of Western historiography, classic historiography found different ways to record the past, each with its own rules, conventions, and focuses. Around the sixth century BC, Greek historiography emerged with the *logographers* – a word compound of *logos*, here meaning 'story' or 'prose' and *grapho*, 'write' – or the *logopoioi* ('story' plus 'to make'), as Herodotus called his predecessors. They wrote in prose to distance themselves from the epic poets of the Homeric tradition. They practised some types of historical writing, perhaps the first of them the genealogy.

Genealogy *as* historical genre (to distinguish it from the more comprehensive approach to the concept that I deal with in the fifth chapter) was originally practised by Hecataeus of Miletus around 500 BC. It seeks to bring order, if not absolute consistency, to the complex tangle of Greek traditions, and to write the history of heroic tradition without falling in mythical history. It aims to distinguish history from myth, as Hecataeus states at the beginning of his *Genealogiai*: 'I write these things as they appear to me to be true. For it seems to me that the accounts [*logoi*] of the Greeks are many and absurd.'[47] This genre is called 'genealogy' based on the title of Hecataeus' text and because of its progression to the ancient myths, but has little to do with medieval and early modern genealogies – based on the genealogies of Matthew and Luke.

Ethnography soon joined genealogy as a historical genre, in its description of foreign lands and people and its presentation of a general picture of a people's mode of life within the setting of its natural and historical environment. It is usually a hybrid, containing both historical and descriptive accounts of a land and its peoples, based on examination and oral inquiry, as pioneered by Dionysius of Miletus's *Persica* and practised later by Herodotus. Greek ethnography functions as the model of the modern fields of cultural history, human geography, and symbolic anthropology.

With the development of Hellenic cities, horography, a combination of chronological and local history and presentation as a record of a city's life year by year, was established as the predominant genre. The organizing principle is chronological, not thematic, ethnographic, or genealogical. It might have been a natural product of the emergence of the Greek city-state. Examples of 'local historians' include

---

[47] Hecataeus of Miletus, *'Genealogies'*, in J. Lake (ed.), *Prologues to Ancient and Medieval History* (Toronto: University of Toronto Press, 2013), 1.

Phaeneas of Eresos, Ephorus of Cyme, Theopompus of Chios, and Hellanicus. They provide a chronological sequence of the city's growth, rather than an explanatory or descriptive history. Horography includes a variety of materials – religious, cultural, and cultic – in addition to political and military events:

> Horography was the Hellenic side of ethnography, a
> product of the same urge to codify the collective lives
> of disparate groups. It owed its distinctive form to the
> fact that an annalistic system of recording events already
> functioned in each Greek city-state, while sufficient
> historical and antiquarian material was preserved to allow
> the writers to flesh out at least a considerable portion of
> the history of the city year by year – something impossible
> for Greeks to do with Persia or Egypt, where the analysis
> naturally became less minute.[48]

Once Greek historiography became more universal in scope, chronography provided a system of time-reckoning, permitting the calibration of events taking place in different parts of the civilized world. Chronographers fixed calendars to arrange events in temporal sequence as they aspired to universal history, though they did not set out a unified framework. Hellanicus of Lesbos built a chronological framework, adding a more imaginative treatment of the genealogical succession.

Chronography survives as a genre in the Roman and medieval annals, and moves modern calendars and the practice of selecting the most relevant events when a year, decade,

[48] Fornara, *The Nature*, 22.

or century finishes. The first of the Roman annals were published by P. Mucius Scaevola around 120 BC, the *Annales Maximi*, and are described by Cicero as follows:

> From the beginning of Rome to the time when P. Mucius was pontifex maximus, the pontifex maximus had every occurrence of each year written down in order to safeguard the memory of the public record. He recorded this onto a white notice-board and displayed the tablet at his house so that the people would be able to know it. Even now they are called the annals maximi.[49]

Rome awoke to its own grandeur around the end of the second century BC, taking annalistic history as the basic and efficient structure – rather than its contents – for their writing of history. The genre was well defined by Tacitus, *De Annals*, 4.71: 'But for my plan of referring each event to its own year, I should feel a strong impulse to anticipate matters and at once relate the deaths by which Latinius and Opsius and the other authors of this atrocious deed perished, some after Caius became emperor, some even while Tiberius yet ruled.'[50] These Roman Annalists, led by Hemina, defined by Pliny the Elder as 'the oldest annalist' (*Natural History*, 13,84), sought the 'earliest time' – an analogous 'quest of the origins' to that of medieval genealogists and nineteenth-century Romantic makers of national myths. This spirit moved Titus Livius to design his *Ab Urbe Condita* ('From the Founding of the City'), around the end of the first century BC.

---

[49] Cirero, *De oratore*, 2.12.52, quoted by Fornara, *The Nature*, 23.
[50] Tacitus, *De Annals*, 4.71 in Alfred J. Church, and William J. Brodribb (eds.), *Complete Works of Tacitus* (New York: McGraw-Hill, 1942).

Finally, the genre of history, as the ancients defined it, emerged, considered that form which provides the description of men's 'deeds,' or praxis: the exposition *rerum gestarum*, 'the narrative of deeds', in Quintilian words. *History* originated in monographs of war, such as those by Herodotus and Thucydides. Whether we like it or not, the Western historiographical tradition has considered this genre as 'the origin of the true history', and of its canon, with Herodotus popularly labelled 'the father of history.' History was born to legitimize a new historical genre, in which their practitioners have to mark a break with the tradition, as Thucydides did in his criticism to the systems of time measurement by horographers and chronograpers:

> People should calculate the actual periods of time; they should not rely on lists of archons or other officials whose names may be used in different cities to mark the dates of the past events. For such methods of calculations are inaccurate in that they leave it unclear whether an event occurred in the beginning, the middle or at some other point, of magistrate's term of office.[51]

At the age of Alexander's journeys, conquests, and expansion, the reports of Greek historians led to an interest in history beyond Greece. Timaeus' writings on Sicily open up the perspective of a more global history, a trend later consolidated by Polybius. As Arnaldo Momigliano explains,

> It was Polybius' most original thought that the virtual unification of the known world under Rome made a new genre of historiography both possible and necessary.

---

[51] Thucydides, 5.20, trans. Simon Hornblower, *A Commentary on Thucydides, Volume II, Books IV–V.24* (Oxford: Oxford University Press, 1996), 492.

For the first time a historian could write authentic universal history with a unified theme – Rome's ascent to world power. What in the fourth century Ephorus had presented as a universal history was to Polybius a mere conglomeration of special histories. The new epoch required a new historiography, and this in turn implied new narrative techniques in order to register the convergence of events.[52]

Later, in the era of Roman consolidation as a superpower, all histories led, literally, to Rome. The prominence of a series of strong leaders culminating in the imperial rulers lends itself to stronger biographical content. History became more global not only in its subject and scope, but also in the origin of the historians, from Greece, Asia Minor, and Africa – and in its global audiences too: Greek speakers of the Eastern Mediterranean and Roman elite.

Roman and Greek historiography knew different forms of autobiography too, especially those related to political memoirs, responding to the rhetorical rules and meaning defined by Cicero in the text quoted above (p. 215), and to the increasing sophistication of political life. Reasoned accounts of one's political career sought to explain and justify one's actions, such as Isocartes' *Antidosis*, Demetrius of Phalerum's *On the Ten Years Rule*, Aratus of Sicyon's memoirs, and, with a more complex form, Caesar's autobiographical writings.[53]

---

[52] Momigliano, *Essays in Ancient*, 70.

[53] Fornara, *The Nature*, 175; for Caesar autobiographical texts, see Andrew M. Riggsby, 'Memoir and Autobiography in Republican Rome', in J. Marincola (ed.), *Blackwell Companion to Greek and Roman Historiography* (London: Blackwell Publishing, 2007), 266–274, here 272–273.

The prose panegyric emerged with other rhetorical prose genres at the end of the fifth century BC, manifested first in the funeral speeches in commemoration of Pericles, as related by Thucydides (2.34–36). Here we find metaliterary reflections, provided by Isocrates around the year 400 BC: to praise, to set an example for emulation, and to enhance the speaker's own reputation. This genre expanded and enjoyed its golden age in late antiquity. Roman imperial panegyrics were typically associated with the emperor's accession, *adventus* (arrival to a city), assumption of the consulship, anniversaries, building work, and gratitude (*gratiarum actio*) such as the bestowal of honour on the speaker, as in the case of Pliny's panegyric of Trajan, still considered an archetypal Latin text for the genre.[54] The genre also developed to praise Roman emperors after their death. They certainly deal with contextual aspects, but their purpose is to shape the recorded memory of the emperor. This genre had significant success with its readership and potential audience, and influenced future Christian hagiography. The context of the translation from ancient Hellenism into Christian Hellenism is textually expressed in historical literature connecting panegyrics with hagiography. Sanctity becomes as important a model for Christian biographies and panegyrics as the function of the emperor had been for the Romans.[55]

Crucially for the development of historical genres in the West, historical and literary works shift from the

---

[54] Mary Whitby (ed.), *The Propaganda of Power: The Role of Panegyric in Late Antiquity* (Leiden: Brill, 1998).

[55] Peter Brown, 'The Rise and Function of the Holy Man in Late Antiquity', *Journal of Roman Studies* 61 (1971): 81–101.

chronological or genealogical ordering principle to the lifespan of an individual. Biography, imperial portrait, panegyric, and hagiography blend in Eusebius' *Life of Constantine*, a historical text with an extraordinary influence on the future.[56] His *Life of Constantine* demonstrated that almost nothing separated panegyric from hagiography, as exemplified in the anonymous *Historia monachorum*, an early version of collective biography and hagiography, that recounts acts of the monks connected with the life of Christ.[57] Eusebius was a literary pioneer here, as he was also in his *Ecclesiastical History* since he 'had started a revolution by inventing the new subject of Christian history', in Pocock's words.[58]

All these historical genres practised in antiquity continued in the Middle Ages, although with three relevant transformations, notably affecting the genres of annals, genealogies, and first-person testimony. Greek horographies and chronologies were absorbed into the thriving medieval genre of the annals, spread in Europe during the ninth century – such as *The Anglo-Saxon Chronicle* – in the context of the revitalization of local powers and the re-emergence of secular history. At their simplest, these annalistic compilations

---

[56] Averil Cameron, 'Eusebius's Vita Constantini and the Construction of Constantine', in M. J. Edwards and Simon Swain (eds.), *Portraits: Biographical Representation in the Greek and Latin Literature of the Roman Empire* (Oxford: Oxford University Press, 1997), 145–174.

[57] Patricia Cox Miller, 'Strategies of Representation in Collective Biography', in Thomas Hägg and Philip Rousseau (eds.), *Greek Biography and Panegyric in Late Antiquity* (Berkeley: University of California Press, 2000), 209–254, here 233.

[58] Pocock, *Barbarism and Religion: Narratives of Civil*, 11.

are the self-conscious construction – even emplotment – of coherent stories, made meaningful by selection, omission, and careful interpretation, and not the mere recitations of events that occurred within a given period.[59]

More crucially, rudimentary Greek genealogies were turned into the complex noble and royal genealogies from the twelfth century, which shaped not only historiography as a genre, but also history and philosophy, as the contemporary commentaries of Nietzsche, Foucault, and Spiegel have shown.[60] This genre developed with the emergence of new noble and royal lineages seeking legitimization. Time was now measured by the succession of *generations* rather than by the chronological progression of *events* (such as the annals) or the duration of a life (such as biographies, hagiographies, and panegyrics). Medieval genealogies usually start by introducing the figure of the founder of the lineage, as opposed to the annals, which begin with references to Scripture, the universal Church, and the Roman Empire. Once the mythical origins are established, they then usually focus on the local lineage.

Shortly after the emergence of noble genealogies, different forms of autobiography expanded throughout Europe. The figure of the chronicler–crusader spread in

---

[59] Janet Nelson, 'The Annals of St-Bertin', in M. T. Gibson and Janet L. Nelson (eds.), *Charles the Bald: Court and Kingdom* (London: Longman, 1990), 23–40.

[60] Foucault, 'Nietzsche', 142–143; Spiegel, 'Foucault and the Problem of Genealogy', 1–14. I pay more attention to this genre of 'medieval genealogies' in the following chapter, because of its obvious connection with the general concept of 'genealogy'.

late-twelfth-century Europe, particularly in France, Italy, and Spain. In the context of the growing value of subjectivity, the emergence of individual authorship, and the re-legitimation of personal testimony as a historical source, these first-person narratives tell the story as witnessed by participants in the crusades against Islam.[61] This new tendency resonates with Greek historiography (Herodotus, Thucydides), where testimony was the only real evidence, as well as with contemporary life writing, where personal memory serves as the basis for an authoritative (and authorizing) narrative. Fulcher of Chartres, one of the first eyewitnesses of the expedition to Jerusalem argued that:

> Having been prompted on various occasions by the exhortations by certain of my companions, I have written a careful account of the celebrated deeds performed in the Lord by the Franks who made a pilgrimage to Jerusalem under arms at God's command, employing an unsophisticated but truthful style, and judging this material worthy to be entrusted to memory, insofar I was capable of doing so and was an eyewitness to what happened during the course of the journey.[62]

Some of the best-known authors and works of this new genre were the chivalric autobiographies written by Geoffrey of Villehardouin, Robert of Clari, Philip of Novara, and Jean of Joinville, all of them active during the thirteenth

---

[61] Peter F. Ainsworth, 'Contemporary and "Eyewitness" History', in Deliyannis, *Historiography in the Middle Ages*, 249–276.

[62] Fulcher of Chartres, *History of the Expedition to Jerusalem*, in Lake, *Prologues*, 174.

century.[63] The autobiographies of kings, especially practised by the Aragonese kings writing in Catalan such as Jaume I, were part of this new generic tradition, and promoted a model of a king according to the new chivalric times and, later, of the authoritatively pre-Renaissance one, as in the case of Peter IV of Aragon.[64]

Historical reliability and authorial authority were based on the character of the witness and participants in the events the authors recount rather than on the weight of written records and oral tradition privileged by monastic and epic historiography. Writing in prose rather than epic poetry increased the *perception* of historical accuracy, reliability, and referentiality, while also expanding the readership for these narratives. With this new development, and the increasing legitimation of the first-person narrative, the author's agency grew stronger and a powerful autobiographical element began to emerge in the writing. Jean of Froissart brought this genre to its peak in the fourteenth century, adapted to a general chivalric narrative rather than to the strict Crusader context, narrating the war between France and England.[65]

In the fifteenth century, a very different generic line appeared in central and northern Italy, where cities came to be virtually autonomous, essentially city-states. The genre of urban history emerged as an expression of cities' self-consciousness, just as ecclesiastical history had been the first self-reflection

---

[63] Michel Zink, *The Invention of Literary Subjectivity* (Baltimore: Johns Hopkins University Press, 1999), 163–219.

[64] Aurell, *Authoring the Past*, 39–54 and 91–108.

[65] Peter F. Ainsworth, *Jean Froissart and the Fabric of History: Truth, Myth, and Fiction in the Chroniques* (Oxford: Clarendon, 2010).

of the Ancient Church and the genealogical genre for the new counties and kingdoms. Yet urban history has a civic and republican air, which contrasts with the previously monastic and royal history of the earlier centuries through annals, genealogies, and chivalric chronicles. Italy was the centre of the emergence of this new genre practised by successful chroniclers such as Giovanni Villani, Leonardo Bruni, Niccolò Machiavelli, and Francesco Guicciardini. It epitomized the country's urban and mercantile development at the end of the Middle Ages. This genre spread in conjunction with the classical revival, which gave it a moral tone based on models of Roman historiography such as Sallust and Livy (whose works, to be sure, were also admired during the Middle Ages), and also Tacitus.[66]

From the sixteenth century, the incorporation of the textual methods of Renaissance humanism and the techniques of archival historical research facilitated the emergence of new historians who were keepers of the public records of the past. There were three historiographical trends in this direction. Firstly, in Spain, some historians and chroniclers such as Florián de Ocampo, Ambrosio de Morales, Jerónimo Zurita, Esteban de Garibay, Antonio de Herrera, and Juan de Mariana were collected by the kings to preserve and control their own histories, and eventually to use them as propaganda, as in the case of Early Modern Spain.[67] Secondly, in Italy and England, some

---

[66] Burrow, *A History*, chapter 18; E. B. Fryde, *Humanism and Renaissance Historiography* (London: Hambledon 1983); Augusto Vasina, 'Medieval Urban Historiography in the Middle Ages', in Deliyannis, *Historiography in the Middle Ages*, 317–352.

[67] Richard Kagan, *Clio and the Crown: The Politics of History in Medieval and Early Modern Spain* (Baltimore: Johns Hopkins University Press, 2009).

historians such as Paolo Sarpi's *History of the Council of Trent* (1619), Enrico Caterino Davila's *The Civil Wars in France* (1630), Clarendon (Edward Hyde)'s *The History of the Rebellion and Civil Wars in England* (1640s), and James Harrington's *Oceana* (1656) privilege political aspects in their narrative to provide moral teachings, emulating the ancient historians.[68] Thirdly, well into the seventeenth century, a new generation of continental ecclesiastic historians such as Louis-Sébastien Le Nain de Tillemont, Ludovico Antonio Muratori, and Jean Mabillon, and erudite English scholars such as Thomas Madox and Thomas Rymer, added a scientific flavour and a critical method to history that would not be abandoned. In the 1930s, David C. Douglas praised this generation of English historians as 'the best sustained and the most prolific movement of historical scholarship which this country (England) has ever seen'.[69] This third genre – particularly practised in Spain, Italy, and England – was defined by Peter Burke as 'more an age of historical scholarship than of historical writing'.[70]

[68] Clarendon is undoubtedly the most famous of them, whose work has been incorporated into the canon of historical works systematically cited by historians of historiography: B. H. G. Wormald, *Clarendon: Politics, History and Religion, 1640–1660* (Cambridge: Cambridge University Press, 1951). For the context of early modern British historiography, see Joseph M. Levine, *Humanism and History: Origins of Modern British Historiography* (Ithaca: Cornell University Press, 1987) and Hicks, *Neoclassical History and English Culture*.

[69] David C. Douglas, *English Scholars 1660–1730* (London: Eyre & Spottiswoode, 1951), 13.

[70] Burke, *The Renaissance*, 142. On this genre, see also Arnaldo Momigliano, 'Ancient History and the Antiquarian', in *Studies in Historiography* (London: Weidenfeld & Nicolson, 1966); Burrow, *A History*, Chapter 19; Grafton, *What Was History?*

In contrast with medieval and early modern historical scholarship, eighteenth-century historiography privileged the genre of philosophical history. The new historiographical type established the particular as an example of the general and demonstrated that the historical events under consideration conformed to general laws. The idea of balance and progress became part of the historian's explanatory equipment. Edward Gibbon, for instance, saw the decline of the Roman Empire as 'the natural and inevitable defect of immoderate greatness'.[71] Historical explanations came to be given more in social and collective, and less in individual and particular, terms. The hegemony of the social, the general, and the essential conquered at the expense of the loss of the chronological, the erudite, and the meticulous. Philosophical history naturally encourages the cosmopolitan history practised by Voltaire and Gibbon. Examples of this new genre were David Hume's *History of England* (1754–1762), William Robertson's *The History of the Reign of the Emperor Charles V* (1769), and, bearing in mind all the nuances highlighted in the commentary on his work in Chapter 3, Edward Gibbon's *The Decline and Fall of the Roman Empire* (1776–89).[72]

Nineteenth-century German historicists created their own particular genre, according to the historiographical revolution they noted, which continues today: the lengthy archival monograph, as modelled by Leopold von Ranke and his successors. This new historical–scientific genre was

---

[71] Edward Gibbon, *The Decline and Fall of the Roman Empire*, J. B. Bury (ed.), 7 vols. (1896–1902), IV: 167.
[72] Burrow, 'Philosophic History', in *A History*, 331–336.

based on different traditions: the antiquarian Renaissance sense of the past, the academicism of the eighteenth-century Enlightenment, and the response to the challenge of building a nation-state, among others. It privileged the political and diplomatic approach, transforming German historical thought from Herder's cosmopolitan culture-oriented nationalism to state-centred expansionist nationalism. It founded the model of the scientific monograph that would be privileged by historical scholarship during the twentieth century, and definitively standardized the practice of history with the other scientific disciplines, decisively contributing to the professionalization of history. It finally separated history from the novel and historical literature, pivoting it into the social-scientific fields:

> Monographic history is the kind of history that most academic historians now write: technical, specialized analysis of particular events or problems in the past. The writing of such historical monographs grew out of the nineteenth-century dream that history might become an objective science, a science that would resemble, if not the natural sciences of physics or chemistry, then at least the social science – economics, sociology, anthropology, psychology – that were emerging at the same time as professionally written history.[73]

The twentieth century witnessed the gradual and successive emergence of new historical genres: impressionist history, organicist history, total history, and new narrative history.

---

[73] Gordon S. Wood, *The Purpose of the Past: Reflections on the Uses of History* (New York: Penguin, 2008), 41.

During the first third of the century, the discipline experienced the consolidation of scientific standardization and the prolongation of the traditional genres, but the practice of history was also strongly influenced by the spread of modernism. In order to remain intellectually current and connect with readers, historians had adapted to modernist ways of thinking through a new genre: *impressionist* history. As Norman F. Cantor explains, historians 'encountered the formidable challenge of writing non-narrative history, a new mode of analytical history that reflected the method of close reading of a segment of past society'.[74] These historians would take a certain moment in time or a specific topic and render practically hundreds of detailed impressions of aspects of the culture, the religion, the art, or the politics without abandoning their aspiration to get the whole picture, in parallel with their counterparts, French impressionist painters. Examples of this genre would be Johan Huizinga's *The Waning of the Middle Ages* (1927), Charles Homer Haskins's *The Renaissance of the Twelfth Century* (1927), Lewis Namier's *The Structure of Politics at the Accession of George III* (1929), Etienne Gilson's *L'esprit de la philosophie médiévale* (1932), Marc Bloch's *La société feodale* (1936), and Ernst Kantorowicz's *The King's Two Bodies* (1957). These books represent, in my view, one of the peaks of historiography: they manage to establish an equilibrium between the analytical monographic approach that follows the strict academic rules of the historical discipline while remaining comprehensive and multidisciplinary enough to avoid disconnection from the non-specialist audience.

---

[74] Norman F. Cantor, *The American Century: Varieties of Culture in Modern Times* (New York: Harper, 1997), 142.

In the interwar period and mid-twentieth century, Oswald Spengler and Arnold J. Toynbee developed *organicist* history, an approach that required its practitioners to seek general laws that would explain the birth, rise, and decline of societies through history, based on an explicit parallelism between these societies and the functioning of organic bodies. They use the seminal concept of civilization, which goes through an organic cycle from its birth to its death. Spengler tried to explain the life of Western civilization (*The Decline of the West*), which during the 1920s was in total collapse.[75] He argued that only charismatic leadership could save it. In the 1950s, Arnold J. Toynbee tried to emulate Spengler's project in his *A Study of History*.[76] His great project identified thirty-one civilizations in history, and analysed their patterns of progressive rise and fall, to determine a general rule for this cycle. These projects, which met with great success among the general readership and a certain amount of resistance among professional historians, were resonances of the traditional genre of universal history practised since antiquity and are connected to contemporary global history.[77]

---

[75] Oswald Spengler, *Der Untergang des Abendlandes* (München: Beck, 1921).

[76] Arnold J. Toynbee, *A Study of History* (London: Oxford University Press, 1951).

[77] On unversal history: for antiquity, Katherine Clarke, 'Universal Perspectives in Historiography', in C. S. Kraus (ed.), *The Limits of Historiography: Genre and Narrative in Ancient Historical Texts* (Leiden: Brill, 1999), 249–279; for late antiquity, José María Alonso-Núñez, 'The Emergence of Universal Historiography from the 4th to the 2nd Centuries BC', in E. De Keyser, G. Schepens, and H. Verdin (eds.), *Purposes of History* (Leuven: Peeters, 1990), 173–192; for the

Some French historians, most of them belonging to the *Annales* School of the 1950s and 1960s, developed a historical genre labelled the '*la terre et les hommes* cycle', based on comprehensive archival research on *one* place, *one* period, and *one* social type. The word *mono*-graph describes it perfectly. These historians were committed to 'total history', which involved a combination of Durkheim's functionalist sociology with Lévi-Strauss structural anthropology and biological environmental determinism. They developed a standard hierarchical arrangement, based on Braudel's triple division of short, middle, and long duration: first, the geographical and demographic context; second, social and economic structure; and lastly, intellectual, religious, cultural, and political developments – the *events*. They adopted a structural approach, using analytical rather than narrative language, and applying social–scientific methodologies to their historical-humanistic research. Some of the most characteristic examples of this form include Fernand Braudel's *La Méditerrané et le monde méditerranéen à l'èpoque de Philippe II* (1949), Georges Duby's *La société aux Xie et XIIe siècles dans la région maconnaise* (1953), Pierre Goubert's *Beauvais et le Beauvaisis* (1960), and Emmanuel Le Roy Ladurie's *Les paysans du Languedoc* (1966).[78]

Middle Ages, Michael I. Allen, 'Universal History 300–1000: Origins and Western Developments', in Deliyannis, *Historiography in the Middle Ages*, 17–42, and Rolf Sprandel, 'World Historiography in the Late Middle Ages', in *Historiography in the Middle Ages*, 157–180. On global history as practised today, see the surveys Bruce Mazlish and Ralph Buultjens, *Conceptualizing Global History* (Boulder: Westview, 1993) and Benedikt Stuchtey and Eckhardt Fuchs (eds.), *Writing World History 1800–2000* (Oxford: Oxford University Press, 2003).

[78] Thomas Bisson, 'La terre et les hommes: a programme fulfilled?', *French History* 14 (2000): 322–345.

In the 1970s, another new historical genre emerged, labelled 'new narrative history' by Lawrence Stone.[79] This genre recovered, in a new way, the storytelling function of earlier texts, giving history a clear narrative tone as an alternative to the structural approach of the previous historical monographs of the *la terre et les hommes* cycle. The narrative became a key feature of these new historical texts, where chronologically organized material was built into a single coherent story, albeit with sub-plots. Its arrangement was descriptive rather than analytical – its central focus being on persons rather than on events and circumstances. Some of the most characteristic examples were Carlo Ginzburg's *Il formaggio e il vermi* (1976), a volume considered the foundation of the subgenre of microhistory, and Natalie Zemon Davis's *The Return of Martin Guerre* (1982). This genre continues to be produced and has been described as a 'cultural narrative' since its topics and methodology connect importantly with the 'new cultural history'.[80]

Today, newly de-centred voices, particularly those that highlight performativity, are emerging in historical writing.[81] We are witnessing a proliferation of new mediums and platforms for the articulation of history, including film

[79] Stone, 'The Revival of Narrative', 3–24.
[80] Sarah Maza, 'Stories in History: Cultural Narratives in Recent Works in European History', *American Historical Review* 101 (1996): 1493–1515; Lynn Hunt (ed.), *The New Cultural History* (Berkeley, 1989).
[81] Ann Rigney, 'When the Monograph Is No Longer the Medium: Historical Narrative in the Online Age', *History and Theory* 49, 4 (2010): 100–117.

and documentaries, social media, graphic narratives, video games and re-enactments, historical novels, and biopics, as well as innovations in first-person narratives such as historical witness, synthetic memories, and travel writing.[82] By creating new ways to represent the past, today's historians seem to be heeding Alistair Fowler's suggestion: 'Genre also offers a challenge by provoking a free spirit to transcend the limitations of previous examples.'[83] Multimodality, re-creation, re-enactment, interactivity, and imagination shape contemporary history; images, social media, games, and films bear the information that produces our perspectives on the present and past.

To understand the historical act, we need to acknowledge these new processes and genres. A key element also involves recognizing a new *democratization* in historical representation: history is no longer the sole property of professional historians but is now also produced by those who experience or engage with it. These new generic modes are challenging the traditional concept of historical authorship and scholarly elitism, inviting us to rethink not only the product we might call history but the *producer* of history – including artists, actors, filmmakers, refugees, average citizens, gamers, social media actors, and autobiographers.

---

[82] Jaume Aurell, 'Rethinking Historical Genres in the Twenty-First Century', *Rethinking History* 19, 2 (2015): 145–157; Jaume Aurell (ed.), *Rethinking Historical Genres in the Twenty-First Century* (London: Routledge, 2016).

[83] Alastair Fowler, *Kinds of Literature* (Oxford: Oxford University Press, 1982), 31. See Vijay K. Bhatia, 'The Power and Politics of Genre', *World Englishes* 16 (1997): 359–371.

Reappraisals

The variety of forms conveyed in this chapter, from classic logographers to modern analytical monographs, from ancient panegyrics to postmodern cultural narratives, proves that genre matters in history. One may give the category of *genre* more or less interpretative relevance, but historians clearly take the task of formulating the appropriate genre strategies very seriously. They search for the genre that fits best with their patrons' demands, the audience's expectations, the rules and conventions of scholarship, the new digital platforms available, or their own principles and tenets.

But this contextualized account of historical genres prompts a question: what do all these genres or types have in common and what is diverse? They actually belong to different taxonomical categories, since some of them are based on the geographical and historical scope of the research while others are based on the narrative structure of time, on the type of a subject treated, on the authorial position, on the formal elements, and, finally, on the aspect of reality approached – military, cultural, political, social, economic, cultural, religious, ecclesiastic. To these divisions, postmodern historiographers have added some more categories, based on the degree of innovation (conventional or experimental), the use of the new platforms or new modes of expression, and those based on the centre-periphery criterion – class, race, gender, postcolonial, history from below, cultural studies.

In this taxonomic context, we should establish some basic organization, to avoid normative classification or a formalist blurring of genres, but to discern those that have generic nature from those that are simply modes, varieties, platforms, or kinds of history.[84] A postmodern theory of genres is shaped by a concept of genre as authors' modes of expression and audiences' horizons of expectations, alternative to the modal categories argued by the traditional theory of history, such as 'the varieties of history' by Fritz Stern or 'the houses of history' by Anna Green and Kathleen Troup.[85] These traditional categories serve the history of historiography, but to reduce the nature of historical genres to them elides the complexities of historical authorship and misconstrues the dynamic relationship between form and content, text and context, and authorship and readership that naturally emerges from the genre.

Following these criteria, I argue that the categories that best fit the historical genres are those based on the geographical scope of the research (local, national, or universal), on the narrative structure of time (annals, genealogies, chronicles or anti-narrative monographs), and on the authorial position (biographies, autobiographies, and scientific monographs), since space, time and authorship are the essential textual/contextual and form/content framework of the historical operation. More recently, the categories based

---

[84] For the distinction between empiricist and formalist theory of genres, see Conte, *Genres and Readers*, 127. Paul Zumthor, *Essai de poétique médiévale* (Paris: Seuil, 1972) considered genres as 'groups or historical families', avoiding normative (*ante rem*) or classificatory (*post rem*) typologies to arrive at a historical-contextual (*in re*) typology.

[85] Fritz Stern, *The Varieties of History: From Voltaire to the Present* (New York: Random House, 1970) and Green and Troup, *The Houses of History*.

on the centre–periphery criterion such as class, race, gender, postcolonial, history from below, and cultural studies have notoriously gained interest and it would be difficult to deny their validity as genres in which authors find specific modes of expression.

Yet, going beyond these taxonomic categories and following the postmodern theory of historical discourse, Alun Munslow proposed a new category of epistemic genres founded on the 'deep narrative strategy' of the historical authors which may enrich the argument:

> Genre in history reflects the epistemological decision of the historian to organize knowledge about the past in ways that satisfy their preferred cognitive, aesthetic (turn), ideological and representational aims. What we might call 'modal history forms' such as economic history, cultural history, race history, social history, intellectual history, military history, gender history, oral history, international history, post-feminist history, political history and postcolonial history, can be cast within any one of the genres of Reconstructionist(ism), Constructionist(ism), Deconstructionist(ism).[86]

Munslow offers a broad expression of genres that transcends a simple empirical or analytical strategy or the way historians read the sources and select the methodology, since it focuses on the kinds of approach to knowledge creation they take. It involves 'the constructed relationships that emerge as a consequence of the different attitudes toward

---

[86] Alun Munslow, *The Routledge Companion to Historical Studies* (London: Routledge, 2000), 125.

epistemology, the utilization of diverse theories and concepts, and the different kinds (bodies) of empiricism invoked by historians'.[87] According to this categorization, other forms of generic classification emerge, particularly those offered by the philosophers dealing with the nature of history: original, reflective, and philosophical history by Hegel;[88] antiquarian, monumental, and critical by Nietzsche;[89] and practical and historical by Michael Oakeshott.[90]

These necessary taxonomic clarifications, and the acknowledgement of the relevance of form in historical production – or, in other words, the impossibility of separating form from its content – allows us to tackle the problem of genre variability and historicity that I address in this chapter, and how these generic transformations work. As Derrida notes, 'at the very moment that a genre or a literature is broached, at that very moment, degenerescence has begun, the end begins'.[91] Todorov describes the process of genre generation in different words but similar terms: 'A new genre is always the transformation of one or several old genres: by inversion, by displacement, by combination.'[92] Consequently, historical genres are conditioned by changing

---

[87] Munslow, *The Routledge*, 124.

[88] G. W. F. Hegel, 'The Three Methods of Writing History', in *Reason in History*, trans. Robert S. Hartman (New York: Bobbs-Merrill, 1953), 3–10.

[89] Nietzsche, 'On the Utility', 124–141.

[90] White, *The Practical Past*.

[91] Jacques Derrida, 'The Law of Genre', *Critical Inquiry* 7 (1980): 55–81, here 66.

[92] Tzvetan Todorov, 'The Origin of Genres', *New Literary History* 8 (1976): 159–170, here 161.

historical circumstances and, conversely, shape our understanding of the times that produced them. Contextualist and textualist positions have emphasized, through the history of historiography, either one of the two sides of this equation. Genre becomes a dynamic rather than static category, and it would be inaccurate or naive to fix texts within a rigid categorization that marks inflexible boundaries between them. As David Baguley puts it, 'every text modifies "its" genre: the generic component of a text is never (except in the rarest of cases) the mere reduplication of the generic model constituted by the (supposedly pre-established) class of texts in the lineage of which it can be situated.'[93] Applying these theories to historical practice allows us to explore historians' strategic choices of genre and to unravel the motivations of the shifting landscape of historical forms developed by them – as well as the consequences these changes have for our understanding of the evolution of our discipline and of the past itself.

The history of the development of historical genres over time reveals their shifting historicity. A genre considered conventional and hegemonic in one period may be updated for the next generation of historians. The succession of historical genres in the Middle Ages – from annals to genealogies in the twelfth century, from autobiographies to chronicles in the thirteenth century, and from universal histories to urban histories in the fourteenth century – illustrates this rhetorical

---

[93] David Baguley, 'Genre and Genericity: Recent Advances in French Genre Theory', in J. Andrew (ed.), *Poetics of the Text: Essays to Celebrate Twenty Years of the Neo-Formalist Circle* (Amsterdam: Rodopi, 1992): 5–6.

reality.[94] In the twentieth century, although we still admire its ability to create a new mental universe in itself, we all experienced the ephemerality of Braudel's *Mediterranée* (1949), considered not so long ago as the epitome of an impeccable scientific approach to history through its *total* history. A genre considered experimental or marginal in one period often becomes the norm for the next generation.[95] The historical genres share with the classical and the canon that paradox so characteristic of the combination of the permanent and the ephemeral that we have mentioned in the previous chapters.

However, historical genres expand by sedimentation rather than by substitution. As Ralph Cohen argues, 'the process of sedimentation involves, in the different genres, elements from other genres that preceded them'.[96] That is, genres do not usually appear and vanish, with new genres substituting their predecessors. Rather, they coexist, although one of them replaces the other in popularity and importance. Mostly, genre innovation consists precisely in the creative adaptation and translation of existing patterns to new needs: '[A] genre does not exist independently; it arises to compete or to contrast with other genres, to complement, augment, interrelate with other genres.'[97] Historical genres are links in the same chain, rather than isolated islands of literary creation.

---

[94] Jaume Aurell, 'From Genealogies to Chronicles. The Power of the Form in Medieval Catalan Historiography', *Viator* 36 (2005): 235–264.

[95] For example, at present, see the collective volume, Munslow and Rosenstone, *Experiments in Rethinking History*.

[96] Ralph Cohen, 'History and Genre', *New Literary History* 17 (1986): 203–218, here 217.

[97] Cohen, 'History and Genre', 207.

The historicity of historical genres and their analogy with the classic may also help us to examine the functioning of their emergence, peak, decline, and, in a few cases,
disappearance. After a given genre's foundational moment,
genres mingle, since they are neither always rigidly nor exclusively compartmentalized, nor stratified horizontally, and
are replaced by others that embody and reflect the changing
times. In those moments, 'old' genres – like 'old' classics – do
not disappear; they are simply reimagined and reformulated
as part of the process of innovation by others.[98] My point is
that we are now in one of these periods, in which the history
of historiography is accelerating and assimilating new genres,
enabled by the development of new technologies, the enriching effect of images, the more active presence of readers in
the process of historical production, and the openness of
audiences to new forms of representing the past. While we
are necessarily open to these new forms of producing history
(with a greater or lesser degree of enthusiasm), we should be
more aware than ever of the benefits of respecting forms of
history practised in the past. Since there are audiences for
every genre, each historian should carefully analyse which
genre best articulates the topic at hand.

Changes in genre reflect different author's choices
and readerly expectations, as generic development reveals
social and cultural changes, confirming Nietzsche's idea that
a new need in the present necessarily opens a new medium

[98] Brian Croke, 'Late Antique Historiography, 250–650 CE', in
John Marincola (ed.), *Blackwell Companion to Greek and
Roman Historiography* (London: Blackwell Publishing, 2007),
567–81, here 580.

of understanding the past.[99] Following Hans Robert Jauss's pioneering task, recent approaches in literary theory have emphasized the function of genres in their social contexts and historical specificity, noting, in particular, that genres are historical assumptions, constructed from the outside (by editors, readers, and critics) rather than by the scholars themselves.[100] Some literary critics have argued that historical genres survive more because of public demand than because of the status of those who write them.[101] Others are convinced that the reader generates meaning by continually putting questions to the narrative, redefining what sort of story it is.[102] A third group holds that it is the expectations of readers and their interpretive communities that are most important in assigning a text to a genre.[103] Finally, Northrop Frye famously argued that genre is determined by the conditions established between the poet and his public.[104]

Nevertheless, I believe that a radical emphasis on the reader rather than the writer, and on context rather than on the text, misrepresents the dialectic on both sides of historical authorship. Historians' authorship and agency should never be underestimated, even in the periods when the historical

[99] Nietzsche, 'On the Utility', 124–141.
[100] Mark S. Phillips, 'Histories, Micro- and Literary', 211–229.
[101] Tomas Hägg and Philip Rousseau, 'Introduction', in *Greek Biography*, 1–28, here 18.
[102] Christopher Pelling, 'Epilogue', in *The Limits of Historiography*, 325–360, here 335.
[103] Robert F. Berkhofer, Jr., *Beyond the Great Story: History as Text and Discourse* (Cambridge: Harvard University Press, 1995), 67.
[104] Frye, *Anatomy of Criticism*, 247.

discipline has promoted monastic collective authorship, has tended to erudite scholarship, has aimed to emulate the experimental and scientific method in the nineteenth century or more recently, has promoted the poststructuralist 'death of the author'. Yet, since historians are not (or should not be) inhabitants of an ivory tower but cultural agents immersed in specific contexts, the interconnection between the author and the reader is (or should be) permanent. As Todorov argues, shared features make genres identifiable for audiences and allow them to harmonically function both as writing models for authors and horizons of expectation for readers.[105] Thus, reflections on historical genre theories and practice may help us understand that, rather than being considered merely circumstantial or obligatory forms, genre choices reflect historians' decisions on how knowledge of the past is authored and organized. This, in turn, embodies historians' cognitive, ethical, and aesthetic aims.

This continuous dialogue between author and reader lies at the heart of the tension between historiographical tradition and innovation so typical of the classics in history. Yet, patrons function as a 'third agent' between authors and readers, and have actually conditioned historians' genre choice in all periods: kings, bishops, and abbots in traditional societies, states, presses, and scholarship, in modern times. Thus, historians have experienced restrictions in choosing or developing genres because of their readers' expectations, their patrons' requirements, their scholarly conventions, and their own training. Nevertheless, I would not defend the idea of the 'death of the author', famously argued by Roland Barthes and

---

[105] Todorov, 'The Origin', 163.

Michel Foucault decades ago.[106] I am convinced that there is still a large space for historical authorship, in which historians may respectfully take the best of the tradition and have no fear of historiographical innovation.[107]

Finally, I argue that the historicity of historical genres and of the classics – and its consequent availability for a critical approach – also offers lessons in historical realities. The emergence of new genres connects with the self-consciousness of historical actors or institutions. As I explain in the analytical section of this chapter, the awareness of the historicity of historical genres helps us understand the latent historical reality behind these texts. The emergence of ecclesiastical history coincides with the first period in which the Church could reflect on itself, after a long period of clandestine existence during the age of persecutions.[108] Historical genealogy became a form of self-exposure of the new noble lineages who became princes of counties and kings of kingdoms – and therefore more able to increase their social self-consciousness – in a post-Carolingian context.[109]

---

[106] Roland Barthes, 'Death of the Author', in *Barthes, Image-Music-Text* (New York: Hill and Wang, 1977), 142–148 and Michel Foucault, 'What is an Author?', in P. Rabinow (ed.), *The Foucault Reader* (New York: Pantheon Books, 1984), 101–120.

[107] Jaume Aurell, 'Autobiography as Unconventional History: Constructing the Author', *Rethinking History: Journal of Theory and Practice* 10 (2006): 433–449.

[108] Sabrina Inowlocki and Claudio Zamagni (eds.), *Reconsidering Eusebius: Collected Papers on Literary, Historical and Theological Issues* (Leiden: Brill, 2011).

[109] See the section 'Noble Self-Consciousness and Historical Writing' in Leah Shopkow, 'Dynastic History', in Deliyannis, *Historiography in the Middle Ages*, 217–248, here 228–229.

Chivalric autobiographies functioned as new self-defining codes of conduct for the nobles.[110] Urban history evidences the political, economic, and fiscal autonomy of cities against feudal power at the end of the Middle Ages. National history was conceived at the moment when modern nations embraced their sense of identity and self-consciousness. The emergence of analytical history in the mid-nineteenth century has been connected with scholarly self-awareness and the subsequent processes of professionalization in history, which 'provided the basis for a self-confident and exclusive self-understanding of the historical profession which now began to distinguish sharply between 'professional historians' and 'dilettantes'. The writing of history became more and more a scientific exercise, while less importance was attached to the literary merits of an historical work.'[111]

Thus, the history of genre development may serve not only for specific historiographical purposes but also to comprehend historical processes. As Peter Burke concludes when dealing with the Renaissance, the sense of the past is shaped by the awareness, and also by the fact, of social change: 'Behind these changes in authorship and readership lay general changes in social and political structures; the rise of humanists, city-states, new monarchies. In other words, the history of the writing of history is itself part of history.'[112]

---

[110] Zink, *The Invention of Literary Subjectivity*.

[111] Steven Berger, Mark Donovan, and Kevin Passmore, 'Apologias for the Nation-State in Western Europe since 1800', in S. Berger, M. Donovan, and K. Passmore (eds.), *Writing National Stories* (London: Routledge, 1999) 3–14, here 4.

[112] Burke, *The Renaissance*, 150.

In the end, the connection between a mode of expression and the nature of truth and meaning raises numerous issues regarding the character and purpose of the representation of the past. The historicity of historical genres compellingly raises the question of what a legitimate mode of historical analysis and meaning creation is, or indeed an illegitimate or non-conventional model of historical analysis. Fitting a form in the present (one specific genre) to a particular body of content (the reality of the past) cuts to the heart of the historical project. The operation of genre choice conveys the epistemological tensions of the historical discipline. We all experience nowadays strict generic rules in the historical discipline that are difficult to break or transgress. This is especially crude when we have to confront professional and peer pressures to publish our articles or when young scholars are applying for a position. *Papers* are, in fact, the most prevalent genre of historical research today. Yet the paper is a very narrow genre that leaves little space for creation and innovation, not to say for developing a lengthy historical argument or connecting with a readership beyond academia.

My research on the historicity of historical genres makes me wonder why historians do not generally think in terms of genre and, indeed, why numerous historians have no concept of genre whatsoever. We seem to prefer to focus on *modes* or *types*, such as social, political, and economic history, but this understanding omits the complexities of creation and the relationship all historical operation establishes between form and content, between authorship and readership, and between creation and reception. This scepticism may be caused simply by the fact that historians think that history is itself a genre like the novel, and therefore does not need to be sub-categorised. But this reluctance to privilege genre categories might be also understood because most historians do not think of history as a literary form, focusing rather on the information, meaning, and content. This attitude can degenerate into autism, hyper-specialization and hyper-annotation of historical narratives that cease to interest the general public and are only followed by a handful of colleagues specialized in the same subject.

To conclude, I propose an ethical purpose that moves beyond the epistemic approach that has governed the structure of this chapter and, more generally, this book: to make historians more attentive to the new developments and possibilities of historical genres, to better adapt the historical form to its content, making it compatible with respect and appreciation for the classics of the discipline. That way, some of these new forms might transcend the constricted rules of academia, as they facilitate a better understanding of the new and changing forms of representation of the past. A more comprehensive and flexible approach to historical genres may facilitate the task of those who envisage a more creative and innovative historical writing and production.

5

Genealogy as Double Agent

Antiquorum nobis relatione compertum est
quod miles quidam fuerit nomine Guifredus.
> Deeds of the counts of Barcelona, *Gesta Comitum
> Barchinonensium*

My curiosity and my suspicion felt themselves betimes
bound to halt at the question,
of what in point of actual fact was the origin of our 'Good'
and of our 'Evil.'
> Friedrich Nietzsche, *The Genealogy of Morals*

The concepts previously discussed in this book – durability, classicism, canon, and genres – are linked in their shared continuity of historical time. It is time now to address the concept of genealogy, which apparently functions as a 'double agent' of continuity and discontinuity. This dual function, however, has never been verified simultaneously. For much of history, from the dawn of Greek historiography to postwar scientific paradigms, genealogy has been synonymous with continuity of origins and blood identity, and therefore closely connected with the concepts of the classic and the canon. Yet, during the last half century, it has shed its narrative garb to become an agent of discontinuity, and thus the nemesis of the classic and the canon.

The invention of the concept of genealogy for academic purposes is usually attributed to Nietzsche, who made it a central notion in his *Genealogy of Morals* (1887). Nevertheless, the term and its associated concepts, meanings, and methods had a long history before he used it – and would have a long history after him. In this complex story, a single signifier ('genealogy') develops a plurality of significances, from its historiographical dimension in classic Greece to the modern Nietzschean and Foucauldian philosophical deployment.

Scholars have analysed the modern development of genealogies after Nietzsche's alleged foundational statement and its prolific Foucauldian reception. They have published many essays on the use of genealogies as a historical methodology and philosophical concept, as those which I will cite throughout this chapter. But, to my knowledge, only one article has focused on the connections between medieval and (post)modern genealogies – Gabrielle M. Spiegel's 'Foucault and the Problem of Genealogy' – and none has provided a systematic history of the trajectory of this concept, from antiquity to the present.[1]

This chapter attempts to fill this gap by providing a history of the concept of genealogy and its associated ideas, delving specifically into its historiographical uses, and connecting it to the four previous concepts discussed in this book. More specifically I will emphasize its polysemy (the intriguing question of how one signifier (*signifiant*) can have encompassed such diverse meanings (*signifié*) throughout history), try to locate what has remained and what has changed in this long trajectory, and explain the (only recently) radically opposed condition (*nemesis*) between the concepts of genealogy and canon – and the implications that this opposition brings to historiography.

[1] Spiegel, 'Foucault and the Problem of Genealogy', 1–14.

My concern, as a scholar myself on medieval genealogies, lies in the fact that the specific meaning of this concept may have been lost in its vast and unquestioned academic circulation.[2] For this reason, I argue that a historicist analysis of this concept may clarify the content assigned to it in each period, and thus avoid the misunderstandings that have arisen from the shifting relationship between content and form that the notion of genealogy has carried over time. In addition, unravelling the internal history of this concept may contribute to a better understanding of the 'classic in history', since it makes direct reference to the issues of permanence and change discussed in this book with reference to historical writings.

From its first explicit use as a historical genre by early Greek historiography to the national history developed in nineteenth-century Europe, the emphasis lay on the etymological sense marked by the first half of the term – a genetic/ historical one: *genesis* and pedigree. In contrast, in late modernity, from the genealogy of the spirit devised by Hegel to its moral application in Nietzsche and discursive approach in Foucault, the concept has pivoted towards the meaning suggested by the second half of the term, etymologically considered – a philosophical/epistemic one: *logos*. In addition, this distinction improves our understanding of the double dimension of the canon – of continuity and discontinuity – to which I referred in Chapter 3.

In the first part of the chapter I will provide a brief history of the concept, from its neutral origins in classical

---

[2] Martin Saar, 'Genealogy and Subjectivity', *European Journal of Philosophy* 10 (2002): 231–245, here 231.

Greece to the emphasis put on the lineage and pedigree in the Middle Ages, its assimilation to national histories in modernity, its Hegelian and Nietzschean philosophical turn, and its use today, inherited above all from Foucault's ideas. My historicist approach to the concept will show its vital polysemy, which has led to many misunderstandings. In the second part, I explain the influence of genealogy on the humanities and social sciences today, with particular emphasis on its implications for the key theme of this book: the ongoing paradox between permanence and change through the analysis of historical texts –precisely what the ambiguous meaning of genealogy reflects.

The Dawn of Genealogy

The relevance of the concept of genealogy, and more specifically its impact on historiography, is clear from the beginning. Since there was no lexical equivalent for history or historiography in any of the languages of the ancient Near East, the ancient Hebrew traditions used *tóledót* ('genealogies') and *divré hayyamim* ('words of those days').[3] The practice of tracing pedigrees is at least as old as the oldest Western literature. Indeed, Book II of the *Iliad* provides a pedigree of Agamemnon's sceptre: 'Powerful Agamemnon stood up holding the sceptre Hephaistos had wrought him carefully. Hephaistos gave it to Zeus the king, son of Kronos, and Zeus, in turn, gave it to the courier Argeiphontes.' For these

---

[3] Piotr Michalowski, 'Commemoration, Writing, and Genre in Ancient Mesopotamia', *The Limits of Historiography*, 70.

genealogies to function, one should trace the ownership of the sceptre – or the county, or the kingdom, or the office – back to Hephaistos to Zeus, the former presumably guaranteeing the quality of the workmanship, the latter the associate claim to political authority, with a hereditary or voluntary donation. The *Rhetoric to Alexandre* – allegedly by Aristotle but probably composed a century after him – contains a justification of genealogy for historical relevance, since giving the eulogy of an individual requires one to mention his lineage: those descended from good backgrounds resemble their ancestors.

Yet, the first proper use of the genealogy for historical purposes – or the first time the recovery of the past is defined with such a name – happens in Ancient Greece by the historian Hecataeus of Miletus' *Genealogiai* [Γενεαλογίαι], c. 500 BC. The genealogy shows a great disruptive capacity from its pre-classical origins. Hecataeus constructed a historical work that sought to bring order to the complex tangle of Greek traditions and sources, and to write the history of heroic tradition without falling into myth. He sought to distinguish history from myth, as he states at the beginning of his work: 'I write these things as they appear to me to be true. For it seems to me that the accounts [*logoi*] of the Greeks are many and absurd.'⁴ The initial sentence of his *Genealogies* – literally, 'the account of the origins' – becomes a deliberate declaration of independence from legendary traditions, as he establishes his own personal perspective as a realistic author, in opposition to previous mythical genres. His genealogies record heroic tradition and seek to bring coherence to the

⁴ Hecataeus of Miletus, *Genealogies*, in Lake, *Prologues*, 1.

sometimes contradictory data of legend, myth, and aetiol-
ogy.[5] It attests to the first rationalizing impulse of the early
Greek logographers.[6] He practices genealogical chronology
and rational explanation of mythical traditions, two basic
instruments for historical discourse.[7] He conceives genealogy
as the study of the family relationships of the high priests and
heroes of mythical times, thus establishing lines of descent,
and often going back to the mythical period.

Beyond his solemn declaration of principles,
Hecataeus also introduces elements of fantasy in his work, so
that he was perhaps inspired by Hesiod's *Theogony* [Θεογονία],
a poem describing the origins and genealogies of the Greek
gods, composed c. 730–700 BC. Hesiod's *Theogony* shows an
early Greek effort to deal with the primeval period by means of
pedigrees that describe the relationships among the gods and
between gods and men. In addition, some seventh-to-fifth-
century BC verse material might have contributed to the way
early prose historiography developed.[8] These include some
longer elegies ascribed to poets writing between c. 650 BC and
the latter part of the fifth century. They recount events in both
the early and recent history of *poleis*: Tyrtaeus, Mimmermus,
Semonides of Amorgos, Xenophanes, Panyassis, and Ion of
Chios. But Hecataeus' option for historical genealogies marks

---

[5] Charles Fornara and W. Fornara, *The Nature of History in Ancient
Greece and Rome* (Berkeley: University of California Press, 1983), 1–2.

[6] J. B. Bury, *The Ancient Greek Historians* (New York, 1909), 13ff.

[7] Lucio Bertelli, 'Hecataeus: From Genealogy to Historiography',
in N. Luraghi (ed.), *The Historian's Craft in the Age of Herodotus*
(Oxford: Oxford University Press, 2003), 67–94, here 76–77.

[8] Even L. Bowie, 'Poetic Ancestors of Historiography', in *The Historian's
Craft*, 67–94.

a new stage in historiographical evolution, one of rationalization and historical criticism, where his use of prose presupposes a different audience than Hesiod's *Theogony*, one ready to accept criticism of genealogical tradition.[9]

Greek genealogy ended as a systematic historical study with the works of Hellanicus of Lesbos and Damastes of Sigeo, circa 400. Later, Thucydides would criticize those genealogists and Hellanicus' method of chronology governed by genealogy, stating that

> people should calculate the actual periods of time; they
> should not rely on lists of archons or other officials whose
> names may be used in different cities to mark the dates
> of the past events. For such methods of calculations are
> inaccurate in that they leave it unclear whether an event
> occurred in the beginning, the middle or at some other
> point, of the magistrate's term of office.[10]

As an alternative to genealogies, Thucydides proposed his method of counting 'by summers and winters', as more suitable to his aim of writing contemporary history, which necessarily had to deal with many more events, needed a detailed structure, and had to include more subdivisions in the passage of time.[11] Chronological accounts thus replaced genealogical structure.

The next golden age of genealogies moves from classical Greece to Israel of Jesus' time. During the second half

[9] Bertelli, 'Hecataeus', 78–79.
[10] Thucydides, 5.20, trans. S. Hornblower, *A Commentary on Thucydides*, ii (Oxford: Oxford University Press, 1996), 492 and Astrid Möller, 'The Beginning', in *The Historian's Craft*, 260–261.
[11] Möller, 'The Beginning', 261.

of the first century, and following a solid rhetorical tradition established in Ancient Israel, the Christian Gospels by Matthew and Luke also made important use of genealogies.[12] They aimed to testify to God's design in the birth of Jesus, his connections with the creation of the world, and the main characters of the history of Israel. They also served to link the Old with the New Testament – functioning as a kind of threshold of the Gospels. The genealogy is called βίβλος γενέσεως (Biblos Geneseos) in the *Genesis* (5: 1), literally 'book of the origins', the phrase used by Matthew at the beginning of his genealogy. Unlike him, however, Luke proceeds directly with the genealogy without giving it any definition.[13]

Genealogies had traditionally been used by the people of Israel to validate the census of the different tribes, to legitimize one's family, to certify their inheritances, and to exclude those who made false claims about belonging to a particular priestly lineage. This was especially crucial after a historical disruption, such as the return after the exile to Babylonia. The prophet Ezra

---

[12] Rodney T. Hood, 'The Genealogies of Jesus', in Allen Wikgren (ed.), *Early Christian Origins: Studies in Honor of Harold R. Willoughby* (Chicago: Quadrangle, 1961), 1–15; Marshall D. Johnson, *The Purpose of the Biblical Genealogies, with Special Reference to the Setting of the Genealogies of Jesus* (Cambridge: Cambridge University Press, 1969); Ernest L. Abel, 'The Genealogies of Jesus', *New Testament Studies* 20 (1974): 203–210; R. Larry Overstreet, 'Difficulties of New Testament Genealogies', *Grace Theological Journal* 2 (1981): 303–326; Herman C. Waetjen, 'The Genealogy as the Key of the Gospel According to Matthew', *Journal of Biblical Literature* 95, 2 (1976): 205–230.

[13] Bartosz Adamczewski, 'The End of Source Theories? The Genealogies in Gen 4:17–5:32 and Their Reworking in the New Testament', *Collectanea Theologica* 90, 5 (2020): 33–64.

recounts that 'the people of the province who came up from the captivity of the exiles, whom Nebuchadnezzar king of Babylon had taken captive to Babylon' (2:1), so that they 'searched for their family records, but they could not find them and so were excluded from the priesthood as unclean' (2:62). This shows that archives or documents were used to prove genealogical origins, at least of the priestly and notable families. These were most probably safeguarded in the temple, but it is more likely that the evangelists did not take these annotations literally. Indeed, their genealogies are more symbolic than literal, emphasizing the most famous characters of the Old Testament, omitting some names, playing with numerical significances, focusing on kings in addition to priests, and including certain women who symbolize the universality of Jesus' message.

Matthew (1:1–7) and Luke (3:23–38) establish the genealogy of Jesus in their Gospels. Matthew starts his narration with the genealogy of Jesus ('This is the genealogy of Jesus the Messiah, the son of David, the son of Abraham': 1:1), while Luke inserts it at the beginning of Chapter 3, after having recounted the circumstances surrounding the birth of John the Baptist and Jesus, his two sojourns in the Temple – the day of his presentation and when, at the age of twelve, his parents found him teaching the teachers of the Law – and his baptism. But both use the genealogy to establish the fact that the coming of Jesus had been expected by the Jews for a long time, and his birth fulfilled this expectation. Matthew highlights his filiation from Abraham and David, while Luke emphasizes the fact that Jesus is 'the son of God'. The differences between the two genealogies lie in their diverse implied readers and the specific objectives of their message.

Gospel genealogies were not, in themselves, a novelty. Pedigrees structure much of the ancient world, among Jews and Gentiles, gods and men, kings and priests, nobles and parvenus. But they provide new historical and symbolic information about the identity of Jesus – even if some of the steps of the chain provided are ahistorical or anachronistic – and an inspiring model for medieval chroniclers. Evangelists intended not only to show *who* Jesus was but also *what sort* of person he was. They recognized the role of genealogies as a vehicle for presenting myths and legends, a method of writing history. The longer one's pedigree and the more illustrious the names in it, the better.

The Rise of Lineage and Pedigree

Greek and biblical genealogies were turned into the noble and royal genealogies of the twelfth century, which shaped historiography as a genre, developed with the emergence of new twelfth-century Western European noble and royal lineages seeking legitimization. The contemporary English chronicler Roger of Wendover established a connection between this new approach to history and the evangelical genealogies, as he states in his *Flowers of History*, 'we have decided to set down for the instruction of posterity a historical epitome together with the complete genealogy of our Savior and the succession of certain kingdoms and kings, so that the diligent listener will be able to learn a great deal from a concise treatment of these things.'[14]

---

[14] Lake, *Prologues*, 275.

As Thucydides' chronological rigour replaced Hecataeus' schematic pedigrees, the annals' strict chronology was replaced by the genealogical narrative. The new key historical concepts now included generation, heritage, and lineage, rather than chronological continuity, outstanding events, or legendary heroic deeds. The genealogical organization of the stories offered both a new vision of aristocratic society through a revised perception of lineage and a new conception of time. Time was now measured by the succession of generations rather than by the chronological progression of events, such as the annals, or the duration of one life – previously articulated in diverse forms of life writing such as biographies, hagiographies, and panegyrics. The rhythmical repetition of the verb *genuit* ('he engendered') served as the grammatical and semantic link of a given history, giving it internal coherence and structure since each link of the chain establishes continuity. Chronological markers typical of the former annals lost their significance since the emphasis on generational succession rendered them worthless. The new genealogies conveyed continuity rather than discontinuity, permanence rather than change, tradition rather than renovation, and gradualism rather than revolution.

Though some of them are pushed back to Adam, many medieval genealogies open by introducing the founder of the lineage. The myth of the founder–hero is reinforced by the chronological distance from the facts of the remote past. The more distant the events, the more malleable – and more easily typified – they are in memory. The selective nature of memory allows the distant past to carry a heavier ideological load than the recent past.[15] The legends of the founders of lineages, well established in the genealogies, enjoy the inexhaustible possibilities of the myth of the origins, while the other events recounted later in the narration are limited by their own historicity. The attributes required for the founder of the dynasty valued chivalric nature over princely ascendancy, a condition he acquires through a clearly exogamic marriage.[16] The re-invention of ancestral heroes, taking parts of their historicity and fictionalizing others, increased the lineage's prestige and created a new genealogical consciousness that took the shape of a tree rooted in the person of the founding ancestor.[17]

These genealogies tended to focus on local lineage rather than on a global past. When this lineage is of royal character, it often became a form of *national history*, which has led to some of these narratives being considered canonical in their respective countries. This is the case of William of Malmesbury's *Gesta Regum Anglorum* in England, the *Grandes Chroniques* in France, the *Gesta Comitum Barchinonensium* for the Crown of Aragon, or the *History of Spain* promoted by

---

[15] William W. Ryding, *Structure in Medieval Narrative* (Paris: Mouton, 1971), 20–21; Marcel Granet, *Danses et légendes de la chine ancienne* (Paris: Alcan, 1926), I: 171–225; and John A. Barnes, 'Genealogies', in A. L. Epstein (ed.), *The Craft of Social Anthropology* (London: Tavistock, 1967), 120.

[16] The ideal traits of the hero-founder in Christine Marchello-Nizia, 'De l'Eneida à l'Eneas: Les Attributs du fondateur', in *Lectures médiévales de Virgile* (Rome: École française de Rome, 1985), 251–266.

[17] Christiane Klapisch-Zuber, 'La Genèse de l'arbre généalogique', in Michel Pastoureau (ed.), *L'Arbre: Histoire naturelle et symbolique de l'arbre, du bois et du fruit au Moyen Age* (Paris: Léopard d'or, 1993), 41–81.

King Alphonse the Wise of Castile, all produced in the twelfth and thirteenth centuries.[18] Medieval genealogies thus prefigured national histories, as Saxo Grammaticus explains in the preface of his *History of the Danes*, written around 1216:

> Just as other nations are accustomed to boast of the glory of their achievements and reap joy from the remembrance of their forefathers, Absalom, archbishop of the Danes, whose zeal ever burned high for the glorification of our land, and who would not suffer it to be deprived of like renown and record, imposed upon me, the least of his followers, since all the rest have refused the task, the work of compiling into a chronicle the history of Denmark, and by the authority of frequent exhortations he spurred my weak faculties to enter upon a labor that exceeded their capabilities.[19]

This way to emphasize 'national' history will continue in modernity. Pierre Nora referred to three historical texts as the main building blocks of France's historical memory: the *Grandes Chroniques*, completed in 1274 by the monks of the Abbey of Saint-Denis, Etienne Pasquier's debunking text *Recherches de la France*, 1599, and the historiography of the Restoration, which created the modern concept of France as a nation-state.[20] The medieval genealogies' long-duration influence lies in the fact

---

[18] For Flanders, Spiegel, 'Genealogy', 43–53; for France, Georges Duby, 'Remarques sur la littérature généalogique en France aux XIe et XIIe siècles', in *Hommes et structures du moyen Âge* (Paris: Mouton, 1973); for Iberia, Aurell, 'From Genealogies to Chronicles', 235–264.

[19] Saxo Grammaticus, *History of the Danes*, in Lake, *Prologues*, 272.

[20] Pierre Nora, 'Between Memory and History: Les Lieux de Mémoire', *Representations* 26 (1989): 21, and Gabrielle M. Spiegel, 'Medieval Canon Formation and the Rise of Royal Historiography in Old French Prose', *MLN*, 108 (1993): 638–658.

that it condenses dynastic memory, the source of future national memory, into an extraordinarily simple structure.

Considering the theoretical and practical potential of this historical genre, and aware of its rhetorical power, historians and literary critics have re-examined medieval genealogies to focus on their political, social, and cultural dimensions.[21] In particular, they study their links with constitutive concepts such as tradition, identity, legitimization, validation, lineage, authority, and power. Anthropologists appreciate the long-term and trans-cultural validity of this genre, practised among very different cultures and periodically renewed, usually under the form of national or ethnic history.[22] Though their interest in the discursive potential of

[21] For the social implications of the continuity of lineages, Duby, 'Remarques sur la littérature généalogique'; Léopold Genicot linked communities of blood with territorial possessions, in *Les Généalogies* (Turnhout: Brepols, 1975); Bernard Guenée emphasized the political consequences of the process of legitimization of the genealogies: Guenée, 'Lés généalogies entre l'histoire et la politque: la fierté d'être capétien, en France, au Moyen Age', *Annales* 33 (1978): 450–477.

[22] Considering the genealogies' political potential, social projection, and ability to promote identity, it is not surprising that this genre has been used in very different cultures and times as diverse as ancient India (Romila Thapar, 'Genealogical Patterns as Perceptions of the Past', in *Cultural Pasts: Essays in Early Indian History* (Oxford: Oxford University Press, 2000), 709–753); modern Hawaii (Valerio Valeri, 'Constitutive History: Genealogy and Narrative in the Legitimation of Hawaiian Kingship', in E. Ohnuki-Tierney (ed.), *Culture through Time: Anthropological Approaches* (Stanford: Stanford University Press, 1990), 154–192); and contemporary Native American (Karen I. Blu, *The Lumbee Problem: The Making of an American Indian People* (Lincoln: University of Nebraska Press, 2001)).

genealogical narratives has produced important critical studies, its content had been largely ignored by positivist historiographers, most probably because of its highly schematic
nature. As Northrop Frye concludes, genealogy, as practised
by medieval chroniclers, becomes a privileged medium for
establishing a rigorous, orderly succession of events and, most
importantly, is viewed as the true foundation for the structure
of history.[23]

Yet one of the fundamental reasons for modern
scholars' interest in genealogies lies in their systematic references to origins – a quality that connects them with Greek and
Gospel genealogies. The potential of narratives of origins as
historical records provides them with a great canonical potential, and is actually harnessed by many cultures, as announced
in the Scriptures: *Laudemus viros gloriosos et parentes nostros in generatione sua* ('Let us now praise famous men, and
our fathers that begot us').[24] As some political scientists have
argued, the study of origins becomes the most powerful site
for the discovery of human diversity.[25] Pierre Bourdieu notes:

> [There] is no more potent tool for rupture than the
> reconstruction of genesis: by bringing back into view
> the conflicts and confrontations of the early beginnings
> and therefore all the discarded possibles, it retrieves the
> possibility that things could have been (and still could
> be) otherwise. And, through such a practical utopia,

---

[23] Frye, *Anatomy of Criticism*, 15.
[24] *Ecclesiasticus*, 44, 1.
[25] Ronald G. Suny, 'Back and Beyond: Reversing the Cultural Turn?',
American Historical Review 107 (2002): 1498.

it questions the *possible* which, among all others, was actualized.[26]

However, to effectively approach medieval genealogies in their own specific context, we must distinguish between the *origins* and the *beginnings*. Foucault, a genealogist himself, confirms the potential of the study of the idealized origins, in front of the solvent effect of the historical beginnings, in these terms:

> The lofty origin is no more than a metaphysical extension which arises from the belief that things are most precious and essential at the moment of birth. We tend to think that this is the moment of their greatest perfection, when they emerged dazzling from the hands of a creator or in the shadowless light of a first morning. [On the contrary], what is found at the historical beginning of things is not the inviolable identity of their origin; it is the dissension of other things. It is disparity.[27]

With the disruption of the legendary origins and the introduction of *historical* beginnings, Foucault suggests that the charm of the myth turns into dissension and disparity. Thus, medieval chroniclers' and modern scholars' interest in mythical origins does not lie in their hypothetical historicity but in their representation of a given culture's self-image, manifested through its social assumptions and worldview.

---

[26] Pierre Bourdieu, 'Rethinking the State: Genesis and Structure of the Bureaucratic Field', in G. Steinmetz (ed.), *State/Culture: State – Formation after the Cultural Turn* (Ithaca: Cornell University Press, 1999), 57.

[27] Foucault, 'Nietzsche', 142–143.

GENEALOGY AS DOUBLE AGENT

The preservation of the mythical power of the origins is one
of the aims of any society. As Mircea Eliade argues, myths
and legends reflect a nostalgia for the origins of human society that evoke a return to a creative era.[28] The figure of the
founder–hero of a dynasty, so characteristic of medieval historiography, demonstrates that the epic is essentially a literary
crystallization of the heroic ideal.

Promoters of this genre were perfectly aware of
the powerful political potential of these texts, based on the
mythical origins of their societies. This reduction of historical
distance brought the past closer, intensifying the emotional
impact of an event. Spiegel summarizes this political potenti-
ality of medieval genealogies in these terms:

> The vital characteristic of genealogy in its medieval phase
> lies in its ability to address not only the historical realities
> of a family's past, but its symbolic aspirations as well. This
> binary capacity of genealogy, to be at once historical and
> symbolic, has its most telling exemplum in the opening
> chapter of the Gospel According to St. Matthew. ... Such
> manipulation of genealogical data for symbolic causes in
> the most fundamental text of medieval society is as good
> an index as any of the range of human action, beliefs,
> and values that could be subsumed within a genealogical
> perspective during the Middle Ages.[29]

During the later Middle Ages, European monar-
chies not only appropriated these 'old' historical texts but also

---

[28] Mircea Eliade, *The Myth of the Eternal Return: Myth and Reality* (New York: Pantheon Books, 1963).

[29] Spiegel, 'Foucault and the Problem', 2–3.

re-created them. In thirteenth-century France, for example, in the light of the Capetian principles of dynastic succession, the ellipses of West Frankish rule were part of a history that was susceptible to correction.[30] In thirteenth- and fourteenth-century Catalonia, the royal family of Barcelona and Aragon ordered successive vernacular versions of the *Gesta Comitum*, updating the original Latin text to consolidate their political status. The vernacularisation of the text became a valuable strategy for the formal alteration of historical writing to obtain political benefits. The text could be understood by a wider audience who was beginning to lose Latin as a vehicular language.[31] In fourteenth- and fifteenth-century Germany, as in the Kingdom of Portugal, the compilation of the most important noble houses of Saxony and of the Empire, and the development of a table of medieval kings and princes reflect the constantly changing construction of the dynastic or institutional past, via genealogies.[32]

Genealogy as National History

The genre of genealogies, as conceived by medieval chroniclers, has had great longevity in the West. In the seventeenth

[30] Andrew W. Lewis, *Royal Succession in Capetian France: Studies in Familial Order and the State* (Cambridge, MA: Harvard University Press, 1981).

[31] For the successive versions of the *Gesta Comitum*, see Stefano M. Cingolani, 'Seguir les vestígies dels antecessors', *Anuario de Estudios Medievales* 36 (2006): 201–240, here 208.

[32] Bernd Schneidmüller, 'Constructing the Past by Means of the Present. Historiographical Foundation of Medieval Institutions, Dynasties, Peoples, and Communities', in Gerd Althoff, Johannes Fried, and Patrick J. Geary (eds.), *Medieval Concepts of the Past: Ritual, Memory, Historiography* (Cambridge: Cambridge University Press, 2002), 167–192, here 176.

century, it was still one of the privileged ways of writing the history of kingdoms. As Orest Ranum explains, 'familial character of monarchical history came to determine the ways in which writers could construct the history of the [French] realm'.[33] French historians tried to perpetuate the memory of the French kings, which implied maintaining the entire realm since there could be no *lignage* without history: '[H]istory provided the mechanism for tying generations together and for transmitting a sense of house and later of nation in the languages and recollections of *gestes* peculiar to them.'[34] The spirit of medieval genealogies is in fact projected into the national histories so typical of the nineteenth century:

> Suger [in the early twelve century] and his successors not only integrated their monastery and their ideology into Capetian family history itself by forging the links between the Capetians, the Merovingians, and the Carolingians. The three-part dynastic family history produced at Saint-Denis in the early twelfth century brought together all the mythical and true elements tying the Capetians to their ancestors and to kingship itself in the *Grandes chroniques de France*. The Dionysian synthesis did not fundamentally differ from that made for other families, except in scope and royalist ideology.[35]

[33] Ranum, *Artisans of Glory*, 3.

[34] Ranum, *Artisans of Glory*, 4; for this idea, see Natalie Zemon Davis, 'Ghosts, Kin, and Progeny: Some Features of Family Life in Early Modern France', *Daedalus* 106 (1977): 87–114.

[35] Ranum, *Artisans of Glory*, 6. See also Ranum, 'Introduction', in *National Consciousness: History, and Political Culture in Early Modern Europe* (Baltimore: Johns Hopkins University Press, 1975): 2 ff.

The emergence of national consciousness was preceded by narrative Romantic history, just as national history was preceded by family and sacred history. Medieval genealogies were retaken by nineteenth-century national histories, inaugurated by Jules Michelet, and soon spread in Europe.[36] In this iteration, it was linked to Romanticism, rooted in national history, and associated with the process of nation-building across Europe. This form of historical writing served to legitimize the nation-state, focusing on the nation-building of the nineteenth century and the subsequent struggle to defend the nation-state against cosmopolitan tendencies such as socialism, communism, anarchism, and Catholic internationalism. If the nation-state stood at the centre of much historical investigation in the nineteenth century, historians focused especially on the role of the state in making the nations, looking for their founders back to the Middle Ages – as the medieval genealogical chronicles did with their founder-fathers.[37]

The sub-genre of *national* history centres on a category that in the nineteenth century was canonized as the informing principle of history and the first category of historical writing. The sub-genre of national histories comes from the genre of genealogies, but we should note the differences between them:

[36] See some examples such as Jules Michelet, *History of France*, Karl Lamprecht, *History of Germany* (1889), P. J. Blok, *History of Netherlands* (1902–18) and Henri Pirenne, *History of Belgium* (1899–1913). Its authors became national heroes and relevant intellectuals for the public debate.

[37] S. Berger and C. Lorenz (eds.), *Nationalizing the Past: Historians as Nation Builders in Modern Europe* (Basingstoke: Palgrave, 2010).

> National history writing, as it arose in the decades of
> Romanticism and the democratic revolutions, involved
> a shift of focus from polity to people, and from the
> realm to its constituent nation. Instead of a succession of
> rulers providing both the focus of the narrative and the
> organizing principle of chapter division, the cohesion
> and organization of the historical narrative was now
> the experience of that collective protagonist called *the
> nation*.[38]

The *older* history dealt with realms and counts, in
which the genealogical leaders provided the continuity of historical events and narrative, taken uncritically by the audience. Now, the collapse of *ancien régime* kingdoms, such
as the monarchy in France or the Holy Roman Empire in
Germany, may have urged historians to look for other, non-
institutional, continuities and an idealized idea of the nation
may well have provided this. Nineteenth-century national
historians tried to represent continuity across institutional
fault lines and revolutions through the abstract, metahistorical, and transcendent Nation. What in the Middle Ages
was the mystical continuity of the transcendent body of the
king, narrativized in the genealogies, was transformed into
the Nation in the nineteenth century, narrativized in national
history. But both actually connect with the reference to the
'myth of origins.'[39] Some historians have also concluded

---

[38] Joep Leerssen, 'Setting the Scene for National History', in *Nationalizing*,
here 71–85, here 74.

[39] Léon Poliakov, *Le mythe aryen. Essai sur les sources du racisme et des
nationalismes* (Paris: Calmann-Lévy, 1994). For the idea of *bodyfication*
of medieval king, see Kantorowicz, *The King's Two Bodies*, 3–6.

that 'it is a serious question whether a political community can achieve political order without developing a foundation myth'.[40] National histories, yesterday as well as today, require genealogical logic.

The Philosophical Turn of Genealogy

Hegel marks the turning point from traditional historiographical to modern philosophical use of the genealogy – from *genesis* to *logos*.[41] He is not usually included in the *genealogies* of genealogy because he does not mention the concept explicitly in his work. But he inspired the later uses of the philosophical concept of genealogy, as Foucault himself explicitly acknowledged.[42]

Hegel's most important contribution to the modern development of the concept of genealogy lies in his emphasis on the second term of the concept (*logos*, the philosophical use and understanding of the concept) over the first (*genesis*, the historical development of a pedigree). Genealogies were deployed as a historical genre from antiquity to Enlightenment, as we have seen in the first part of this chapter, but Hegel introduces it in his project on the history of the spirit, adding a philosophical dimension that would

---

[40] Carl J. Friedrich, *Man and his Government: An Empirical Theory of Politics* (New York: McGraw-Hill, 1963), 96,
[41] Montserrat Herrero, 'Genealogical Practices: Three Ways to Consider the Presence of History in Philosophy', *Giornale di Metafisica* 2 (2016): 575–597, here 575.
[42] Michel Foucault, 'The Order of Discourse', in Michael J. Shapiro (ed.), *Language and Politics* (Oxford: Blackwell, 1984), 108–139, here 134.

remain. Consequently, medieval genealogies were considered anachronistic by contemporary historians and essentialist by philosophers.

In his historical–philosophical project, Hegel admits three historiographical styles such as original history, reflective history, and philosophical history, but he also proposes a genealogy of the spirit that unravels the rational process dominating history.[43] However, while Hegel is concerned with questions of meaning and significance, genealogists like Nietzsche and Foucault shifted to issues of use, time, function, discourses, and power.[44] Nietzsche transforms Hegel's genealogy of spirit into a genealogy of morals; Foucault turns it into a genealogy of power. But something has been lost in translation, since both Nietzsche and Foucault emphasize the use of the concept for methodological rather than epistemological purposes.

Nietzsche's interest in philosophy and history lies not only in truth and reality themselves, but in their evaluation, as he emphasizes in his work, especially in his *The Birth of Tragedy* (1872) and the second *Untimely Meditation*, 'On the Use and Abuse of History for Life' (1876). He argues that an approach to the past must be governed by our desire to improve the present rather than by a purely conceptual objective. For this reason, he applies the concept of genealogy to

---

[43] G. W. F. Hegel, *The Philosophy of History*, John Sibree (ed.)(Kitchener: Batoche, 2001), 14 (on the three styles) and 22 (on the genealogy of the spirit).

[44] On the intellectual genealogy of this shift, see Michael S. Roth, *Knowing and History: Appropriations of Hegel in the Twentieth Century France* (Ithaca: Cornell University Press, 1988), 190.

morality in his *Genealogy of Morals* (1887), written some years after the two other works just mentioned, as opposed to the Hegelian development of the spirit in history.

Nietzsche's genealogy examines the historical origin of values.[45] His critical history – which he contrasts with the monumental and the antiquarian – is already in itself a genealogy and becomes a tool for destabilizing traditional values. Genealogical practice produces a past *a posteriori* through the evaluation of values inherited by tradition. Nietzsche's genealogy implies the differential element of values from which their value itself derives.[46] He was, after all, writing about morals and explaining why morality has a history that is not necessarily connected to morality, just as the meaning of words is often bound up with an arbitrary or contingent history, as is clear from philology. His general project in his *Genealogy of Morals* is the critique of traditional values by their entire re-evaluation. He assumes that values – legal, moral, or rational – can never be appreciated in and for themselves, since they always presuppose a previous evaluation. From this perspective, genealogy becomes a philosophical method rather than a historical genre, a scientific technique of questioning traditional ideas and aporias in order to deconstruct and, eventually, re-construct them. It offers the possibility to develop new ethics of action, belief, thought, and desire.[47]

This new use of genealogy provides Nietzsche with a platform from which to tell a story of the genesis of

[45] Brian Lightbody, *Philosophical Genealogy. Volume I: An Epistemological Reconstruction of Nietzsche and Foucault's Genealogical Method* (New York: Peter Lang, 2010), ix.
[46] Gilles Deleuze, *Nietzsche and Philosophy* (London: Continuum, 1983), 2.
[47] Lightbody, *Philosophical Genealogy*, I: 2–3.

contemporary ethical beliefs and practices.[48] He adopted a genealogical perspective to render problematic the values of his/our culture as embodied in our morals, science, religions, and philosophy, and in the political, spiritual, and ideological assumptions that have been dominant from antiquity. Few concepts used by scholars and intellectuals have ended up being so polysemous and ambiguous. And this is largely because of Nietzsche's enormously influential use of it at the end of the nineteenth century.

Gilles Deleuze was the first to interpret Nietzsche's critical project as a genealogy in his persuasive *Nietzsche and Philosophy* (1962), in contrast not only with Hegel but also with Kant:

> Nietzsche creates the new concept of genealogy. The philosopher is a genealogist rather than a Kantian tribunal judge or a utilitarian mechanic … Genealogy is as opposed to absolute values as it is to relative or utilization ones. Genealogy signifies the differential element of values from which their value itself derives. Genealogy thus means origin or birth, but also different or distance in the origin.[49]

The conceptual dimension of Nietzsche's genealogy pivots on his repudiation of the notion of the *substratum* – as substance, subject, and thing-in-itself – which had dominated

---

[48] Robert Guay, 'The Philosophical Function of Genealogy', in Keith A. Pearson (ed.), *A Companion to Nietzsche* (London: Blackwell, 2006), 353–370, here 353.

[49] Deleuze, *Nietzsche*, 2. Another version of this use of Nietzsche's genealogy, in Alasdair MacIntyre, *Three Rival Version of Moral Inquiry: Encyclopaedia, Genealogy and Tradition* (London: Duckworth, 1985).

the Western history of philosophy before him. The methodological dimension lies in the initial quest – a critical search
for the past oriented towards the service of present life and
activity – which links his perspective to the previous uses of
the term. What began as a classical philosophical project, an
attempt to trace the unity, permanence, and continuity of
an invisible essence, the discovery of which is based on the
analysis of its perceptible manifestations, ended up reinforc-
ing rupture, subversion, contingency, contestability, change
and discontinuity – the qualities with which the concept of
genealogy has since become associated.[50] Genealogy is here
used to discover the hidden principles of morality, metaphys-
ics, and religion by revealing its origins, meanings, and worth.

As we see, the history of the concept and its historiographical and philosophical use shifted after Nietzsche's use of
it, diverging completely from the one we have seen in Greek
historiography, gospel pedigrees, medieval genealogies, and
romantic national histories. After Nietzsche, the link between
signifier and signified disappears from the concept of genealogy, since during the twentieth and twenty-first centuries
genealogy will come to mean many different things – some
of them complex, but all of them moving away from its most
apparent meaning. Paradoxically, the term *genealogy* had
hardly been mentioned by medieval historical genealogists,

---

[50] Mark Bevir, 'What is Genealogy?', *Journal of the Philosophy of History*
2 (2008): 263–275, here 266–268; David Couzens Hoy, 'Genealogy,
Phenomenology, Critical Theory', *Journal of the Philosophy of History*
2 (2008): 276–294; Colin Koopman, *Genealogy as Critique: Foucault
and the Problem of Modernity* (Bloomington: Indiana University Press,
2013), Chapter 3.

while contemporary philosophers use it freely, with very varied meanings, and not always attendant to its full conceptual projection.

Some critics doubt that Nietzsche introduced a new method called genealogy.[51] Others argue that 'genealogy simply is history correctly practised'.[52] Indeed, Nietzsche actually never explicitly states what he means by it, so we have to infer the traces of his notion from his historical studies and passing remarks on methodology. But these traces demonstrate that genealogy, as Nietzsche conceives it, 'is a historically contingent anti-realist representation set within and constructed to convince a specific and terminate type of perspective'[53] that provides us with keys to understanding the reality. As Nietzsche states in the introduction of his essay, he was obsessed with 'what in point of actual fact was the *origin* of our "Good" and of our "Evil". Indeed, at the boyish age of thirteen the problem of the origin of Evil already haunted me'.[54] Yet, unlike ancient, medieval, and early modern genealogists, he thinks that

> no thing is to be found at the origin. While others
> [i.e. medieval genealogists] search out origins to
> find something in its pristine purity, untarnished by

[51] Christoph Schuringa, 'Nietzsche's Genealogical Histories and His Project of Revaluation', *History of Philosophy Quarterly* 31 (2014): 249–269, here 256.

[52] Alexander Nehamas, *Nietzsche as Literature* (Cambridge: Harvard University Press, 1985), 246.

[53] Anthony K. Jensen, *Nietzsche's Philosophy of History* (Cambridge: Cambridge University Press, 2013), 157.

[54] Friedrich Nietzsche, *The Genealogy of Morals* (Mineola, NY: Dover, 2003), 3.

culture and history, Nietzsche denies the notion of the substratum in all the forms it has taken in the history of philosophy (substance, subject, the soul, the thing-in-itself, etc.). Any thing, person, event is construed by Nietzsche to be a matter of historical, cultural, practical interpretation, and beneath the series of interpretations there is nothing, no thing.[55]

Nietzsche reveals the corrosive critical power of genealogy and its efficient mode of questioning. It reveals historical conditions of existence and criticizes the events that have led us to constitute ourselves and to recognize ourselves as subjects of what we are being, doing, thinking, and saying.[56] His genealogy, as a form of valuation, provides a more plausible and well-supported account of our history than other available alternatives, such as conventional history.[57] Behind this questioning of traditional history lies a susceptibility to historicism and contemporary Germanic positivism, hegemonic in university departments, analogous to the traditional philology that Nietzsche had tried to demolish with his *Birth of Tragedy* (1872).

After Nietzsche, much of the responsibility for the polysemy that the concept of genealogy has assumed since the 1970s, as the *mythical* condition that modern scholars have assigned to the term, lies in the work of Michel Foucault.[58]

[55] Michael Mahon, *Foucault's Nietzschean Genealogy: Truth, Power, and the Subject* (Albany: State University of New York Press, 1992), 82.

[56] Mahon, *Foucault's*, 82.

[57] Raymond Geuss, *Morality, Culture, and History: Essays on German Philosophy* (Cambridge: Cambridge University Press, 1999), 23.

[58] Foucault, 'Nietzsche, Genealogy, History', 139–164.

In his resistance to conventionality, Foucault emphasized the disruptiveness of the concept, which contrasts with the continuist projection of medieval genealogies. His genealogy dissolves historical continuity and linearity, potentially disruptive, subversive, and delegitimizing. As Spiegel explains, Foucault's genealogy, 'demands a battle of knowledge against the 'power effects' of scientific discourse and takes its place in this battle as a tactic, deployed to put into play the forms of knowledge (*savoirs*) thus engaged, as a result of which they are 'desubjugated' and rendered free.'[59]

Foucault promotes a very diverse use of the concept, from a methodological tool to a simple statement of his historical–philosophical project, through its analogy with the concepts of 'history', 'genesis', or 'rupture'. Martin Saar summarizes these meanings in three aspects: as a mode of writing history (method), as a model of evaluation and critique (value), and as a textual practice or genre (style).[60] Among these meanings, perhaps the most specific in Foucault is genealogy as the undermining of all forms of historically grounded truth claims, based on the recuperation of lost origins and simple lines of development. He reconceptualizes Nietzsche's notion of genealogy and emphasizes his radical critique of the origins and conventions of knowledge in three ways: (1) parodic, that is, directed against reality and opposing the theme of history as a reminiscence of recognition; (2) dissociative, that is, directed against identity, and opposing history understood as continuity or the representative of a tradition;

---

[59] Spiegel, 'Foucault and the Problem of Genealogy', 10.
[60] Saar, 'Genealogy and Subjectivity', 232.

and (3) is sacrificial, that is, directed against the truth, and opposing history as a body of knowledge.[61]

Similar to medieval genealogists, and despite his anti-historical use of genealogies, Foucault focuses on the quest for origins, referring to the distinctions among various terms typically translated as 'origin'. He attempts to capture the exact essence of things, one that reveals the primordial truth or original identity beneath the masks accumulated in history. But, he argues that there is no essence behind things, and that uncovering an essence results from the fabrication of alien forms. Yet his concept of genealogy should be approached differently from Nietzsche's, since Foucault uses it as a method, a strategy, a critical tool, and a form of interpretation rather than simply meaning. His version becomes an epis-temic tool rather than an ontological inquiry. Foucauldian genealogy deconstructs and constructs the essence of histori-cal and temporal realities. It asks, 'what has been given to us as universal, necessary and obligatory' and proposes instead 'whatever is singular, contingent, and the product of arbitrary constraints'.[62] In his anti-essentialist and anti-metaphysical project, the Hegelian spirit and the Nietzschean moral disap-pear in favour of individuals telling stories without spirit and morals – the field of discourse becomes hegemonic.

---

[61] Benjamin Sax, 'Foucault, Nietzsche, History: Two Modes of the Genealogical Method', *History of European Ideas* 11 (1989): 769–781, here 789.

[62] Jim Tully, 'To Think and Act Differently', in Samantha Ashenden and David Owen (eds.), *Foucault Contra Habermas* (London: Sage, 1999), 90–142, here 94, and David Owen, 'On Genealogy and Critical Theory', *European Journal of Philosophy* 10 (2002): 216–230, here 221.

Foucault distinguishes between critical and genealogical methods. He explains that, while the 'critical side of the analysis deals with the system's enveloping discourse, ... the genealogical side of the analysis, by way of contrast, deals with series of effective formation of discourse'.[63] The use of genealogy allowed him to focus on discontinuities rather than continuities, since for the genealogist there are no fixed essences, fundamental laws, or metaphysical finalities. The deepest truth that the genealogist has to reveal is 'the secret that [things] have no essence or that their essence was fabricated in a piecemeal fashion from alien forms'.[64] Genealogy deals with explanations and discourses rather than events and historical facts, so that the universals are revealed as the result of the contingent emergence of constructed (and imposed) interpretations rather than the previous existent essences. Foucauldian genealogies thus seek to demolish the primacy of origins, of unchanging truths, of doctrines of development and linear progress.

This explains why genealogy, as articulated by Foucault, has had such an immense influence on history and social sciences, since it can effectively demolish the supra-historical, teleological, unquestioned, or meta-disciplinary perspectives underlying all academic fields.[65] In this sense, the genealogist

[63] Michel Foucault, 'The Discourse of Language', in *The Archaeology of Knowledge* (New York: Harper, 1972), 234.

[64] Michel Foucault, 'Nietzsche', 142.

[65] Hayden White best unravelled these unconscious and unquestioned realities that underlie all disciplines when he applied them to the historical discipline and defined them as containing a 'deep structural content, which is generally poetic, and specifically linguistic, in nature,

becomes a scholar, avoiding any generalization, essentialism, ideal significance, or typological analysis. In a 1983 retrospective interview, he assigned to genealogy an essential function in his work, since it was present in the three major areas of his interest as a thinker: truth, power, and ethics:

> Three domains of genealogy are possible. Frist, an historical ontology of ourselves in relation to truth through which we constitute ourselves as subjects of knowledge; second, an historical ontology of ourselves in relation to a field of power through which we constitute ourselves as subjects acting on others; third, an historical ontology in relation to ethics through which we constitute ourselves as moral agents.[66]

Each of these areas is connected with one of his major works: truth in *The Birth of the Clinic* (1963), power in *Discipline and Punish* (1975), and ethics in *The History of Sexuality* (1976).[67] In this sense, Foucault moves away from genealogy applied to morality, as Nietzsche does, and focuses on the genealogy of ethics, because moral codes seemed to him too stable and formal.

and which serves as the precritically accepted paradigm of what a distinctively a "historical" explanation should be. This paradigm functions as the "metahistorical" element in all historical works that are more comprehensible in scope than the monography or archival report' (White, *Metahistory*, ix).

[66] Michel Foucault interview in Hubert L. Dreyfus and Paul Rabinob, *Michel Foucault: Beyond Structuralism and Hermeneutics* (Chicago: University of Chicago Press, 1983), 237.

[67] Dreyfus and Rabinob, *Michel Foucault*, 237. On Foucault's intellectual itinerary, see Allan Megill, 'Foucault, Structuralism, and the Ends of History', *The Journal of Modern History* 51 (1979): 451–503 and Stuart Elden, *Foucault: The Birth of Power* (London: Polity, 2017).

The Legacy of Genealogy

The creation of the concept of genealogy has been assigned to contemporary philosophy, especially to Nietzsche and Foucault, who have provided the term with dense epistemic meaning and vigorous subversive projection. These philosophers have certainly proposed new ways to define and use genealogies, with different meanings and methodologies from those genealogies and pedigrees traditionally practised by ancient historians, medieval chroniclers, early modern scholars, and modern nationalists. But Nietzsche's and Foucault's concept of genealogy did not emerge from a historiographical vacuum. It developed from a long process of comings and goings, verifiable at least since antiquity, as I argue in this chapter.

Yet, beyond its shifting use through time, what is perhaps more relevant is the conceptual ambiguity of the genealogy, which has derived from a continuous interplay between the inheritance and the rational, between the methodological and the ontological, between the historical and the philosophical, between the *genesis* and the *logos*. This perpetual semantic and semiotic flux has resulted in a permanent inconclusiveness of the legacy of genealogy. Its malleability has endowed it with a remarkable polysemy, efficacy as an academic tool, source of social change, and permanent potential for renewal. This has provided relevance to its project, which we cannot understand without the recognition of the paradox which results from the juxtaposition of its permanence and transience as an academic tool, analogous (and contrasting) to the subversive quality that Nietzsche and Foucault assigned to the term.

In the context of these semantic and methodological debasements of the concept, I would now like to address what are – if they exist – the continuities of the concept through time. The question is: can we consider the genealogy just as a polysemic concept or are there some permanencies and continuities? And so, what function can be assigned to 'genealogy' for a better understanding of the concepts of the classic and the canon as they have been articulated in this book?

There is at least one continuity that allows us to speak of *one* concept over time: the genealogy's permanent appeal to the origins, irrespective of its aim to either idealize the past – as the traditional chroniclers and historians did – or to reject it, as modern philosophers have done. Turning to origins is the main paradigm of genealogy, the basic subject of its narrative, the key of its methodological use, the condition of its efficacy, and as Montserrat Herrero has argued, the privileged point of convergence between the *logos* and the *genesis*.[68]

Aviezer Tucker distinguishes four types of origins: mythical, rationalist, genealogical, and scientific.[69] Genealogists have used one or another depending on their epistemic objectives. Medieval genealogies, for instance, are mythical in their content and objectives, especially in their projection of the legendary origins of the dynasties and nations. They search for the essences which persist continuously. They base their effectiveness on the conviction of certain societies in which time and history confer authority, legitimacy, and honour.

[68] Herrero, 'Genealogical Practices', 575–597.
[69] Aviezer Tucker, 'Origins and Genealogies', in A. K. Jensen and C. Santini (eds.), *Nietzsche on Memory and History* (Berlin: De Gruyter, 2021), 57–75, here 57.

Since we cannot accurately establish its chronology, mythical origin stories are necessarily anachronistic, since their
epistemic foundation contain deliberately non-chronological
accuracy. The move towards rational and scientific origins,
however, emerged in the eighteenth and nineteenth centuries.
Both were established when scholar and scientific criticism
spread among biblical, historical, and textual studies.[70] Finally,
modern and postmodern philosophers such as Nietzsche and
Foucault deploy genealogical origins: 'As much as mythical
origins transmit essences through ontological continuity and
scientific origins transmit information signals, Nietzsche's
genealogical origins should transmit values through collective
non-episodic memories that preserve values that resulted from
traumatic historical events.'[71]

In fact, the practice of genealogy referring to origins
has had some recent, perhaps unexpected, sources among
political scientists. In the 1990s, cultural and social diagnoses by Francis Fukuyama and Samuel P. Huntington, among
others, were based on an almost literal application of genealogy to legitimize the dominant political order of the present.[72]
They used the concept not only to understand the word but
also to intervene in it. All of them share the assumption that
traumatic historical events affect political values and behaviour across generations. Notably, both diagnoses were produced after the collapse of the Soviet Union in the 1990s.

[70] Tucker, *Our Knowledge of the Past*, 46–91.
[71] Tucker, 'Origins', 66.
[72] Francis Fukuyama, *The End of History and the Last Man* (New York:
Free Press, 1992) and Samuel P. Huntington, *The Clash of Civilizations
and the Remaking of World Order* (New York: Touchstone, 1996).

The second line of continuity of the concept posits that genealogy always involves a historical element. This is obvious in the *genesis* phase of the genealogy, from fifth-century BC Greek genealogists to nineteenth-century national historians. This permanent historicist condition of the genealogies provided Hegel's, Nietzsche's, and Foucault's philosophical projects with a historical condition not shared by many of their colleagues, but welcomed by part of historians. A genealogist – historian, philosopher, or social scientist – is a historian too, or, at least, proceeds historically. One of the more influential economists, Thomas Piketty, has evolved from a pure economist to a genuine genealogist, as he admits in the introduction of his *Capital and Ideology* (2020):

> The earlier book [his *Capital in the Twenty-First Century*, 2014] tended to treat the political and ideological changes associated with inequality and redistribution as a sort of black box. ... But I never tackled head-on the question of how inegalitarian ideologies evolved. In this new work I attempt to do this much more explicitly by examining the question in a much broader temporal, spatial, and comparative perspective.[73]

Yet, perhaps less paradoxically than it may seem, the historical dimension of genealogy is compatible with its continuous appeal to the present: 'Genealogy at its best involves a practice of critique in the form of the historical problematization in the present'.[74] All forms of genealogy engage the

[73] Thomas Piketty, *Capitalism and Ideology* (Cambridge: Harvard University Press, 2020), ix.
[74] Koopman, *Genealogy as Critique*, 2.

present because the understanding of the past provides us with keys to the present and about ourselves. This may be questionable for historical scholars since genealogy tends to play with time categories more freely than historians usually do. When Nietzsche and Foucault used the concept of genealogy to deconstruct the past – or to re-semanticize it – they broke with the traditional contextualist approach to history and an essentialist approach to philosophy. They do not necessarily fall into the fallacy of presentism, since one cannot study the current institution or concept in the past without negotiating with that idea or institution in the present. But they evaluated the past trying to intervene in the present.

In contrast to these continuities – remission to the origins, historical condition, and appealing to the present – other discontinuities in the use of genealogies by chroniclers and critics exist. First of all, traditional and modern genealogies are both driven by power, but they differ in the way they approach it:

> Whereas more traditional forms of historiography focus on explaining the rise and fall of kingdoms or the origin and transmission of ideas or customs for examples, the principal purpose of a genealogical investigation is to unmask how discourses, ideas and institutional systems are byproducts of power. Power, but more specifically the struggle for greater power, so argues the genealogist, is responsible for creating the very objects, discourses and institutions of history itself. Power produces what we, as investigators, deem to be important historical 'events' according to our agendas.[75]

---

[75] Lightbody, *Philosophical Genealogy*, I: 133.

Another discontinuity between traditional and modern genealogy is its opposing inquiry processes. While ancient, medieval, and early modern genealogies trace a pedigree to search for origins and emphasize established tradition, modern and postmodern genealogies use the form to question and subvert. The pedigree always starts from a singular origin, which is an actual source of that value and cannot be broken in any part of the chain – continuity is essential – so that the series of steps may preserve whatever value is in question. The older, the better: the passage of time itself is a value.[76] Yet Nietzschean and Foucauldian genealogies differ from this tracing of pedigree because they do not intend to legitimize any present person, family, practice, value, or institution, nor enhance the status of any contemporary item. They are not necessarily projected to the *last* step of the chain. They are not linear, as the whole point of *Genealogy of Morals* shows: Christian morality is not the fruit of a single line of development but a conjunction of a contingent number of a larger number of separate series of social and psychological processes – from the resentment of slaves directed against their masters to a certain desire on the part of a priestly caste to exercise dominion over others. Nietzsche's appeal to origins is not historical but properly genealogical.

Finally, there is a relevant difference between approaching any given past genetically or genealogically. We use genealogy when we examine a period that undeniably belongs to history, but it does not as yet – for us – belong

---

[76] Geuss, *Morality*, 1–3.

to 'the past'.[77] Yet, nineteenth-century national history is also genetic in nature. By providing for the nation an equivalent of what ancient and medieval genealogists offered for the lineage, professional historians of the nineteenth century not only established the purity of the group's bloodlines but also confirmed the claim of the dominant ethnic group within the nation to the land it ruled.[78] The medieval lineage genealogists, the early modern monarchical and dynastical genealogists and the modern national genealogists have evident parallelisms. As Orest Ranum concludes, 'as family and sacred history, history had preceded the rise of national consciousness, but the latter could build upon these and be integrated into family history'.[79]

Beyond these continuities and discontinuities, and assuming the semantic shifting of the concept through history, I conclude that genealogy is always playing with the two opposites of the equation inserted in the DNA of the genealogy-as-signifier. It, therefore, builds a narrative that deals with the convergence between *logos* and *genesis* consisting of a specific connection between meaning and events through discourses.[80] One period certainly put more emphasis on one or the other side of the equation. But the balance – and the tension – between both remain consistent: for genealogy to function as a tool of knowledge and power, it must make at least some reference to origins (*genesis*) or their

---

[77] White, *The Fiction of Narrative*, 244.
[78] White, *The Fiction of Narrative*, 316.
[79] Ranum, *Artisans of Glory*, 13 and Ranum, *National Consciousness*, 2–10.
[80] Herrero, 'Genealogical Practices', 577.

rational treatment (*logos*), in spite of the emphasis placed on one or the other end of the equation.

This leads us, as a final point, to question the relationship between genealogy and history. Both activities/disciplines share the same object – the inquiry into the past – but they approach that past *differently*. Bernard Williams defines genealogy as a 'narrative that tries to explain a cultural phenomenon by describing a way in which it came about, or could have come about, or might be imagined to come about'.[81] According to this, genealogy is not simply a matter of 'real history', since it encourages authorial intervention, and may include a role for a fictional narrative and an imaginary developmental history, which helps to explain a concept, value, or institution based on a supposed line of genealogical coherence. Once developed, modern philosophical genealogy differs from traditional historiography on the level of its *subject*, since it focuses on tracing the stories of values and practices that relate to subjectivities and self-formations rather than in politics and institutions. Second, it contrasts in its *explanation* too, its mechanism relating historical data to discourses rather than events. And, finally, it is divergent in its *textuality*, with its use of hyperbole, allegorization, and exaggerations and a complex implication of the audience rather than a more symbolic use of the language.[82]

Whatever these differences, however, there is a continuous interaction between history, philosophy, and

---

[81] Bernard Williams, *Truth & Truthfulness: An Essay in Genealogy* (Princeton: Princeton University Press, 2002), 20–21.

[82] Martin Saar, 'Understanding Genealogy: History, Power, and the Self', *Journal of Philosophy of History* 2 (2008): 295–314, here 312.

genealogy, whose links are closely related by the kind of our approach to the past, whether this is understood as a foreign country, as a source of wisdom, an instrument of power and domination, or as the familiar home to which we can always return. But a problem remains: when genealogists make the past immediately usable, they may undermine the integrity and the pastness of the past.[83] For this reason, a crucial distinction between the three concepts – history, philosophy, and genealogy – can contribute decisively to avoiding some misunderstandings about the past and the present.

Ultimately, the complex semantic and morphological itinerary of the genealogy examined in this chapter confirms the formal definition suggested by Spiegel: a 'complex of metaphoric structure'.[84] This explains why genealogy has been able to embrace such different realities – semantically and semiotically – over time, as has been applied to the narration of the legendary origins of Rome, the pedigree of Jesus, the mythical origins of the most prestigious lineages of medieval Europe, the dynastic history of early modern Europe, the national histories of modern Europe, the Nietzschean critique of the traditional values of Western morality, or the Foucauldian subversive tool in postmodern criticism.

These diverse uses reveal the peculiar tension of the unsettling character of a concept through time, and the normalizing power of disciplinary histories that today marks one of the most visible agendas of genealogy – one that takes

[83] Gordon S. Wood, *The Purpose of the Past* (New York: Penguin Press, 2008).
[84] Spiegel, *The Past as Text*, 110.

advantage of its charismatic character to make us rethink the ways we engage the past. In the end, genealogy's metaphoric structure allows history to absorb much of the literary flow accumulated by previous historical books. Applied to historiography, genealogy connects rather than disintegrates, since it is capable of turning historical works of all times into common milestones on the same road.

Conclusions

Non aspettar mio dir più ne mio cenno:
libero, dritto e sano è tuo arbitrio,
e fallo fora non fare a suo / senno:
per ch'io te sovra te corono e mitrio
('I do not give you sign or word;
free, upright and whole is thy will;
'twere a fault not to act according to its prompting;
wherefore I do crown and mitre thee over thyself').

Dante, *Divina Commedia*

As the great classicist Roland Syme put it, 'men and dynasties pass, but style abides.'[1] Syme aimed to give a free interpretation of Tacitus' exhortation in favour of the sublimity of writing as opposed to the mediocrity of the ephemeral: 'meditation et labor in posterum valescit'. But he also inspired me to write this book, with the intention of rescuing the historical texts that have overcome the corrosive power of time and whose value remains, irrespective of the circumstances surrounding their writing. Crucially, the understanding of these classics contribute to answering François Hartog's recent anxious question: 'When only the present seems to be available, when time has no reference point but itself, how is life or action thinkable?'[2]

---

[1] Ronald Syme, *Tacitus* (Oxford: Clarendon Press, 1958), II: 624.
[2] Hartog, *Chronos: The West*, ix.

I argue that the ability of some history classics to transcend time stems from their literariness, as it supports the text's historicity. I analysed some of the visible qualities of these classics which include features shared with the classic in literature, such as endurance, timelessness, universal meaningfulness, resistance to historical criticism, susceptibility to multiple interpretations, and ability to function as models. But I introduced other specificities of the historical operation such as the surplus of meaning, historical use of metaphors, effect of contemporaneity, and a certain appropriation of literariness without damaging the pastness of the past. These observable qualities can be systematically examined. Yet the conditions required for becoming a classic or entering the canon in history remain in part difficult to define because all historical operation contains – or should contain – the unpredictability and unsystematic of art.

One clear similarity between literature and historical writing is that, while both are bound to the period of their writing, classic literature and classic historical writing manage to overcome their context. They transcend limiting epistemological conditions, a consensus among authors on the basic rhetorical rules of writing, a certain social context, and specific inclinations of the potential audience at a given historical moment. Yet, while great literature maintains its integrity with the passage of time, great historical writing must acknowledge the fact of additional data and shifting interpretations of the past. Thus, while Gibbon's *Decline and Fall* certainly is a classic, the specialists have been able to complete or enrich some of its historical data. So, we read Gibbon if we are interested in his global account of the fall of the Roman Empire illuminated by the Enlightenment and in his ability to address the great questions of humanity, but hardly for its scientific and empirical value. The same may be said for Pirenne's *Mohammed and Charlemagne*, since most current research does not hold that the Mediterranean was as closed off by the rise of Islam as he argues. Readers do, however, continue to appreciate his brilliant account and captivating ideas of a difficult period for Europe, the relationship he established with the present, and his echoing of the comparative method of Plutarch's *Parallel Lives*, as encoded in the title.

We appreciate in these and the other historical writings analysed in this book that 'timeless fascination of the historiographical classic to the content that it shares with every poetic utterance cast in the mode of a narrative', in Hayden White's words, so that 'the classical historical narrative continues to fascinate as the product of a universal human need to reflect on the insoluble mystery of time'.[3] Only the literary elements of these historical texts – and, crucially, the analogy with the past itself which this figurative language contains – remain, giving them their deserved place in the pantheon of historical classics. These classic works of history – and the others I have referred to in this book without aiming to be exhaustive, normative, canonical, or systematic – deploy metaphorical and figurative language rather than mimetic or literal discourse. Scholars do not agree to what extent historians must pay a price for this *figural* operation: while critics such as Hayden White argue that historical texts may lose part of their historicity in this process of figuration, others such as Frank Ankersmit are

---

[3] White, *The Content of the Form*, 180.

convinced that this process enriches the historical representation of the past. Yet, this process of de-historicization, de-
contextualization, and contemporaneity of certain historical
texts constitute the inescapable – and, sometimes, painful –
part of the process of becoming a classic. Experience has shown
that the risk is worthwhile. Here lies the paradox of historical
writing, a practice that crosses the boundaries between science
and art, between academic presentation and narrative form,
and between the past (the content of this narration) and the
present (the form in which this past is represented).

The study of the classic and the canon also raises
questions related to the present, such as the assignment of
authority or the essential mechanisms governing the historiographical transmission, the relations between the centre
and the periphery of the profession, the dynamics of historiographical paradigm shifts, and the tensions between tradition
and innovation. The very existence of the classics of history,
and their ability to combine sedimented authority with modern accommodation, make us keep thinking on the nature of
historical interpretation, and with our present.

Gadamer has explained the mysterious connection of
the classic with the present, which is independent of all the
circumstances of time – a kind of timeless present that is contemporaneous with every other present. Its effective medi-
ating status between past and present should be given more
attention by critics:

> The general nature of tradition is such that only the
> part of the past that is not past offers the possibility of
> historical knowledge. The classical, however, as Hegel

says, is 'that which is self-significant and hence also self-interpretive.' But that ultimately means that the classical preserves itself precisely because it is significant in itself and interprets itself; i.e., it speaks in such a way that it is not a statement about what is past – documentary evidence that still needs to be interpreted – rather, it says something to the present as if it were said specifically to it. What we call 'classical' does not first require the overcoming of historical distance, for in its own constant mediation it overcomes the distance by itself. The classical, then is certainly 'timeless,' but this timelessness is a mode of historical being.[4]

The recognition of the presentism of the classic and the canon unmasks the hypocrisy of overemphasizing criticism of the dominance of historiographical centres that exercised hegemony in the past, since there is always someone who occupies that place – and an aspirant fighting to take that place. The authors of the established historical works had to fight, at some point, for a place in the pantheon of the classics or on the podium of the canon themselves. The resistance of the old canon is as defensible as the struggle of the new one to become valuable, so it seems advisable to maintain a balance between respect for the historiographical tradition and the search for new paths. The recognition of the classics and of the canonical can contribute precisely to the awareness of the need for this flexibility, and a dynamic dialogue between tradition and innovation in the historical discipline and practice.

---

[4] Gadamer, *Truth and Method*, 289–290.

Edward Said's, Ankhi Mukherjee's, and postcolonial studies' dispute against the canon, considered inextricably implicated in colonial power, embodies the most relevant arguments in the contemporary contestation of canons, but also illustrates the challenges of conducting cultural and intellectual exchanges without them in the present. By examining the dynamics of the classic and the canon, and its respective connection with the concept of genre and genealogy, I have tried to show that these concepts are not only related to continuities, permanence, and essence, as their critics claim, but also to discontinuities, change, context, and conjuncture. This has led me to argue that criticisms of the canon as essentialist, hegemonic, and normative are weak because experience has shown that, in reality, this aspiration to demolish the canon has culminated in its revision or substitution by others, rather than its disappearance.

In fact, this continuing vitality and dynamism of the canon is ensuring a growing presence of women historians and a more global authorship of what in the future might be perceived as a classic or included in the canon. This augurs that, in the not-too-distant future, another author will be able to undertake a new study of the classic in historiography which, with the right perspective, may already include some of the works, coming from a postcolonial sphere, that are gaining durability in historiography.[5] As the passage of

[5] This will be actually possible thanks to the most recent histories of historiography that I have quoted throughout the book: Jayapalan, *Historiography*; Dirlik, Bahl, and Gran, *History after the Three Worlds*; Fuchs and Stuchtey, *Across Cultural Borders*; Sharma, *Historiography*; Wang and Iggers, *Turning Points in Historiography*; Woolf, *A Global*

time is necessary to verify the durability of a historical work, I hope that in a few decades it will be possible to discern which of these works included in the new global histories of historiographies can be included in a study as the one I am now proposing. But we do not have sufficient time perspective to discern which of these historical narratives – and others of the more recent ones cited in this book – will have continuity and gain durability in historiography.

* * *

I would like to end this book by emphasizing two conclusions. First, I hope to have contributed in some measure to demystifying the idea that 'classic' and 'canon' are two notions that imply normativity, rigidity, traditionalism, uncritical inertia, or cultural supremacism. The data I have provided, especially in the chapters on canon and historical genres, show that enduring books have usually opened up a new field of study, a new methodology, a new way of approaching the analysis of the past, or a new way of representing it.[6] What

---

History of History; Duara, Murthy, and Sartori, *A Companion to Global Historical*; Iggers, Wang, and Mukherjee, *A Global History of Modern Historiography*. See also the ambitious collective work *The Oxford History of Historical Writing* (Oxford: Oxford University Press, 2011–2012).

[6] I have always found it relevant to delve into the meaning of the new and the old in history, the relative nature of these concepts, and the continuous paradoxes of their itineraries: see Peter Burke, 'Overture: The New History, Its Past and Its Future', in P. Burke (ed.), *New Perspectives on Historical Writing* (Cambridge: Polity, 1991), 1–23 and Ignacio Olábarri, '"New" New History: A Longue Durée Structure', *History and Theory* 34 (1995): 1–29.

made the works of some historians great and lasting is their ability to open new fronts. Thucydides created the concept of 'history' which was not available before, as Polybius proposed the concept 'the writing of history.' On the modes of emplotment, Michelet was a master in casting all his histories in the romantic mode, as Ranke in comic, Tocqueville in tragic, and Burckhardt in satire. On the ideological implication, Nietzsche is a typical example of an anarchist approach, as Macaulay of conservatism, Braudel of radicalism, and Croce of liberalism. On the formal argument, the Formist model of explanation is to be found in Carlyle, as the Organicist typically in Theodor Mommsen, Mechanicist in Hippolyte Taine, and Contextualist in Burckhardt. On the great schools of historical thought in modern historiography, Michelet founded the Romantic school, as Ranke the historicist, Charles Seignobos the positivist, Bloch and Febvre the Annals, Thompson and Hobsbawm the Marxist, Braudel the structuralism, Carlo Ginzburg the microhistory, Natalie Zemon Davis the narrative history, and Hayden White the philosophy of history recovered by historians.[7]

This list, necessarily schematic but nevertheless illustrative, shows that all these classical and/or canonical historians have achieved the durability of their historical writings

---

[7] Three of the categories that I distinguish in this paragraph – the modes of emplotment, the ideological implication, and the formal argument – are inspired by White, *Metahistory*, 7–22. White takes Northrop Frye's *Anatomy of Criticism* as a model for the first; Karl Mannheim's *Ideology and Utopia* (New York: Harcourt, 1946) for the second; and Stephen C. Pepper's, *World Hypotheses* (Berkeley: University of California Press, 1966) for the third.

not so much by their tendency to preserve certain disciplinary conventions, but rather by confronting them through an innovative approach to the past. This is another of the many paradoxes of history writing: classicism arises from discontinuity rather than continuity, from innovation rather than preservation, and from nonconformism rather than conventionality. Critics of other fields will have to decide to what extent this fact has its counterpoint in literature or art. But in historiography, it appears as a fact that has been possible to demonstrate thanks to the perspective of centuries of historical practice.

The recognition of the possibility of being able to carry out such a study is precisely what leads me to the second conclusion. I hope that this research will contribute to consolidating the field of 'historical criticism', or 'critical analysis of historical texts', complementary to but distinct from the theory of history and the history of historiography, which has begun to flourish in historiography in recent decades. The exploration of the artistic and literariness portion of the historical works has already been carried out in various ways and approaches by Leo Braudy, Peter Gay, John Clive, Jack Hexter, and more recently, by Ann Rigney, Paul Ricoeur, Alun Munslow, Frank Ankersmit, Philippe Carrard, Lionel Gossman, and, perhaps the most influential of them all from a strictly historiographical perspective, Hayden White.

Most of these critical historians of history have carried out this critical task, making it compatible with their own historical work. This is the spirit that inspired this book, since, while admitting that this may not apply to other fields, I find it difficult to offer a critical approach to historical writing without having practised it at the same time. My aspiration has been to contribute to add onto the historians' agenda the criticism and the meta-criticism in the field of history, not in order to regulate, standardize or normalize the discipline but to increase its creativity, literarity, and art.[8]

More than half a century ago, Hayden White debunked the myth of the hegemony of epistemological and methodological questions in the historical operation over literary and formal ones, something fostered by those who, during the previous two centuries, had tried to reduce history to a scientific activity. As he explains, 'The demand for the scientization of history represents only the statement of a preference for a specific modality of historical conceptualization, the grounds of which are either moral or aesthetic, but the epistemological justification of which still remains to be established.'[9]

In addition to the obvious advantage of serious scrutiny in any historical operation, I argue that the field of historical criticism also contributes decisively to increasing the theoretical perspective of any historian. Theoretical reflection allows historians to delve into the reality of historical authorship and practice, connecting them to the present from which they try to access the past. When they are well equipped with a theoretical armoury, as most of the 'durable' historians who have appeared in this book have been, historical practice brings them closer to the protagonists of the past, trying at the

---

[8] Hayden White, 'Foreword', in K. Pihlainen (ed.), *The Work of History: Constructivism and a Politics of the Past* (New York: Routledge, 2017), ix–xii, here x–xi.

[9] White, *Metahistory*, xii.

same time to improve the world they live in. When historians engage both theory and practice, they are immunized from an archaeological history that is not relevant for its society as well as from a critical history conditioned by ideological, reductionist, or manipulative presentism. In this sense, being open to practicing history and theorizing the practice of history makes historians more realistic in their approaches to the past and in their theories of *how* to approach that past. History is then not reduced to an ideological or narcissistic exercise, but to an aesthetic operation well rooted in the epistemology that every activity of historical category requires.[10] This theoretical enrichment, arising from the acknowledgment and exploration of the classics, has already been fruitfully experimented with in other disciplines, especially in sociology. As Jeffrey C. Alexander concludes, 'the functional necessity for classics develops because of the need for integrating the field of theoretical discourse'.[11]

In the end, this book would not have been possible without the process experienced by historiography in the final decades of the twentieth century: the shift from the epistemology of history to the poetics of history, and from the question of whether our knowledge of the past could be reliable to the question of *how* we represent this past. Language and rhetoric were no longer tools to understand reality but became part of the reality.[12] One of the pioneers of this turn in historical criticism, John Clive, summarized the content of the

[10] I have developed some of these ideas in Aurell, 'Practicing Theory and Theorizing Practice', 229–251.

[11] Alexander, 'The Centrality of the Classics', 27.

[12] Liakos, 'Historicising', 145 and 146.

permanent attraction that the classics of historiography have always maintained:

> One can learn from the great historians: first of all, about the nature of genius. Reading masterpieces like Gibbon's *Decline and Fall of the Roman Empire* or Burckhardt's *Renaissance Italy*, one encounters that mixture of learning, personal voice, view of the world and human nature, and knowledge of the past filtered through mind and art out of which great history emerges.[13]

Clive makes it clear that the classics of historiography have been able to convey more than just a mimetic description of the past they sought to recover. They also managed to say figuratively something about the permanent conditions of the human condition, about our present. Clive agrees here with Frye, who argued that the quality of the form (the beauty of narration) is what remains timeless in the historical work, since its content is patrimony of its own time: 'Nearly every work of art in the past had a social function in its own time, a function which was often not primarily an aesthetic function at all.'[14]

Trying to learn from those great classics (authors of the past and critics of the present), and paraphrasing Eliot, my concern in this book has been with the progressive provincialism, belittling, and formalism of historiography. Accompanied by some historical, literary, art, and philosophical critics' comments and interpretations, I hope I have been able to provide some insights into the richness of the classics of historiography, or at least to raise some theoretical

[13] Clive, *Not by Fact Alone*, ix.
[14] Frye, *Anatomy of Criticism*, 344.

and practical interest in the concept itself applied to historical writing. One of the most instructive lessons we have learned from them is that creative writing may reformulate and challenge conventional rules without radically breaking with tradition. To my delight, my approach to history classics has not only provided conventions for interpretation but also inspiration for creation. Accordingly, I hope that the reflections presented in this book will encourage not only new theoretical explorations of these concepts but also contribute to the production of sublime historical narratives, in the present and the future.

At the beginning of this book, I quoted Eliot's, Kermode's, and Coetzee's seminal essays on the classic. They, significantly, deploy Virgil – the most classic author in the most classic period – as a model of classicism. Dante chose Virgil too as his classic guide on his journey through the Inferno and Purgatory. Even if the pagan Virgil could not enter heaven, he 'crowned and mitred' Dante just before leaving him at the threshold of the *Paradiso*.[15] Dante showed us

---

[15] Non aspettar mio dir più ne mio cenno:/ libero, dritto e sano è tuo arbitrio, / e fallo fora non fare a suo / senno: / per ch'io te sovra te corono e mitrio ('I do not give you sign or word;/free, upright and whole is thy will;/'twere a fault not to act according to its prompting;/wherefore I do crown and mitre thee over thyself') (Dante, *Divina Commedia, Purgatorio*, Chant 27, vers 139–142). On this, Dante's mysterious and sublime passage, see Kantorowicz, *The King's Two Bodies*, 491–495. To me, this verse epitomizes the concept of the classic itself, since it 'is pregnant with implications and allusions, and that its fullness, radiating into so many directions, is an exhaustible as that of any work of art charged with life' (Kantorowicz, *The King's Two Bodies*, 494).

the way: trust the classics and they will lead you faithfully, even though you might have to leave their guidance and at a certain point continue alone.

I once read that the book that deserves to be called a 'classic' is the one that is worthy not simply to be read but rather to be reread. In this spirit, reading and re-reading the classics of history helps historians improve our historical thinking and representing. Perhaps we will not attain the category of classic that Dante achieved after his expedition with Virgil, but at least these classics of history are going to provide our texts with that universal spirit they – and our audience – deserve. In the meantime, the inexhaustible source of inspiration from the classics of history will continue enriching our cognitive (opening multiple interpretations and stimulating new research), ethical (moving to action), and aesthetic (inspiring beauty) work.

Works on Historical Criticism

Ankersmit, Frank. *Sublime Historical Experience* (Stanford: Stanford University Press, 2005).

Baker, Herschel. *The Race of Time* (Toronto: University of Toronto Press, 1967).

Braudy, Leo. *Narrative Form in History and Fiction* (Ann Arbor: University Microfilms International, 1970).

Brown, Peter. *Society and the Holy in Late Antiquity* (Los Angeles: University of California Press, 1982).

Carrard, Philippe. *History as a Kind of Writing: Textual Strategies in Contemporary French Historiography* (Chicago: University of Chicago Press, 2017).

Carrard, Philippe. *Poetics of the New History* (Baltimore, MD: Johns Hopkins University Press, 1992).

Clive, John. *Not by Fact Alone: Essays on the Writing and Reading of History* (New York: Alfred A. Knopf, 1989).

Gay, Peter. *Style in History* (New York: Basic Books, 1974).

Gearhart, Susan. *The Open Boundary of History and Fiction* (Princeton: Princeton University Press, 1984).

Gossman, Lionel. *Between History and Literature* (Cambridge: Harvard University Press, 1990).

Hartog, François. *The Mirror of Herodotus* (Los Angeles: University of California Press, 2009).

Hexter, Jack H. *On Historians* (Cambridge: Harvard University Press, 1979).

Himmelfarb, Gertrude. *The New History and the Old* (London: Harvard University Press, 1987).

Levine, Joseph M. *The Autonomy of History* (Chicago: University of Chicago Press, 1999).

Momigliano, Arnaldo. *Essays in Ancient and Modern Historiography* (Oxford: Blackwell, 1977).

Pocock, J. G. A. *Barbarism and Religion* (Cambridge: Cambridge University Press, 1999–2015).

Rigney, Ann. *The Rhetoric of Historical Representation* (Cambridge: Cambridge University Press, 1990).

Spiegel, Gabrielle M. *Romancing the Past* (Los Angeles: University of California Press, 1995).

White, Hayden V. *Metahistory* (Baltimore, MD: Johns Hopkins University Press, 1973).

White, Hayden V. *The Content of the Form* (Baltimore, MD: Johns Hopkins University Press, 1987).

White, Hayden V. *Figural Realism* (Baltimore, MD: Johns Hopkins University Press, 1998).

White, Hayden V. *The Fiction of Narrative* (Baltimore, MD: Johns Hopkins University Press, 2010).

Chapter 1 – The Conditions for Durability

Bakhtin, Mikhail. *The Dialogic Imagination* (Austin: University of Texas Press, 1981).

Bourdieu, Pierre. *Homo Academicus* (Paris: Minuit, 1984).

Fritzsche, Peter. *Stranded in the Present* (Cambridge: Harvard University Press, 2004).

Hartog, François. *Regimes of Historicity* (New York: Columbia University Press, 2015).

Hartog, François. *Chronos: The West Confronts Time* (New York: Columbia University Press, 2022).

Jameson, Fredric. *The Political Unconscious* (Ithaca: Cornell University Press, 1981).

Koselleck, Reinhart. *The Practice of Conceptual History* (Stanford: Stanford University Press, 2002).

Koselleck, Reinhart. *Futures Past: On the Semantics of Historical Time* (New York: Columbia University Press, 2004).

Kuhn, Thomas S. *The Essential Tension* (Chicago: University of Chicago Press, 1977).

Nietzsche, Friedrich. *On the Advantage and Disadvantage of History for Life* (Indianapolis: Hackett, 1980).

Oakeshott, Michael J. *Rationalism in Politics* (Indianapolis: Liberty Fund, 1991).

Oakeshott, Michael J. *On History and Other Essays* (Indianapolis: Liberty Fund, 1999).

Steiner, George. *Language and Silence* (London: Faber and Faber, 1985).

White, Hayden. *The Practical Past* (Evanston: Northwestern University Press, 2014).

Chapter 2 – The Dynamics of the Classic

Ankersmit, Frank. *History and Tropology* (Berkeley: University of California Press, 1994).

Aristotle. *Poetics*, eds. John Baxter and Patrick Atherton (Montreal: McGill-Queens University, 1997).

Calvino, Italo. *Perché leggere i classici* (Milan: Oscar Mondadori, 1995).

Coetzee, John M. 'What Is a Classic?', in *Stranger Shores: Literary Essays*, ed. John M. Coetzee (New York: Viking, 2001), 1–16.

Culler, Jonathan. *On Deconstruction* (London: Routledge, 1983).

Eliot, T. S. 'What Is a Classic?', in *On Poetry and Poets*, ed. T. S. Eliot (London: Faber and Faber, 1957), 53–71.

Felton, Henry, *A Dissertation on Reading the Classics, and Forming a Just Style* (Menston: Scholar, 1971 [1709]).

Gadamer, Hans-Georg. *Truth and Method* (London: Sheed & Ward, 1989).

Gombrich, Ernst H. *Ideals & Idols: Essays on Values in History and in Art* (London: Phaidon, 1979).

Johnson, Mark, ed. *Philosophical Perspectives on Metaphor* (Ann Arbor: UMI, 1997).

Kermode, Frank. *The Classic: Literary Images of Permanence and Change* (London: Harvard University Press, 1983).

Leeuwen, Theodoor Marius van. *The Surplus of Meaning* (Amsterdam: Brill, 1981).

Levin, Samuel R. *The Semantics of Metaphor* (Baltimore, MD: Johns Hopkins University Press, 1977).

Löwith, Karl. *Meaning in History* (Chicago: University of Chicago Press, 1949).

MacCormac, Earl R. *A Cognitive Theory of Metaphor* (Cambridge: MIT Press, 1990).

Mukherjee, Ankhy. *What Is a Classic?: Postcolonial Rewriting and Invention of the Canon* (Stanford: Stanford University Press, 2014).

Ortony, Andrew. *Metaphor and Thought* (Cambridge: Cambridge University Press, 1993).

Ricoeur, Paul. *Interpretation Theory* (Fort Worth: The Texas Christian University Press, 1976).

Ricoeur, Paul. *The Rule of Metaphor* (Toronto: University of Toronto Press, 1977).

Ricoeur, Paul. *Time and Narrative* (Chicago: University of Chicago Press, 1990).

Chapter 3 – The Inescapability of the Canon

Alter, Robert. *Canon and Creativity* (New Haven: Yale University Press, 2000).

Altieri, Charles. *Canon and Consequences* (Illinois: North-Wester University Press, 1990).

Baehr, Peter. *Founders, Classics, Canons* (New York: Routledge, 2002).

Barker, John. *The Superhistorians: Makers of Our Past* (New York: Charles Scribner's Sons, 1982).

Barton, John. *Holy Writings, Sacred Text: The Canon in Early Christianity* (Louisville: Westminster John Knox Press., 1997).

Blenkinsopp, Joseph. *Prophecy and Canon: A Contribution to the Study of Jewish Origins* (Notre Dame: University of Notre Dame Press, 1977).

Bloom, Harold. *The Western Canon* (New York: Harcourt Brace, 1994).

Cohen, Richard. *Making History: The Storytellers Who Shaped the Past* (London: Simon & Schuster, 2022).

Crowther, Paul. *Defining Art, Creating the Canon* (Oxford: Clarendon, 2007).

Dionysius of Halicarnassus, *Critical Essays*, ed. Stephen Usher (Cambridge, MA: Harvard University Press, 2014).

Fleming, Mike. *The Literary Canon: Implications for the Teaching of Language as Subject* (online, access 1 January 2022).

Franke, William. *On the Universality of What Is Not* (Notre Dame: University of Notre Dame Press, 2020).

Gossman, Lionel. *The Empire Unpossess'd: An Essay on Gibbon's Decline and Fall* (Cambridge: Cambridge University Press, 1981).

Guillory, John. *Cultural Capital: The Problem of Literary Canon Formation* (Chicago: University of Chicago Press, 1993).

Katz, Elihu, et al. *Canonic Texts in Media Research* (Cambridge: Polity, 2003).

Kermode, Frank. *Pleasure and Change: The Aesthetics of Canon* (Oxford: Oxford University Press, 2004).

Marcuse, Herbert. *The Aesthetic Dimension* (Boston: Beacon Press., 1979).

Matijasic, Ivan. *Shaping the Canons of Ancient Greek Historiography* (Berlin: De Gruyter, 2018).

McDonald, Lee M. and Sanders, James A., eds. *The Canon Debate* (Peabody, MA: Hendrickson, 2002).

McDonald, Lee M. *The Formation of the Biblical Canon* (London: Bloomsbury, 2017).

Morrissey, Lee, ed. *Debating the Canon* (New York: Palgrave Macmillan, 2005).

Vasari, Giorgio. *The Lives of the Artists* (Oxford: Oxford University Press, 1991 [1550]).

Chapter 4 – The Canonical Function of Historical Genres

Aurell, Jaume. *Authoring the Past* (Chicago: University of Chicago Press, 2012).

Burrow, John W. *A History of Histories* (London: Allen Lane, 2007).

Cohen, Ralph. 'History and Genre', *New Literary History* 17 (1986): 203–218.

Conte, Gian Biagio. *Genres and Readers* (Baltimore, MD: Johns Hopkins University Press, 1994).

Deliyannis, Deborah M., ed. *Historiography in the Middle Ages* (Leiden: Brill, 2002).

Derrida, Jacques. 'The Law of Genre', *Critical Inquiry* 7 (1980): 55–81.

Fowler, Alastair. *Kinds of Literature* (Oxford: Oxford University Press, 1982).

Gervase of Canterbury. *The Historical Works of Gervase of Canterbury*, ed. William Stubbs (Cambridge: Cambridge University Press, 2012).

Grafton, Anthony. *The Footnote: A Curious History* (Cambridge: Harvard University Press, 1997).

Green, Anna and Troup, Kathleen, eds. *The Houses of History: A Critical Reader in Twentieth-Century History and Theory* (Manchester: Manchester University Press, 1999).

Hecataeus of Miletus. 'Genealogies', in *Prologues to Ancient and Medieval History*, ed. Justin Lake (Toronto: University of Toronto Press, 2013).

Jacoby, Felix. 'Über die Entwicklung der griechischen Historiographie', *Klio* 9 (1909): 80–123.

Jauss, Hans R. *Toward an Aesthetic of Reception* (Minneapolis: University of Minnesota Press, 1982).

Kraus, Christina Shuttleworth, ed. *The Limits of Historiography: Genre and Narrative in Ancient Historical Texts* (Leiden: Brill, 1999).

Lucian of Samosata. *How to Write History*, trans. K. Kilburn (Cambridge: Harvard University Press, 1959).

Munslow, Alun and Rosenstone, Robert A., eds. *Experiments in Rethinking History* (London: Routledge, 2004).

Spiegel, Gabrielle M. *The Past as Text* (Baltimore, MD: Johns Hopkins University Press, 1994).

Stern, Fritz. *The Varieties of History: From Voltaire to the Present* (New York: Random House, 1970).

Todorov, Tzvetan. 'The Origin of Genres', *New Literary History* 8 (1976): 159–170.

Wood, Gordon S. *The Purpose of the Past* (New York: Penguin, 2008).

Woolf, Daniel. *A Global History of History* (Cambridge: Cambridge University Press, 2012).

Zink, Michel. *The Invention of Literary Subjectivity* (Baltimore, MD: Johns Hopkins University Press, 1999).

Zumthor, Paul. *Essai de poétique médiévale* (Paris: Seuil, 1972).

Chapter 5 – Genealogy as Double Agent

Deleuze, Gilles. *Nietzsche and Philosophy* (London: Continuum, 1983).

Foucault, Michel. *The Archaeology of Knowledge* (New York: Harper, 1972).

Foucault, Michel. *The Order of Things* (New York: Vintage, 1973).

Foucault, Michel. 'Nietzsche, Genealogy, History', in *Language, Counter-Memory, Practice* (Ithaca: Cornell University Press, 1977), 139–164.

Genicot, Léopold. *Les Généalogies* (Turnhout: Brepols, 1975).

Herrero, Montserrat. 'Genealogical Practices', *Giornale di Metafisica* 2 (2016): 575–597.

Jensen, Anthony K. and Santini, Carlotta, eds. *Nietzsche on Memory and History* (Berlin: De Gruyter, 2021).

Johnson, Marshall D. *The Purpose of the Biblical Genealogies* (Cambridge: Cambridge University Press, 1969).

Koopman, Colin. *Genealogy as Critique* (Bloomington: Indiana University Press, 2013).

Lightbody, Brian. *Philosophical Genealogy* (New York: Peter Lang, 2010).

MacIntyre, Alasdair. *Three Rival Version of Moral Inquiry* (London: Duckworth, 1985).

Mahon, Michael. *Foucault's Nietzschean Genealogy* (Albany: State University of New York Press, 1992).

Nietzsche, Friedrich. *The Genealogy of Morals* (Mineola, NY: Dover, 2003).

Ranum, Orest. *Artisans of Glory* (Chapel Hill: The University of North Carolina Press, 1980).

Roth, Michael S. *Knowing and History* (Ithaca: Cornell University Press, 1988).

Sax, Benjamin. 'Foucault, Nietzsche, History', *History of European Ideas* 11 (1989): 769–781.

Spiegel, Gabrielle M. 'Genealogy: Form and Function in Medieval Historiography', *History and Theory* 22 (1983): 43–53.

Spiegel, Gabrielle M. 'Foucault and the Problem of Genealogy', *The Medieval History Journal* 4, 1 (2001): 1–14.

Thapar, Romila. 'Genealogical Patterns as Perceptions of the Past', in *Cultural Pasts: Essays in Early Indian History* (Oxford: Oxford University Press, 2000), 709–753.

Williams, Bernard. *Truth & Truthfulness: An Essay in Genealogy* (Princeton: Princeton University Press, 2002).

genealogy (cont.)
   Nietzsche, Frierich, and, 258, 281,
      284, 286, 290, 294
   of Jesus, 266
   pedigrees, rise of, 267–275
   philosophical turn of, 279–289
   relevance of, 261
   senses of, 193
genres. *See also* historical genres
   annales, 219
   autobiography, 49
   biography, 49
   chronicle, 13, 219, 223
   city history, 149
   genealogies, 13, 275–279
   hagiography, 232
   plurality of, 38
   universal histories, 218, 249
   urban histories, 13, 249
   variability of, 207
gentiles, 267
Geoffrey of Monmouth
   History of the Kings of Britain, 148
Geoffrey of Villehardouin, 148, 234
Geoffrey of Viterbo, 219
geography, 52, 80
Germany, 28, 116, 154, 275, 278
German historicism, 116, 221, 239
Gervase of Canterbury, 22, 219, 220
   on genres, 214
Gesta Imperatorum (Thomas of
   Pavia), 221
Gesta Regum Anglorum (William
   of Malmesbury), 269
Gibbon, Edward, 15–17, 25, 44, 57,
   67, 88, 90, 96, 109–111, 113,
   125, 129, 133–135, 150, 151, 153,

155, 159–167, 169, 170, 186,
   197, 199, 238
   *Decline and Fall of the Roman
   Empire*, 17, 34, 44, 57, 96, 110,
   111, 127, 133, 159–161, 163–167,
   170, 172, 175, 176, 180
   Rise and Decline, 195
Gilson, Etienne, 240
   *L'esprit de la philosophie
   médiévale*, 240
Ginzburg, Carlo, 72, 78, 96, 135, 156,
   171, 186, 190, 307
   Il formaggio e il vermi, 243
   The Cheese and the Worms, 17,
   96, 101, 156
Giotto di Bondone, 185
Goldman, Lucien, 192
Gombrich, Ernst, 139, 185, 186, 192
   on canon, 139
goodness, 29, 75
Gorak, Jan, 140
Gospel genealogies, 267, 272
Gospel of Luke, 265, 266
Gospel of Matthew, 265, 266
Gossman, Lionel, 15, 16, 25, 129, 308
Goubert, Pierre, 242
Grafton, Anthony, 23, 195
Gran, Peter, 159
Great West colonization, 123
Greco-Roman period, 143
Greek civilizations, 63
Greek ethnography, 226
Greek genealogy, 233
Greek historiography, 40, 41, 222,
   225, 227, 230, 234, 258,
   260, 283
Greek horography, 232

Namier, Lewis
  *The Structure of Politics at the
    Accession of George III*, 240
narrative form in history, 24
national history, 41, 169, 255, 260,
    261, 270, 277, 278
  genealogy as, 41, 169, 255, 260,
    261, 270, 277, 278
natural time
  disruptive *vs.* asynchronic
    relationship, 55
nature, concept of, 38
Nelson, Benjamin, 51, 126
new historicism, 59
new narrative history, 128
new narrativism, 130
New Science (Giambattista Vico), 128
New Testament, 265
Niccolò Machiavelli
  History of Florence, 149
Nietzsche and Philosophy
    (Gilles Deleuze), 282
Nietzsche, Friedrich, 40, 45, 61, 68,
    92, 106, 174, 198, 233, 248,
    251, 260, 280–284, 286, 287,
    289, 290, 292–295
  Genealogy of Morals, 258, 281, 295
  on genealogy, 280–285
  The Birth of Tragedy, 280
  Untimely Meditation, 280
Nora, Pierre, 270
Novick, Peter, 10, 23

Oakeshott, Michael J., 75, 77, 154, 248
  on practical past, 74
Oceana (Harrington), 237
Old Testament, 265, 266

On the Ten Years Rule (Demetrius
    of Phalerum), 230
On Thucydides (Dionysius of
    Halicarnassus), 216
oral history, 247
Orientalism (Edward W. Said), 158
Otto of Freising, 148
  Deeds of Emperor Frederick, 148

Palmer, Bryan, 73
panegyrics, 231
Panyassis, 263
Parallel Lives (Plutarch), 302
Paris, Matthew
  Chronica Majora, 148
Parkman, Francis, 166
Past as Text, The (Gabrielle M.
    Spiegel), 56
Pasquier, Etienne, 270
past's contemporary relevance,
    122–129
patriotism, 73
Paulinus of Venice, 219
Peloponnesian War (Thucydides),
    42, 44, 200
Persian Wars (Herodotus), 34, 44, 111
Persica (Dionysius of Miletus), 226
Peter IV of Aragon, 149, 235
Phaeneas of Eresos, 227
Philip of Novara, 148, 234
Phillips, Mark S., 212
philosophical concept, genealogy,
    279–289
philosophical history, 19, 190, 238,
    248, 280
philosophy, discipline of, 19
philosophy of history, 20, 116

INDEX

Picasso, Pablo, 179, 185
Pihlainen, Kalle, 21, 99, 101, 108
Piketty, Thomas
    Capital and Ideology, 293
Pirenne, Henri
    Mohammed and Charlemagne, 302
Pliny the Elder, 228, 231
Plutarch, 17, 62
    Parallel Lives, 302
Pocock, J. G. A., 134, 163, 164, 172,
    180, 232
poetics of history, 24
political biography, 67
political history, 247
political theology, 58, 127
politics, 118
    agency, 127
    military, 127
    power, 127
Polybius, 17, 31, 62, 66, 96, 145, 151,
    153, 190, 217, 218, 229
    Histories, 96
Porter, Roy, 160
positivism, epistemology of, 103
postcolonial criticism, 36, 140
postcolonial history, 247
post-colonialist denunciations, 141, 157
post-feminist history, 247
post-modernism, 36, 140, 173, 211
post-structural genealogy, 189
practical past, 74–81
Prescott, William, 166
presentism, 46, 59, 71, 75–77, 79, 81,
    125, 196, 204, 294, 304, 310
professionalism, 10
professionalization of history, 77,
    143, 151, 239, 255

provincialism, 3, 46, 158
Provincializing Europe
    (Chakrabarty), 158
psychology, 60, 239

quantitative approach, 78, 135
quantitativism, 95

race history, 247
radicalism, 307
Ralph de Diceto, 219
Ranke, Leopold von, 16, 31, 48, 53,
    67, 73, 77, 111, 112, 117, 124,
    125, 133, 150, 153, 174, 186,
    190, 199, 238, 307
    History of the Reformation, 17, 31
Ramon Muntaner, 149
Ranum, Orest, 14, 276, 296
rationalizations, 82, 264
Ravaisson, Felix, 154
realism
    magical, 179
    naïve, 104
reality of the past, 13
reductionism, 7, 125, 140
religion, 118
Rembrandt's eyes (Simon
    Schama), 101
Renaissance, 153, 255
Renaissance humanism, 236
*Renaissance of the Twelfth Century,
    The* (Charles Homer
    Haskins), 240
Return of Martin Guerre, The
    (Natalie Zemon Davis),
    17, 59, 61, 79, 96, 130, 156,
    178, 243

338